# Redemptive Faith

## "How to Know that You Know You are Going to Heaven"

*A Reference Book for Growing & Sustaining Your Faith*

## by: Glenn Leonard

I dedicate this book to my loving wife Linda who has inspired me to be the man God designed me to be. Her support, her encouragement, and yes, her patience in giving me the time to write this book has allowed me to pursue this worthy goal. I am truly among the most blessed of all men.

# Table Of Contents

# Introduction

You may recall the story that after the crucifixion, Thomas stated that he would not believe that Jesus was resurrected unless he saw for himself the nail marks in Jesus' hands. When Jesus appeared a week later to Thomas Jesus said, "Because you have seen me, you have believed; blessed are those who have not seen and yet believed" (John 20:24-29). Hebrews 11:1 teaches us that "faith is being sure of what we hope for and certain of what we do not see." The rest of Hebrews chapter 11 gives a wonderful presentation of some of the heroes of the Bible and how faith worked in their lives. <u>Faith requires the existence of belief, trust, and commitment even when there is an absence of observable proof.</u> From the verses in Hebrews 11 we learn that faith is not something which merely requires contemplation; it demands action. God wants us to take action in the form of being obedient and submissive in our behaviors to His will, in spite of not having sensory confirmation of the reality of His being. This is a hard concept for many. It is not something you can merely mull over. It gets even more challenging because it involves an intimate, daily relationship. The relationship is further complicated because it is with an ethereal Being who makes claims and prophecies in a book which can be hard to read at times.

Ostensibly educated people will make fun of you if you choose this course of action. Others will say you are seeking a crutch in order to explain the inexplicable. Still others will say you are being close-minded and simple. They think the world is too big for just one God. For them science, society, and the government have all the answers. The enlightened elite declare that theology is merely mystical philosophy. Who are we, as Christians, to think we have this special revelation about eternal life? We also learn in Hebrews 11:39-40 that the ultimate pay off for faith does not even come in this lifetime. The promise is that God has something "very special" planned for those of us who believe and trust in Him solely on the basis of faith. What if the minute after you die, nothing happens? All of that time you spent reading the Bible and praying to this God will have been for nothing. Will you feel robbed? This is where faith has to drive your life. We have no absolute proofs. In addition, being faithful to God will require both your time and your money. Are you up to the challenge of putting your faith into action? The heroes of the Bible were up to the challenge and they are still leading the way for us today.

Look at these great men and women of the Bible. Only one of them was perfect. However, <u>God does not depend on having perfect people to accomplish His plans. What He needs are "willing" people.</u> Each of us is targeted by the enemy. Satan wants us to have self-doubts. Satan wants us confused. He wants our faith to be watered-down. He wants us to question ourselves and God. Satan would prefer that we not even acknowledge God. If we must, then he wants us to be ineffective in our witness to others. If he can stop you from taking that first step, then he wins.

This is why the topic of redemptive faith has become my spiritual passion. It guides my biblical studies and my life. Redemptive faith reflects the spiritual status of your soul which, in turn, is revealed by an action component in your behavior. As a young boy of 8, I asked Jesus to be my Lord and Savior. There have been many times in my life where I have led a solid Christian life. Shamefully, there have also been periods where if being a Christian were a felonious act, there would not have been sufficient evidence against me for a conviction. This saddens me. I had faith but I was not living it out in the way God desires. My spiritual life was something of varying priorities. Thankfully I did not die in the meantime. What a waste of opportunities I lived. Out of this sadness comes praise. I praise God Almighty for being patient with me and allowing me to live long enough so I could come to my senses. I praise the Lord God Almighty that He, in His grace, has allowed me to live long enough that I forevermore desire a close personal relationship with Him. Through this I have made a more steadfast commitment to have Jesus the Lord of my life and have established the Holy Spirit as the Commander of my soul. I put my total faith in God's holy righteousness. I am certain that the God of the Christian Bible is the one true God. I am reminded of Romans 8:28, "And we know that in all things God works for the good of those who love Him, who are called according to His purpose." Jehovah Jireh has been true to me. He has provided me with experiences which have molded my faith into being unshakeable. God is good.

I am writing this book for a number of reasons. This has become my reference book for teaching redemptive faith in my Sunday School class. <u>As a resource guide, this book is targeted at anyone who is concerned with helping themselves and others to grow in their faith</u>. The Scriptures quoted in this book form the bedrock of my biblical understanding. I have referenced many scriptural verses so that when these topics come up in class, I will have the wisdom of the Holy Scriptures to guide me. If others read it, I am hopeful these discussions will be valuable to them as they strive for a more meaningful life with God. I hope everyone will take up the habit of reading His Holy Scriptures on a daily basis. Perhaps the Scriptures quoted in these discussions will make you seek a greater understanding of our Lord. As a note, I reference much of the teachings of the Bible and particularly Jesus in the present tense. These lessons, along with our Savior are still alive. He is not to be relegated to this world's past. The Good Shepherd guides us in the present and reveals our future. Our Jesus is risen, so He is to be treated as being present.

My goal is to encourage people to be more active in their faith. For too long I was content to sit in church and be a sponge. It was okay with me that others did everything. I thought that by my mere presence, I was doing something. That is not what the Bible teaches though. In addition, I want to be bold in my faith. I love Simon Peter. There have been times in my life when I have been brash and impetuous. There have also been times in my life where I have failed miserably to live as God intends for me to live. It is so encouraging to read about the transformation of Peter from the night of his denials and then progressed to later in his life when he lovingly instructed the family of believers on how to live as Christ would have them to live. I love the gentle boldness he displayed in his faith as reflected in 1st and 2nd Peter. He gives me hope. The apostle Paul is another giant in my eyes. If I had the ability to memorize an entire book of the Bible, it would be Romans. If young Christians would take the time to study the life of Paul, they would never think that after asking Jesus into their hearts, life should be a bowl of cherries. Quite the contrary proved to be the case for Paul. What a tower of faith Paul was (and still is). You will see that I quote extensively from the New Testament. Though these books were written almost 2000 years ago, they are still relevant and powerful today.

The Old Testament is not to be neglected either. <u>Mankind has not changed much in its spiritual nature over the entirety</u>

of human history. We still fight much the same battles (just our clothes are a little nicer and we have a lot better transportation). Stop and think, where would we be without the books given to us by Moses, Joshua, David, Solomon, Job, Isaiah, Jeremiah and all the other old saints? All of these heroes had the monumental faith that God is who He says He is – The Great I Am. Through the Old Testament we learn a lot about the character of Jehovah God. Any Bible study which minimizes (or worse yet, excludes) the Old Testament misses much of the revealed character of El Elyon, the Most High God. It is by way of the Old Testament where the New Testament can be most properly understood.

The New Testament goes on to teach us about the life and sacrifice of Christ Jesus. He is the Word, the Way, the Truth, and the Life (John 1:1, 14:6). The Holy Spirit is introduced to us through Jesus as being His agent to guide and guard us, to keep us as His (John 14:16-26). The New Testament teaches us that the Holy Spirit is the seal (2 Corinthians 1:21-22) which helps us to "know that we know" that we belong to El Elyon, The Most High God. Not only are we more fully introduced to our Messiah and the Spirit of God in the New Testament, it also reveals the closer, more personal relationship we get to have with our heavenly Father as the result of the loving sacrifice of our Lord and Savior. The apostles teach us of the great truths which our religion brings to this world through the life of Christ Jesus. There are many reasons why we can call the Bible the Book of Ultimate Truth. We will explore the vast evidence which supports our faith that God is who He says He is and He does what He says He will do. The writers of the Holy Scriptures have taught me a lot about what a Christian walk should be. Now I am dedicated to living it. I no longer want to be guilty of being some lukewarm Christian who blends in with all of the rest of the world (Revelation 3:15-16).

This book hopefully will be a resource guide for you as well as an encouragement. Additionally, it is intended to be a call to action. The tone is meant to be loving while still calling us into an awareness of approaching accountability. While I am secure in my personal salvation, I am afraid we, as a body of church goers, do not take God's righteousness seriously. Where is the fear of God's wrath in our society? <u>We talk so much about His love that we gloss over Him being a Holy God</u>. Casual believers would have us asking "How can a loving God treat us in any manner other than how we have come to expect our grandparents to treat us?" Our heavenly Father is no doting grandparent! Above all else, He is holy. This holiness requires Him to be righteous. In His righteousness, He holds us accountable for our deeds (Jeremiah 17:10). He has no favorites. God will not be mocked nor deceived. All will face His judgment. Prepare yourself.

<u>Although we do not always clearly see God's plan unfolding in our daily lives, we can rest assured Jehovah God is always at work, making sure His plan is progressing according to His prophecies</u>. Many challenges in life come our way and we do not always understand why they happen to us. We need to try and see God's fingerprints on our daily lives. We need to thank God for our insights, our refinement, and our chastening. I fear that if I had not had some of the life experiences which I have had, I would still be lax in my faith. I previously felt that since I was saved, I really had nothing to worry about. The proverbial "fire insurance" was in my name and I was safe. I have come to realize that does not constitute the kind of relationship with God which He desires. I fear the spiritual battles which are ahead for our country and our world. There are too many people who have the old attitudes which I fell into. My fear is we are not as resolved as my father's generation to combat evil in this world. The battle is engaged. The time is now. I intend to be prepared.

To get the greatest value from your reading, you may want to have your Bible handy as you read these discussion points. I have tried to relate Scriptures to each of these points. I used both the New International Version Disciple's Study Bible (NIVDSB) and the King James Version Life Application Study Bible (KJVLASB) for this project. I also referred to The New Unger's Bible Dictionary and William MacDonald's Believer's Bible Commentary for additional resource materials. Other authors I have used extensively are Rick Warren, Charles Stanley, D. James Kennedy, C. S. Lewis, Henry Blackaby, and Martin Luther. Read the verses being cited for yourself and see what treasures the Holy Spirit and these men of renown will reveal to you.

As an author I make no claim to having a theological pedigree. Modern biblical scholars are an invaluable asset to us as we seek to grow in our relationship with this Triune God of ours. Yes, He is ours and we are His. It is a beautiful, yet mystifying relationship at times. Scholars help to explain difficult passages. They open our eyes to the interrelated nature of various biblical verses spanning both the Old and the New Testaments. They guide us through the various nuances of translations of words which can be cryptic to our understanding. Furthermore, they explain the meaning of the original language used in the writing of God's Holy Word. At times, there are verses in different books of the Bible which seem to be directly contradictory. How Matthew, Mark, Luke, or John may have been moved by the Holy Spirit to record the same event will be, nonetheless, a little different. These men certainly did not look over each other's shoulders to make sure they said the exact same things about the events surrounding the life of Christ.

When such discrepancies occur, no, the scoffers have not surreptitiously discovered passages filled with minor and major errors thereby providing them with the potentially embarrassing evidence that the Bible is actually inaccurate.

What our biblical scholars point out is that these verses often merely reflect the differences in perspective which the writer had on that particular event. As we know, multiple people can view a situation and each come out with an accurate, albeit different take on the event. The commentators help guide us through a reconciliation of how these verses support rather than contradict the message God is presenting through the various books of the Bible. Our Lord has used these gifted theologians mightily in growing His family of believers. Our heavenly Father also has a place for those of us who are of the "common man" status. To those who are faithful to their biblical studies, they will know that only a few of the great men of faith had any extensive formal training in theology. One of the amazing aspects of our God is that He uses everyday people all over this world to accomplish His purposes. He did that from the start and He continues in it today.

I make no claims to having special knowledge which can only be found in the pages of this book. There are many fine Christian writers for this subject matter; some probably deal better with this issue of redemptive faith than I have done. I have only my personal Bible studies, years of attending Sunday School and worship at a church whose pastor is a gifted biblical scholar, and most importantly, having the privilege of being raised in a Christian home – all of which have guided me in my biblical understanding. As I would embark on writing a section, I would pray that the Holy Spirit guide me in revealing whatever it is that God would have me say about the topic. If anything sounds particularly noteworthy in what I have written, then credit the Holy Spirit. If anything is off-based, then blame me for not correctly sensing what the Spirit was trying to convey. There is nothing especially noteworthy about me. I am much like many of you. I struggle. I also believe. My college degree is in psychology though I have never practiced it as a profession. I am a businessman.

I try each day to live out the teachings of God's Holy Word. Each morning during my prayers, I ask the Lord to use me in a way which brings honor and glory to Him. Sometimes I fail. *Even in my failures, God continues to bless me. He is forever faithful, even when I am not.*

Life is better now than it has ever been for me. I have a precious wife who I absolutely adore and two remarkable daughters who are the lights of my life. I am blessed with many warm and caring friends. However, it is not because of whom I am but Whose I am that I rejoice. <u>I believe Jehovah God is the one true God</u>. <u>I believe Jesus Christ is His Son and through my abiding faith in Him I have eternal life</u>. <u>I believe the Holy Spirit is my seal that proves I belong to El Elyon, the Most High God, who created the heavens and the earth</u>. I believe all of this with the utmost of my heart, my soul, and my mind. It is my hope that I have correctly expressed my understanding of redemptive faith and that you will grow in your love and understanding of God Almighty as the result of reading the following pages. Lastly, it is my greatest desire that I have expressed myself in a way which is pleasing to our heavenly Father. I no longer have the pleasure of hearing my earthly father and mother speak to me. Thankfully, whenever I open the pages of the Holy Bible, I get to hear my heavenly Father's voice instructing me, edifying me, encouraging me, and yes, rebuking me. We serve a truly awesome God. He is forever faithful to those who seek Him.

This book was written with the awareness that not everyone reads a book in chapter order. May I urge you to start with Chapters One and Two. Then you can skip around and read various topics which speak to your immediate interests. I have tried to make each chapter capable of intertwining the related concepts and discussions so that one will not be lost if they choose to skip around with the chapters. I want to encourage the reader to eventually read all of the chapters. If they are followed in chapter order, I think the reading flows a little better. Nonetheless, it is your book. Use it in whatever manner you prefer in your quest to seek a closer relationship with God Almighty. I have tried to make this an engaging book which prompts you to explore the Bible more fully. Lastly, this book should be approached as a series of Sunday School lessons. As with such lessons, you may disagree occasionally with some of the points but hopefully the overall message will be worthy of the time you spend reading this book.

# Chapter One What is Redemptive Faith

※

In a discussion of redemptive faith, one might ask, "How much faith is sufficient for salvation? How much faith must we have to be assured of an eternity with God Almighty?" Perhaps we should turn to Matthew 17:20 to see what our Lord says about this matter. Jesus proclaims, "I tell you the truth, if you have faith as small as a mustard seed, you can say to this mountain, 'Move from here to there' and it will move. Nothing will be impossible for you.'" As tiny as a mustard seed is a good starting point. While the mustard seed is in fact very tiny, it is pure in its constitution. It is 100% mustard seed. Nothing is phony; nothing is for show. It is not confused about what it is. Neither does it remain a tiny seed. With proper nourishment and cultivation, it becomes useful. A mustard seed in itself is of little use. Put in the right soil and nurtured by a caring gardener, it becomes a productive tree.

Obviously the quantity of one's faith is not the question. The quality is what brings glory to God. Keep in mind what Jesus teaches us in Luke 18:15-17, "People were also bringing babies to Jesus to have Him touch them. When the disciples saw this, they rebuked them. But Jesus called the children to Him and said, "Let the little children come to me, and do not hinder them, for the kingdom of God belongs to such as these. I tell you the truth, anyone who will not receive the kingdom of God like a little child will never enter it." Little children and excited new believers may not have yet built up great reservoirs of faith but they do have a purity of faith which makes them mighty.

The term "redemptive faith" will be used by me because I want there to be a clear distinction in mind between faith in Jesus Christ as our Lord and Savior which leads to eternal salvation as contrasted to casual faith which is commonly used to reference head knowledge or nominal acceptance of something. I have faith that the bank has my money safely accounted for and is processed correctly. I have faith that the medicine I take is not something which will lead to my death. I have faith that the laws of our society will protect me rather than imprison me. These usages of the word faith connote an expectation. Faith such as this will not lead to my soul being secured in the arms of El Shaddai, our Lord God Almighty. Redemptive faith does. Redemptive faith is more than an expectation. It is based on a belief system which is so steadfast in us that it defines the very fabric of our being.

While there are many excellent definitions of faith, I find this one very simple and direct: ***Redemptive faith involves having the heartfelt inner confidence that God is who He says He is and He does what He says He will do*** (King James Version Life Application Study Bible p. 31). This definition comes out loud and clear in Exodus 3:13-17, "Moses said to God, "Suppose I go to the Israelites and say to them, 'The God of your fathers has sent me to you,' and they ask me, 'What is His name?' Then what shall I tell them?" God said to Moses, "I AM WHO I AM. This is what you are to say to the Israelites: 'I AM has sent me to you.'" God also said to Moses, "Say to the Israelites, 'The Lord, the God of your fathers—the God of Abraham, the God of Isaac and the God of Jacob—has sent me to you.' This is my name forever, the name by which I am to be remembered from generation to generation. Go, assemble the elders of Israel and say to them, 'The Lord, the God of your fathers—the God of Abraham, Isaac and Jacob—appeared to me and said: I have watched over you and have seen what has been done to you in Egypt. And I have promised to bring you up out of your misery in Egypt into the land of the Canaanites, Hittites, Amorites, Perizzites, Hivites and Jebusites—a land flowing with milk and honey." God obviously links who He is with what He does. His words carry action. We can trust that He is who He says He is by what He does.

As a side bar, I will be using many of the various names for God, Jesus, and the Holy Spirit in this book. These names have a great value for us. Each of these names for the various members of the Triune Godhead carries a special message about an attribute of the God in whom we place our faith. By Divine design, Jehovah God is known to us by His various acts and characteristics. As you learn a new name for God, you grow in your understanding of who He is. This is one of the reasons why I like the above definition of faith. God is who He says He is and His various names increase our awareness of this God who we serve. You may go to the Blue Letter Bible online at www.blueletterbible.org to research these various names. I also have them listed in the Appendix of this book. I want to encourage you to visit this website. It is an extremely helpful place for biblical research and commentaries.

### *Why Faith*

On page 1105 of the NIV Disciple's Study Bible commentary it gives us this insight into possibly why God chooses faith as the avenue for our redemption: "God did not send the Messiah with overwhelming evidence so everyone would follow Him automatically. He sent His Son to give true fulfillment of Scripture so that people truly seeking God's will in faith would repent and follow Him even to death". I often quote these commentaries verbatim rather than paraphrasing them because I want my readers to know exactly how valuable these commentaries are. They have greatly increased my understanding of the Holy Scriptures and I thank God for the people who wrote these commentaries. I want these writers to get all of the credit for their diligent scholarship and illuminations.

I use the term "redemptive" as a point of emphasis because I am directing our attention to a very specific, conditional use of the word "faith". I am not referring to faith in general, nor am I referring to redemption in general. The faith I am highlighting leads to our redemption out of a life of sin and into a secured life for all eternity with the Holy Trinity. The New Unger's Bible Dictionary defines redemption as: "A comprehensive term employed in theology with reference to the special intervention of God for the salvation of mankind. Its meaning centers in the atoning work of Christ as the price paid for human redemption, and on account of which Christ is called the Redeemer...Redemption implies antecedent bondage. Thus the word refers primarily to man's subjection to the dominion and curse of sin" (Unger, page 1068). Paul writes in Galatians 3:13, "Christ redeemed us from the curse of the law by becoming a curse for us". In Galatians 4:4-6 Paul further states, "But when the time had fully come, God sent his Son, born of a woman, born under law, to redeem those under law, that we might receive the full rights of sons. Because you are sons, God sent the Spirit of His Son into our hearts..."

So, where do we begin in this search for how we can "know that we know" that we are going to heaven? There are many fine verses which can start us on this path to eternal salvation. One of the most commonly cited can be found in John 3:14-18, "And as Moses lifted up the serpent in the wilderness, even so must the Son of man be lifted up: That whosoever believeth in Him should not perish, but have eternal life. For God so loved the world, that He gave His only begotten Son, that whosoever believeth in Him should not perish, but have everlasting life. For God sent not His Son into the world to condemn the world; but that the world through Him might be saved. He that believeth on Him is not condemned: but he that believeth not is condemned already, because he hath not believed in the name of the only begotten Son of God." You either accept this as God's truth or you do not.

That is not to say though that we believers do not have evidence to substantiate our faith. <u>There is ample evidence that God is who He says He is</u>. There is ample evidence that Jesus is who He says He is. The evidence is not like DNA evidence which can scientifically ascertain the parentage of a child. If it were, then it would not require the essential element which God desires: as already quoted, Hebrews 11:1 "faith is being sure of what we hope for and certain of what we do not see." Adonai (our Lord and Master) wants us to believe "just because He said so". Can we, as humans, humble ourselves to accept the word of an ethereal Being who we cannot see, touch, or smell? This faith has many avenues of evidence for those of us who have placed our faith in Jehovah God. Much is largely *historical* in nature. It relies on the testimony of witnesses to certain events. It also relies on our *observations in nature*. Open your eyes; look around you. God's handiwork is all around us. There are no intelligent explanations of life on this earth outside of the creation story. Additionally, the evidence comes to us at times through our *intuitions*. When we are in sync with our spiritual nature, we can sense His holy presence. Most cultures have an awareness of a Creator. They sense His presence even though they do not correctly identify Him. Paul teaches us that these intuitions has been genetically encoded into us by Elohim, God the Creator (Romans 1:18-20, 2:13-15). Some of the best evidence is through *the accuracy of the prophecies* which El Elyon gave to His chosen prophets. This evidence will be more thoroughly discussed in the following pages. For now, I want to establish that redemptive faith which has eternal consequences is unique from faith which surrounds many of our common, everyday experiences.

### *The Role of Repentance*

The Greek word for repentance means "to change the mind". The Hebrew word denotes "to turn" or "to return". The implication is that a repentant person returns to God's teachings and rejects the path of sinfulness. Faith and repentance are intertwining biblical concepts and should be studied together in order to better understand God's intentions for our lives. Repentance promotes humility, which opens us to greater faith. The New Unger's Bible Dictionary gives an insightful treatment to our discussion of redemptive faith. "Faith is not saving faith unless it includes repentance. Saving faith may therefore be properly defined for those who have the light of the gospel as such belief in the Lord Jesus Christ as leads one to submit completely to the authority of Christ and to put complete and exclusive trust in Him for salvation"(p 397).

What modern man often thinks of as faith is actually a casual awareness. This may even extend to a nominal acceptance. This sort of noncommittal faith is not what I am presenting as being acceptable to El Shaddai, the Lord God Almighty. Redemptive faith involves both a belief in and a transformation into being like Christ Jesus. Anything less is not genuine, redemptive faith. It is something but it is not what will secure you a place in heaven. This is where Satan's deception is at work. As our Lord teaches us in

Matthew 7:13-14, "Enter through the narrow gate. For wide is the gate and broad is the road that leads to destruction, and many enter through it. But small is the gate and narrow the road that leads to life, and only a few find it." Satan loves to deceive people into thinking incorrectly about God. He wants to confuse you and then have you confuse others.

Probably one of the most underemphasized teachings of The Holy Bible is spiritual repentance. Satan wants us to be confused about God's nature and how we are to maintain this lifelong relationship with the Most High God. He wants us to be unclear on what is required of us by the Lord. Many are deceived into believing they only need to intellectually acknowledge who Jesus is. This is why Unger brings up the aspect of repentance. He defines repentance as: "In the theological and ethical sense a fundamental and thorough change in the hearts of men from sin and toward God. Although faith alone is the condition for salvation (Eph. 2:8-10; Acts 16:31), repentance is bound up with faith and inseparable from it, since without some measure of faith no one can truly repent, and repentance never attains to its deepest character till the sinner realizes through saving faith how great is the grace of God against whom he has sinned. On the other hand, there can be no saving faith without true repentance. Repentance contains as essential elements: (1) a genuine sorrow toward God on account of sin (2 Cor.7:9-10; Matt.5:3-4); (2) an inward repugnance to sin necessarily followed by the actual forsaking of it (Matt.3:8, Acts 26:20; Heb.6:1); and (3) humble self-surrender to the will and service of God (Acts 9:6)" (Unger, p. 1073).

### *Who has Faith*

Hebrews is an excellent book to study when you want to learn more about faith. In Hebrews 11:3 the writer teaches us, "By faith we understand that the universe was formed at

God's command, so that what is seen was not made out of what was visible." The commentary in the NIVDSB gives the following insight for this verse. "The world had a beginning point when out of nothing God created an ordered universe. The Christian experience of faith begins by accepting a personal Creator as the foundation of life. We do not prove a divine Creator through human logic but rather we come by faith to the conviction that God created the world by His word." Christians make no pretense whatsoever that we have scientific proof that creation happened as described in the Bible. It is our faith which guides us in this understanding. We are smart enough to know that not everything can be explained with our current knowledge. Enlightened people are discovering new things about our world every day. By our powers of observation and the internal wisdom which God put in each of us (Romans 1:18-20; 2:14-15), we come to the understanding of God's divine powers in creation. To us, the biblical explanation of creation makes more practical sense than any other out there today.

We must realize however that all people have some measure of "faith". Furthermore, most people with a conscience have been repentant at various times in their lives. Christians do not have a corner on the market for faith or repentance. People in all different cultural groups all around the world have these qualities. The crucial factor is the object of one's faith and the direction of their repentance. Even atheists have faith. They tend to believe in an evolutionary explanation of this world. To believe in the evolutionary theory, since it is a theory and not proven fact, requires faith. There are many fundamental assumptions which this theory requires one to make.

As much as evolutionists deride Christians for the lack of scientific evidence that our God created the heavens and the earth, many of their so-called theoretical assumptions are more comical than they are good science. From the earliest of data, this poorly constructed theory has been fraught with deceptive assertions. With its widely recognized flaws and the growing clamor against the outright falsehoods in its data, evolutionary theory does not even qualify as good science. Talk about fairytales. Where oh where on this earth is this magical species which is half way between leaving what it was and becoming what it will be? If evolutionists cannot find an actual living, breathing animal, at least show us some acceptable fossils of this ever happening? Did evolution across species just suddenly stop? Where is this mythical monkey which is on its way to being a man? They try to claim the reason none of this shows up in nature is because evolution takes a long, long time. How convenient. None of us will live long enough to disprove their theories. Since none of us can disprove it, that is their proof. Now that's a nice racket.

Do you remember from high school biology the phrase "ontogeny recapitulates phylogeny"? Ernst Haeckel drew what was to represent the embryonic development of a fish, salamander, tortoise, chick, hog, calf, rabbit, and human. The similarities were amazing. Haeckel submitted this to Darwin as proof that all animals start out looking very similar during their embryonic development. Darwin was greatly impressed by these sketches. However, it was all a hoax. Ernst Haeckel had faked his data in order to give support to Darwin's theory (Nancy Pearcey, Total Truth, Crossway Books, Wheaton, 2005, pages 163-165). With current research technology, scientists have found Haeckel's assertion to be completely false. Even with this knowledge, somehow these falsified sketches continue to this day to appear in biology textbooks. Worse yet, many scientists at that time knew he had faked his sketches. Why do you suppose they kept quiet? This book by Nancy Pearcey does an excellent job of exposing the pseudo-science behind evolutionary theory.

By the way, remember Darwin's famous study of the finches on the Galapagos Islands? Subsequent studies revealed an incorrect interpretation by Darwin of the data (Pearcey, Total Truth, pages 158-160). Darwin purposed the variations in the lengths of the finches' beaks showed genetic adaptation as the result of environmental changes. These transformations were suggested to be the result of rainfall shortages triggering genetic changes for the more adaptive finches. Thus, survival of the fittest had its champions. Fortunately for scientific truth, later studies by unbiased researchers showed these were merely seasonal variations in beak length and not an act of evolutionary development. So many questions and so little empirical data. So much for the noble evolutionary scientists. Why do the evolutionists continue in their ruse? Admitting the truth would be abhorrent to them. Then they would have to face the God they have spent so much time defacing. This sends chills down their backs.

There are so many unanswered questions with the theory of evolution. From where did the first cell which supported life come? How did it align with the next cell? How did these cells happen to come together in such close proximity that they were able to combine? How did this planet's elements originally come together to support life? How is it that the sun and the moon are exactly aligned to provide our earth with warmth and gravity without destroying it? No, most people think that religion is not being taught in our public schools. The evolutionary theorists know better. Evolution has become their religion. It is what they turn to when trying to explain life. Their most insurmountable problem is they try to offer an explanation of creation which, according to them, started without a creator. Who or what began the whole process is a tremendous stumbling block for them. In my opinion, it requires more faith to believe in the evolutionary explanation of creation than it does to believe in

Yahweh. As you think about it, this flawed explanation of life does not even qualify as a good religion. A good religion offers hope. With this theory all you get is a meaningless life where you become an insignificant cog in the machinery of nature. Think about that for a moment. No wonder most of these people end up bitter. Man has a natural yearning for meaning and personal significance. This is so universal that each culture has its own stories about how they seek to discover the deeper meaning to life. Evolutionary theory totally destroys this. Their souls are cut off from the One True Source which can elevate them to spiritual fulfillment. For this, they are to be pitied.

In the interest of appeasing everyone, please do not think that you can combine the story of creation as given in the Bible with evolutionary theory and in so doing think you have come up with a compromise explanation. God does not work that way. God says He created the heavens and the earth. Evolutionary theory denies God completely. The two are competing religions. No combination of the two is possible without completely disemboweling both in the process. There is no hyphenated Creationism-Evolutionary Theory. God's Word is to be sufficient for us. We need not go any further. Christian scientists help us to better understand our world. They do not explain God; they help us to recognize His handiwork.

All I have to do for my mind to accept Jehovah God as the Creator is to look up at the heavens, admire the stars, watch a mountain stream teeming with trout as it flows along its journey to the valley below, gaze upon the spectacle of a beautiful landscape where the sun is setting just above the trees as they stand so majestically and all of nature comes together at that moment in amazing wonderment, or better yet, to hold a precious baby in my arms, look into its eyes, see it smile, listen to it laugh, and then I know that the mysterious feeling stirring in my heart is there to help me know that God Almighty designed all of this. My mind is sufficiently rational to recognize that the harmony of our universe did not just happen. It has to be the handiwork of a Master Designer. There is way too much intelligence in its design for these things to have happened by mere chance. Adonai designed all of this for us. We are His and He is our Creator. I have to admire the evolutionists for their tenacity though. At least they are willing to fight for what they believe (unlike many of our Christian lawmakers). Please support your local lawmakers and Christian scientists who are starting to battle with these evolutionists in our schools. They need our prayers and support.

A large number of people place their faith in government and its various agencies. Some are very proud. They lust for power. Government is an avenue for them to attain this power. Recognition, status, and prestige drive them to aspire to political office. Big government replaces God in their minds. They become the ones wielding the power. This allows them to mistakenly feel like they are in charge. Power like this is a fleeting thing. Sadly, they will have been using their talents to aggrandize themselves rather than our Lord Jesus. Others realize how vulnerable they are in this difficult world, so they turn to other people to provide them with protection and sustenance. The social group expands to become the government. The government becomes the one thing they turn to when confronted with life's problems. They feel powerless, so they seek the power which is found in government to reassure themselves. In their eyes, the government is to care for them, protect them, and give them the assurance that their life matters. Wrongs are made right; people are given their basic needs. Can you not see how some have come to view the government as their god? Here the person is making an assumption that those in government are worthy of their faith. Personally, I find it easier to believe in an ethereal Being than to believe that governmental bureaucrats and politicians hold my best interests at heart.

When atheists, agnostics, Buddhists, Hindus, Islamics, etc. determine they have gone down the wrong path in life, they are said to be repentant if they: (1) are sorrowful for what they have done, (2) turn from the bad behavior and (3) toward an acceptable behavior. The difference is when we come to such a point in life, we orient ourselves towards El Shaddai, The Lord God Almighty. He is the target of our faith and repentance. Other groups have something else as their target. It is important that we recognize other people will have similar practices to us. This is where Satan is so masterful. He makes them look so close to us with regards to certain behaviors and moral codes that it makes us look like a bunch of exclusionists for questioning them. Are they not doing what we are doing? Does not their worship process follow much the same as our worship practices? Do they not believe with all their hearts that they are right, just like we believe we are right? It does not matter though that they follow our behaviors. It does not matter how strongly they hold to their beliefs. What matters is the object to which we are oriented. There is only one true God. To be more precise, there is one Triune God. <u>Without all *three* members of the Godhead, the religion is rendered false because it is incomplete</u>. Rather than Christians being exclusionists, it is they who are excluding someone – Christ Jesus. Sadly for the nonbelievers, the One and only One who can save them is being rejected by them.

The work of the Holy Spirit is to point us to Christ as the Savior to the world. Matthew 1:18-20 teaches that Mary conceived Jesus through the Holy Spirit. From that start, the Holy Spirit continues to point people to Christ. In John 14:26 Jesus reveals the work of the Holy Spirit, "But the Counselor, the Holy Spirit, whom the Father will send in my name, will teach you all things and will remind you of everything I have said to you." Hebrews 10:10-18 declares that the Holy Spirit directs us to the saving power which can only be found in Jesus.

No other religion has a source for salvation like we do. Our salvation is freely given us by grace from Adonai because He is our loving Lord and Creator. Grace is given without merit. Better still, it is open to *all* who will believe in the Son of God (John 3:14-18). All other religions require works and adherence to countless rules. It is my understanding that none of the other world religions allow you to know with absolute certainty while you are still alive here on earth that your redemption is secured for all eternity. They do not have this assurance. This faith in Christ Jesus and this alone is what determines whether you live inside of God's blessings or outside of them. You can be a good person. You can be a great person. You can pay your taxes. You can obey all of this country's laws and be a good neighbor. You can give to charities. You can feed the homeless. You can donate your time and money to helping children who are disadvantaged. None of this matters though in terms of your spiritual salvation. <u>If you do not have Jesus Christ as your spiritual center-point, then you are lost</u>. God does not demand that we be "good little boys and girls" each and every day of our lives. What He does demand is that we accept His Son as our Lord and Savior. In John 14:6 Jesus makes this strongest of emphatic statements concerning our path to salvation, "I am the way and the truth and the life. No one comes to the Father except through me." God sent Jesus to us for our redemption and we are to receive Him as our Redeemer. Anything less will be rendered insufficient on Judgment Day (Revelation 19:9, 20:11-15).

Redemptive faith is believing that God is who He says He is and believing that He does what He says He will do. In John 3:16 God teaches us what? That if we will believe in His Son, we will have everlasting life. God says Jesus is His

Son, therefore Jesus is God also. Jesus is part of the essence of God the Father. That is what we are to believe. God also says we are to believe in His promises. His promise here is eternal life for those who accept Jesus Christ as their Lord and Savior. Do you believe with all your heart and soul that God's words in John 3:16 are true? If so, then your soul is safe.

### *Temptation Either Refines or Tarnishes Our Spirit*

Do not be mistaken, there is constant spiritual warfare going on between the forces of good and evil in this world. I know this sounds like something out of the 19th century but it is nevertheless true. Satan does not stop trying to influence you the moment you become a Christian. Remember the story of the temptations of Christ (Matthew 4:1-11). Satan even tried to negate the mission of Jesus for this world through his temptations. If he tried it with Jesus, why would it not seem plausible that he would be constantly trying these deceptions with us? If he cannot win you to his side, he at least wants to neutralize you. He wants as many lost souls to accompany him to hell as possible. He hates Adonai (Our Lord and Master) for the punishment God has sentenced him to serve. It appears he is still quite upset about being kicked out of heaven.

C. S. Lewis in <u>Mere Christianity</u> gives an excellent explanation for the spiritual battles going on in our world. He states, "Christianity thinks this Dark Power (Satan) was created by God, and was good when he was created, and went wrong. Christianity agrees with Dualism that this universe is at war. But it does not think this is a war between independent powers. It thinks it is a civil war, a rebellion, and that we are living in a part of the universe occupied by the rebel. Enemy-occupied territory – that is what this world is. Christianity is the story of how the rightful king has landed, you might say landed in disguise, and is calling us all to take part in a great campaign of sabotage" (pages 45-46). To continue with this line of thought, we Christians are part of the counterinsurgency. It is our job to try to take back what God originally designed in the Garden of Eden. Some day we will be part of a victorious celebration, but until then, we must recognize our enemy for the cunning which he possesses.

To be accurate, actually the victory has already been won. When Christ died and then was resurrected, the victory over death and sin was achieved (1 Corinthians 15:55-57). Dr. Henry Blackaby in Experiencing the Cross gives us some wonderful insight on this topic. He warns us that not all that we face is spiritual warfare. Some of it is the chastening of our heavenly Father. Blackaby says, "if you can't tell the difference between spiritual warfare and God's discipline of His children, you're in serious trouble" (p. 89). I have to admit, sometimes I am confused. I tend to think that Satan is tempting me when I am struggling. If I remember back to my prayer requests, I can usually trace it back to asking God to help me with certain behavioral or character flaws. How can God help me to improve if He does not give me tests? When I do wrong during these tests, it is certainly in my best interest that my loving heavenly Father disciplines me. My earthly father certainly disciplined me. Dad never did it out of meanness or hostility. He knew that for me to grow to be the person I should be, occasionally firm discipline was required. I love him for loving me enough to take on the hard task of being a parent. Our heavenly Father is even more so.

Blackaby is very helpful here in reminding us that God is more in the business of refining us than the devil is in the business of tripping us up. One way to tell is by the severity of the situation. Blackaby states, "When God disciplines His children, it's far more severe than anything Satan ever does to us. Nowhere in Scripture do I see that Satan ever destroyed the people of God, but when you look at the biblical record of God's discipline, He *did* destroy His people. In Old Testament times He crushed the nation of Israel and sent them into captivity. So we need to be very consciously aware of the seriousness of attributing the activity of our Father God to Satan. <u>If we keep on blaming everything negative or painful in our lives on the devil, we may very well miss the good and loving work of discipline and training God seeks to accomplish in our lives</u>" (p.90). I am so very thankful for these profound words from Dr. Blackaby. I have to admit that I fall into this trap at times. With his instruction, I will work harder to make sure I reflect on negative events and try to see where the hand of God may be. To think Satan is tempting me is one thing. In a way, that is a badge of honor. To realize that God is disciplining me is a whole other story. It sends chills down my spine. I certainly do not want to confuse these events. As I have said before, I am so very thankful for the godly men who have written books which had added to my understanding of the sanctification process. Their service to the kingdom is to be praised.

With regards to temptation, Satan relishes accusing believers before God of our weaknesses and our failures. As in Job 1:6-12, the devil roams the earth, along with his band of lesser demons trying to destroy our relationship both with God the Father and with all mankind. Once you are sealed with the Holy Spirit because you have pledged your faith in Jesus Christ as your Lord and Savior, that is not the end of Satan trying to discourage you. It is only the beginning of him trying to neutralize the effectiveness of your witness to others. He wants weak Christians. He wants timid Christians. He wants believers who are not active in their faith. His henchmen are everywhere. Their jobs are to constantly try to trip up the faithful. How do they do this? By presenting temptations to you and trying to influence your choices. Just as we have angels all around ministering to us (Matthew

4:11, Daniel 6:22, Hebrews 1:14), Satan has his evil spirits trying to counteract our influence with others. Perhaps our ministers should preach a few more "hell fire and brimstone" message so what I am trying to communicate here would not sound so far out.

Temptation is Satan's instrument of enticement to encourage us to live his kind of life. <u>God does not consider it a sin if we are tempted</u>. <u>What we *do* as the result of Satan's temptations determines whether we are sinful or obedient</u>. To resist temptation we should follow Jesus' example (Matthew 4:1-11): (1) pray for the Holy Spirit to strengthen and guide us, (2) quote favorite Scriptures to defend us from Satan's attempts to sway us away from obedience to God, and (3) remove ourselves from that situation. Being obedient to God requires focus and commitment.

Pride, gratification of our sexual lusts, and greed are three of Satan's favorite instruments of temptation. God wants us to counter these impulses with (1) humility, (2) service, and (3) compassion. These latter three take the emphasis off ourselves and places it on our relationship with God and our fellow man. Refer to 1 Corinthians 10:13, "No temptation has seized you except what is common to man. And God is faithful; He will not let you be tempted beyond what you can bear. But when you are tempted, He will also provide a way out so that you can stand up under it." Now read 2 Timothy 2:22, "Flee the evil desires of youth, and pursue righteousness, faith, love and peace, along with those who call on the Lord out of a pure heart." Paul gives excellent advice here. I have followed it many times. Unfortunately, there have been a number of times where I seem to have forgotten these words of wisdom. As I grow in my faith, I try not to forget them any more.

What is the purpose for God allowing Satan to tempt us? <u>When we are tested, if we resist the temptation this will strengthen our character and deepened our commitment</u>

to God. Paul and Peter both speak extensively about how resisting temptations build perseverance, character, and holiness (Romans 5:3-4 and 1 Peter 1:13-16). Remember what Peter admonishes us for in 1 Peter 1:15-16. "But just as He who called you is holy, so be holy in all you do; for it is written: 'Be holy, because I am holy.'" Therein is the purpose of testing – to refine our relationship with God. He is holy; therefore He calls us to pursue holiness. Testing is one of the tools God uses in the process of refinement. All of this is to help us pursue holiness. When we fail, that means there is more work to be done. Call on the Holy Spirit to give you the perseverance sufficient to continue the fight. Do not give up on yourself. Remember, Elohim never gives up on us. I know – it's what I'm counting on.

With reference to resisting temptation, you cannot have cherished sin (Psalm 66:18) in your life and expect forgiveness. Cherished sins are willful sins which you know even before committing them that these are wrongful acts. Moreover, these are sins which you cherish (you value them, you take pleasure in them). I am not referring to the daily sins we inadvertently commit. Cherished sins are intentional sins which we give greater value to than we value pleasing God. With these sins present, your request for forgiveness would be insincere, thus unacceptable. If you are not willing to turn away from that sin, then your repentance of the sin is disingenuous. Some mistakenly have the audacity to beseech God with a laundry list of prayer requests, while holding on to coveted sins. This is a very hard lesson for many. When our backs are to the wall (as in the case of illness or financial hardships), we want to cry out to God. We expect Him to hear our prayers. The problem is, if we have perpetual sin in our lives at that moment, God has to say 'No' to our request. Why? God takes sin seriously. This is due to His character of being holy and righteous. Rewarding us with blessings while we are unrepentant would go against His character.

Although this world may be confused about sin, God is not. Although this world shows a great proclivity towards minimizing sin, God does not.

Psalm 51 is an excellent account of repentance by David after his coming to grips with his sinful actions with Bathsheba. David displayed his conviction of the sin when he cried out, "For I know my transgressions, and my sin is always before me. Against you, you only, have I sinned and done what is evil in your sight" (v. 3-4). David revealed his repentance when he begged God, "Create in me a pure heart, O God, and renew a steadfast spirit within me" (v. 10). David showed he wanted to turn away from his sin and re-center his life on God. The NIV Disciple's Study Bible commentary on these verses states, "The proper function of guilt is to lead us to take full responsibility for our sin, to recognize that sin ultimately relates to God and alienates us from Him, and to confess God's justice rather than trying to justify ourselves. Those who repent trust God's love, seek to get rid of sin and guilt, acknowledge that all sin is against God, do not try to justify themselves in any way, and ask for new dedication and a new start." Read this again. It will make a difference in your prayer life.

God knows the heart of man. David knew this and that is why he did not try to justify his sin in Psalm 51. To try to explain our sins to God is an affront to His holiness and omniscience. Listen to the sagacious advice David gave to Solomon in 1 Chronicles 28:9, "And you, my son Solomon, acknowledge the God of your father, and serve Him with wholehearted devotion and with a willing mind, for the Lord searches every heart and understands every motive behind the thoughts. If you seek Him, He will be found by you; but if you forsake Him, He will reject you forever." So there is no use in thinking you can spin your story hoping Jehovah God accepts your words at face value. Repentance is where

God deals with the hypocrites, the insincere, and those who do not turn from their wicked ways.

## *The Nature of Faith*

What is the nature of faith? As I have stated, I do not have a seminary degree so I do not know what the intellectuals espouse but I do know what I have experienced in life. I believe faith has both qualitative and quantitative aspects – somewhat like ice cream, if you will. My wife and I enjoy a small bowl of ice cream at night. We watch our weight, so a little ice cream doesn't hurt. Some brands of ice cream are better than others. Ice cream has both qualitative and quantitative components. When the quality is not so high, I find myself eating more just to satisfy my sweet tooth. I might even add some chocolate syrup just to give it a little more pizzazz. Of course, this adds considerably to the calories. Now that's my justification for my wife buying the premium brand – works for us.

Jesus scolds the disciplines for having little faith in Matthew 8:23-27. "And when He was entered into a ship, His disciples followed Him. And, behold, there arose a great tempest in the sea, insomuch that the ship was covered with the waves: but He was asleep. And His disciples came to Him, and awoke Him, saying, Lord, save us: we perish. And He saith unto them, 'Why are ye fearful, O ye of little faith?' Then He arose, and rebuked the winds and the sea; and there was a great calm. But the men marveled, saying, 'What manner of man is this, that even the winds and the sea obey Him!'" These same men grew not only in the amount of their faith but in the quality of their faith as the New Testament stories of their lives unfold.

The qualitative component of faith is shown in us when our faith becomes so steadfast that we are willing to charge the gates of hell armed only with water pistols, if He commands us. Peter and John had that kind of faith. In Acts 4:1-21 it teaches us about the boldness of Peter before the Sanhedrin. He defended his belief that Jesus is the Messiah and that the Jews unjustly crucified Him. Peter was not willing to allow the Sanhedrin to intimidate him and thereby stop him from preaching the Good News. Go to your Bible and read these verses. This is the same Peter who denied Jesus three times only two months earlier. Peter's faith was transformed into a higher quality by his gut-wrenching repentance for denying Christ that fateful morning. This transformation continued with his subsequent restoration by Jesus before our Lord's ascension. Peter then became "the rock". God took a failure and then strengthened the believer. What a remarkable testament this is for Romans 8:28, "And we know that in all things God works for the good of those who love him, who have been called according to his purpose." As then, God is still in the business of maturing our faith. Is your faith getting better with age?

It seems to me a person's quality of faith is in direct proportion to their repentance. The result of having a greater determination to rid yourself of any immoral behavior (repentance) will produce a greater quality of faith. Does the sorrow over your sins weigh you down? Do you feel burdened by the wrongs you have done (Matthew 5:4)? Or do you just hate that you got caught? Are you embarrassed but probably you will repeat these offenses again? What separates a casual believer from genuine believers is genuine believers are more sincere and more determined to turn away from their sins and turn towards God. They are more God-oriented and less self-directed.

Most people however have a measure of repentance. An alcoholic may repent of this disease and turn away from ever drinking again. If that alcoholic is a nonbeliever, then they turn away from a life of drinking in excess and toward a life of sobriety. If the alcoholic is a believer, then they turn away from a life of drinking in excess and toward a life which is God-centered. The difference is that Christians have God as their point of orientation for faith and repentance whereas nonbelievers focus on something other than God. Spiritual repentance is a key determinate of whether your faith is acceptable to God for your eternal salvation.

### *The Three Components of Faith*

As I see it, saving faith has three basic components: belief, commitment, and trust. You must *believe* that God is who He says He is. In other words, you accept the numerous attributes which the Bible reveals to us that our heavenly Father possesses. Each time you read a Bible story or hear a sermon, ask yourself what that teaches you about the character of God. Some of Jehovah's attributes are Him being: holy, righteous, loving, wise, forgiving, glorious, majestic, prophetic, omnipotent, sovereign, stern, tender, kind, patient, redeeming, resourceful, healing, faithful, timeless, creative, compassionate – get the picture? All things which are good, God is. For your beliefs to grow to where they support a resolute faith, you have to know God. Prayer is an excellent thing to do but it does not replace biblical studies and attending corporate worship. For you to know that you know you are going to heaven, you have to first know who it is offering this plan of salvation. Working on incomplete knowledge can lead you to making an unwise decision.

How do we develop a rock solid belief in our Triune God? The psychological progression of thoughts and ideas becoming attitudes has long captured the interest of social scientists. Emotions play a major role in transforming basic thoughts into the cohesive mental structures which we refer to as attitudes. At the core, these thought patterns unite around a topic – religion, sexual identity, politics, economics, social interactions, family dynamics, national identification, education, work ethics, leisure activities, etc. The list is almost endless. What make attitudes resistant to change are the emotions which surround them. These emotions denote a measure of like or dislike. Psychologists refer to this as the approach/avoidance paradigm. We become attracted to things which we like. Things which we dislike, we tend to avoid. Attitudes and beliefs are supposed to help steer us into successfully interacting with our world. Of course, we do not always correctly process these mental constructs. Here is one of the obstacles for faith. Our culture often promotes attitudes which are contrary to God's will. When believers encounter this, they must approach the situation with as much love as possible in order to defuse the negative emotions which some have built up concerning Christianity.

Good missionaries tend to be excellent social psychologists (whether they know they are or not). On the mission field, you have to become rather proficient at sizing up people and situations. Missionaries know love and fear are the strongest of emotions. They know attitudes and beliefs flow along the continuum for approach (like/love) and avoidance (dislike/fear). As more confirming experiences arise, these attitudes group themselves into primary, secondary, and tertiary beliefs (more about this in Chapter Five). The point here is that beliefs are supported by well cultivated mental and emotional frameworks. They are slow to develop and, likewise, very resistant to change. This presents a fundamental challenge when working with nonbelievers.

Beliefs play a very important role in our lives. Our beliefs guide us in helping us to better understand the world. They assist us in processing new information as it relates to previous experiences or knowledge. More importantly, they direct us in making decisions and judgments. The better we feel about our track record in making decisions based on these attitudes and beliefs, the more credence we place in them. Belief in God is the result of a series of confirming experiences where our knowledge of Jehovah is in agreement with what we hear, see, and read about God. Our daily life experiences either confirm or reject the notion of the Christian God. When someone is living in a culture filled with darkness, it is very difficult for their life experiences to confirm the existence of a loving, holy God. This is where they have to be willing to listen to the urgings which God places in each of us to seek Him.

As these mental frameworks of what we think about God become engrained in our minds, our beliefs filter any new messages which relate to God. The more we understand the true nature of God, the stronger our steadfastness becomes. Contradictory and inaccurate information confuse our beliefs. People who learn a little about Jesus but then reject Him are those who have had difficulty in assimilating the truths of the Scriptures. Their cultural or social network may have been in great contrast to the teachings of our Lord. Basically, beliefs have to be cultivated. God gave us the Holy Bible in order to cultivate these beliefs.

This is where reading all 66 books of the Bible have a great advantage. You get to see the common threads of God's many characteristics being woven together so that those who seek Him will truly find Him (Deut. 4:29, Psalm 9:10, Matthew 7:7). A believer cannot fully know who God says He is if they only read the New Testament. Please make it a part of your daily Bible studies to turn to the clean white pages of the Old Testament. They certainly will turn better when you are in church if they have been turned by you at home. There are many, many great stories in the Old Testament. In addition to it being an indispensable part of the Bible, it is great literature. The wisdom of the Proverbs, the solace of the Psalms, the battles of the Israelites, the frustrations of the Old Testament prophets – all of these make great reading. Learn how God dealt with His chosen people when they were leaving Egypt. Read of the kings of Israel and how they prospered and failed. Each story gives us additional insights into the character of Yahweh. God reveals Himself to us as we read these biblical stories and we ask ourselves, "What does this lesson teach me about who God is?" These lessons not only strengthen our faith but they give us valuable evidence that God really is who He says He is. The bottom line is, once we know the character of God, we get a very good profile of how God wants us to live.

Next, we must *trust* that God does what He says He will do. This means we trust in His sovereign plan as the *only* source for our eternal redemption. Like beliefs, trust takes time. With trust, there is a certain predictive validity which must be achieved. By this I mean, a person has to be comfortable in feeling they can anticipate what a person or thing will do in a particular situation. This is why God gave us prophets. He wants us to know we can predict what will happen by knowing God's will in our lives. Here is the challenge – it is hard to be committed to someone we do not trust. It is hard to trust someone we do not know. The more our beliefs confirm that God is who He says He is, the more we can trust that He does what He says He will do. Often this trust is tested because we do not always see the evidence of God in all aspects of our lives. Only as you mature in the sanctification process can you see God's fingerprints on every situation, even those which cause us great pain or disappointment.

In addition, there is an action component to our faith. We must make a *commitment* to seeking God's kingdom, worshipping and praising Him as the only true God, and living a righteous life which reflects the teachings of our Lord Jesus. We must be obedient to the commands and instructions which God presents to us in order to fulfill this commitment. This is to be a total commitment – partial commitments are not acceptable to God. He is a jealous God (Joshua 24:19-20) and wants all of our allegiance. By this I mean our Triune

God is to be the *only* God we worship and praise. We are not to have God first and then money, status and personal enjoyment are to follow as lesser gods. No, commitment means absolutely no divided loyalty between Jehovah God and any other object for our worship and praise.

As we grow in our faith, we come to the realization that our commitment to being obedient to God's will is a sign of wisdom rather than a lack of freedom of our own will. Obedience reflects commitment. We commit to Jehovah God that He is the object of our faith and we promise to be steadfast in our service to His kingdom. Our commitment to God's will is often challenged by our own selfish interests, desires, and priorities. As we mature, our faith helps to encourage us to follow our godly commitments, even when our own desires conflict. The sanctification process is a constant refinement of our beliefs, trust, and commitment to God.

Just as faith has multiple elements (belief, trust, and commitment), each of these components has their own special mixtures of the following ingredients: our thoughts, attitudes, motivations, emotions, and experiences. Developing a steadfast faith in God requires time because so many ingredients must coalesce in order for this faith to become a defining part of our life. A transformed life is a process, not an immediate status. New thoughts and attitudes are dynamic. Our faith is ultimately to be rock solid, right? In order for this to happen, all of these ingredients must bond together to form a mental network supporting a united spiritual framework.

For this to be achieved, we must have a series of confirming experiences which validate the accuracy of our burgeoning belief system (more on this in Chapters Five and Six). For this validation to occur in our spiritual life, God's Word has to "come alive" in our lives. Why do you think the Holy Spirit inspired these 40 men to record the various books of the Bible? So we can experience God in a variety of ways and settings to enable our faith in God's Word to be substantiated by what we each experience as individuals. Certainly there are individual differences, but at the core, we all face many of the same spiritual issues. Each of us should identify with the spiritual landscape of the Bible. The interwoven thread throughout the Bible is that the human spirit faces very similar challenges across all the generations. This is why the message of God is as pertinent today as it was 2000 years ago. The Bible is an indispensable guide for your life. These stories are about issues which continue to happen today. Of course there are cosmetic differences, but the basic nature of man has not changed over our recorded history. Prayer and Bible reading are essential to the maturation of our faith. As Peter said in 1 Peter 4:12, we should not be surprised by the things happening to us. They have all happened before.

Basically, this phenomenon we call life is a very complicated journey where a collection of people can experience the same thing yet come away with very different thoughts and impressions. Nowhere is this difference more evident than in the Parable of the Sower. This is because the dynamics of all the above mentioned ingredients flavor each person's perception of an event differently. People process the same bit of information in their own way, based on their existing thoughts, emotions, attitudes, desires, and beliefs. This is why it is so important to reach young people. They have less conflicting experiences and beliefs which act as a filter for new thoughts and ideas. You can see the truth in this each Sunday morning. A congregation can hear a sermon and each will take away whatever their minds seized on and what spoke to their particular interests and needs. This is why we are all unique. Our own set of beliefs filters each new experience. Moving someone along the path to redemptive faith requires patience and wisdom in helping them to process this unmerited gift our Lord is offering us. Keep in mind, the message of the Good News is radically different from anything else they have ever heard.

Precisely for this reason is why missions minded churches will send mission groups into the same area year after year. Some will plant the seeds of Christianity while others will harvest the crop which someone else planted many years prior. Is this not what Paul is saying in 1 Corinthians 3:5-9? Unshakeable faith requires many confirming experiences. Quick success in the mission field often yields deceptive results. Listen to what Jesus is trying to teach us in the Parable of the Sower. This parable highlights the validity of our discussion on the components of faith.

### *Matthew 13:3-9, 18-23 "The Parable of the Sower"*

The focal passage of this book can be found in Matthew 13:3-9, 18-23 (the focal message is Romans 3:21-28). Please read these verses carefully. Feast on them. Savor them like a fine meal. Read the commentaries so you can grow in your understanding of the basic truth which Jesus wants His followers to attain. Remember the promise which Jesus made: God will bless the person who hungers for His Word (Matthew 5:6).

Jesus was sitting by a lake and the crowd grew so large that He had to get in a boat in order to be seen and heard. Matthew 13:3-9, "Then He told them many things in parables, saying: "A farmer went out to sow his seed. As he was scattering the seed, some fell along the path, and the birds came and ate it up. Some fell on rocky places, where it did not have much soil. It sprang up quickly, because the soil was shallow. But when the sun came up, the plants were scorched, and they withered because they had no root. Other seed fell among thorns, which grew up and choked the plants. Still other seed fell on good soil, where it produced a crop—a hundred, sixty or thirty times what was sown. He who has ears, let him hear."

In our Lord's Parable of the Sower, Jesus teaches us about faith and the human condition. Jesus explains this parable in Matthew 13:18-23. <u>The sowing of the seeds represents the truth of God as sown by Jesus, His Son</u>. This story reveals the truth about how various people receive the word of God. Those who walk with the Lord produce fruits from their labors of love. This walk demonstrates to others their genuine, redemptive faith. Faith always has an action component. In this parable, the seeds (the Gospels) are received in four different ways: 1) total rejection, 2) casual head knowledge which produces joy but is not yet life transforming, 3) passive acceptance but is not yet heart knowledge, which would produce action; more like nominal belief but nothing steadfast, and 4) mature, life transforming faith which produces fruitful Christian behavior. This passive acceptance or nominal belief is what some may call moderate faith. Moderate faith is the battle grounds for our discussion because it can be so deceptive. The people who represent this group are what I call CINO's (Christians In Name Only). Our commitment to Christ Jesus has to produce fruit in order to be considered mature faith. By fruit, it is meant that our character traits reflect the fruits of the Spirit (Galatians 5:22-23). These traits enable us to do the work of our Lord. They allow us to be a light to the world. Therefore, passive acceptance is no faith at all – it is masquerading as faith but it really is not redemptive faith. <u>Faith is to be considered redemptive only when it moves you to become like Jesus, not just to know Him in an intellectual sense</u>.

Read your Bible. It is 66 books by 40 authors filled with wonderful stories which will inspire you. All kinds of fascinating things are there, ready for you to learn. You will gain enlightening knowledge of yourself and of mankind. Intriguing stories of heroes and villains can be found in each book. There are stories of people just like yourself who did not have special knowledge or skills but they did have a willingness to seek God's plan for their lives. There is another amazing thing to learn – the demons know more about Jesus than many of us do. They know His power. They know from where He came. Yes, they know Him but they do not place their faith and obedience in Him. They have head knowledge of Him but they follow Satan. Acts 19:13-17 gives a humorous account of a demon possessed man giving a severe beating to 7 men who claimed to exorcise demons in Jesus' name. The evil spirit said, "Jesus I know and I know about Paul, but who are you?" He then overpowered them and gave them a good thrashing. Their mistake was they presented themselves as persons with authority through Jesus but they did not know Jesus as their Lord and Savior. The point to this passage is that after that incident, the name of Jesus was treated with more respect and honor throughout that region. <u>Passive acceptance in the form of nominal faith is very dangerous for people who think they have their eternal salvation secured by such faith</u>. Nominal faith deceives others into thinking you are something you are not. You misrepresent Christ to them. That is something which is very unwise to do. It also can deceive you into thinking you have made an adequate life decision when you actually have not.

# Chapter Two The Object of Our Faith – the Holy Trinity

———∞∞∞———

How do we know that God is who He says He is? Read Isaiah 46:9-11. In this passage God proclaims, "Remember the former things, those of long ago; I am God, and there is no other; I am God, and there is none like me. I make known the end from the beginning, from ancient times, what is still to come. I say: My purpose will stand, and I will do all that I please. From the east I summon a bird of prey; from a far-off land, a man to fulfill my purpose. What I have said, that will I bring about; what I have planned, that will I do." As Dr. D. James Kennedy in his book <u>Why I Believe</u> on page 2 tells us, "It is a matter of predictive prophecy" which allows us to know that God is who He says He is. Dr. Kennedy goes on to assert on that page, "The biblical prophecies are quite specific, real, and genuine; they are unique because they do not exist anywhere else. In all the writings of Buddha, Confucius, and Lao-tse, you will not find a single example of predicted prophecy." Dr. Kennedy continues on page 12-13, "Predictions are also promises. <u>I believe that God gave us more than two thousand predictions in order that we may learn to believe His promises</u>. God promised that the walls of Jerusalem would be rebuilt; that the walls of Babylon would never be rebuilt; that Tyre would be destroyed; that Sidon would continue – so that we may believe His promises. He also promised that he that believeth on the Son shall never die, but have everlasting life..." Dr. Kennedy wrote a beautiful book explaining the fundamentals of what he believes. This book is excellent in addressing the issues of faith and I encourage you to read it.

*The existence of God explains the inexplicable.* Things far too wondrous for us to fully comprehend are rendered tenable when we look to see God's creative signature on them. People have the need to know, to understand, to make sense of our world. Man is not wired for chaos. We try to bring order to our lives. We study molecules to better understand how the human body functions. We study the body to better understand life. We go back full circle to the molecular components of life to better understand how we began. The creative splendor of God shows up in *all* these endeavors. The pure majesty of DNA, the double helix structure in the nucleus of cells which supports the fundamental core of life, draws us to God's creative force. Here is His signature. No rational mind can look at this fundamental building block of humanity and not come away with an amazing appreciation for our Creator. Only those who are confused by their prideful rebellion can look at the biology of life and not see evidence of El Shaddai. God does not leave us to our own designs to gain an understanding of Him. We are not without evidence of Him.

How can we be so sure of this belief in God? **Our steadfast belief combines the evidence of His Truth as found in the Holy Scriptures, coupled with the urgings in our heart as it is being drawn by God to worship Him, to produce the assurance Christians have that our faith is correctly established in the Triune God – the Father, the Son, and the Holy Spirit**. El Elyon (The Most High God) put this longing for Him in all people, so we are without excuse (Romans 1:19-20). We will be held responsible by how we respond. It is my firm conviction that <u>belief in God is based on a reasonable assessment of all the evidence</u>. There are over 2000 prophecies in the Old Testament which have been fulfilled (D. James Kennedy, <u>Why I Believe</u>, p 3). As for the man we know as Jesus, 333 prophecies were fulfilled (Kennedy, p.109). The evidence is strong and substantial. The rejection of this evidence reveals an unwilling mind to carefully weigh the truth. <u>No other book in all the world has the Bible's accuracy for prophecy</u>. No, we are not mindless sheep being led around because we have weak souls and have the need for a spiritual crutch. We have healthy minds which know the Truth, regardless of what the scoffers might assert.

### *By His Prophecies We Know Him*

By the accuracy and fulfillment of His prophecies we not only learn that God will do what He says He will do but we also learn a lot about His character (His attributes). Let us start with Isaiah 42:1-9 for a short review of some of these prophesies. Please turn in your Bibles to this passage. Pay particular attention to v. 9, "See, the former things have taken place, and new things I declare; before they spring into being I announce them to you." <u>God is telling us He reveals Himself as the only true God through the accuracy of His prophecies</u>. This particular passage introduces us to Jesus' righteousness. It also lets Israel know that the Messiah is not going to be a great military conqueror like David but rather a suffering servant who "will bring justice to the nations" (v. 1). Israel totally missed the value of this prophecy because they rejected the nature of the prophecy. They wanted military might. In these verses God is trying to let them know that He is more interested in building a future kingdom of believers who have a steadfast faith in His Word and not an earthly nation of great wealth and power. They did not hear

His prophecy because it was not what they wanted to hear. Such was life for Isaiah.

This passage provides us with an excellent example to guide our prayer life. God did not answer the prayers of the Israelites as they prayed for military conquests because He had something better in mind for them. Elohim was offering them an eternal kingdom which would surpass anything imaginable on this earth. It was to be a kingdom established on righteousness. Not by might but by what is right is how God intends for us to live. When the Israelites did not receive the answer to their prayers as they had wished, they totally disregarded God's provision. Does this ever happen with you? The sad thing is that God provided prophets to reveal this to them but they were so caught up in the affairs of this world that they refused to accept this Godly message.

We will continue with Isaiah by turning to chapter 43:10-13. Here El Shaddai proclaims, "You are my witnesses," declares the Lord, "and my servant whom I have chosen, so that you may know and believe me and understand that I am He. Before me no god was formed, nor will there be one after me. I, even I, am the Lord, and apart from me there is no savior. I have revealed and saved and proclaimed—I, and not some foreign god among you. You are my witnesses," declares the Lord, "that I am God. Yes, and from ancient days I am He. No one can deliver out of my hand. When I act, who can reverse it?" God wanted Israel to reflect back on its history and come to repentance. His past prophecies had come to fulfillment, so they should trust in His new prophecies. How many times was Jehovah God to prove Himself to them?

Now go to Isaiah 53:2-12. Unfortunately for the Jews they missed this message as well. Fortunately for the Gentiles, we recognize with humble hearts to whom God is pointing us. This is such a poignant prophecy that I feel compelled to quote it in its entirety. "He (Jesus) grew up before Him

(God) like a tender shoot, and like a root out of dry ground. He had no beauty or majesty to attract us to Him, nothing in His appearance that we should desire Him. He was despised and rejected by men, a man of sorrows, and familiar with suffering. Like one from whom men hide their faces He was despised, and we esteemed Him not. Surely He took up our infirmities and carried our sorrows, yet we considered Him stricken by God, smitten by Him, and afflicted. But He was pierced for our transgressions, He was crushed for our iniquities; the punishment that brought us peace was upon Him, and by His wounds we are healed. We all, like sheep, have gone astray, each of us has turned to his own way; and the Lord has laid on Him the iniquity of us all. He was oppressed and afflicted, yet He did not open His mouth; He was led like a lamb to the slaughter, and as a sheep before her shearers is silent, so He did not open His mouth. By oppression and judgment He was taken away. And who can speak of His descendants? For He was cut off from the land of the living; for the transgression of my people He was stricken. He was assigned a grave with the wicked, and with the rich in His death, though He had done no violence, nor was any deceit in His mouth. Yet it was the Lord's will to crush Him and cause him to suffer, and though the Lord makes His life a guilt offering, He will see His offspring and prolong His days, and the will of the Lord will prosper in His hand. After the suffering of His soul, He will see the light of life and be satisfied; by His knowledge my righteous servant will justify many, and He will bear their iniquities. Therefore I will give Him a portion among the great, and He will divide the spoils with the strong, because He poured out His life unto death, and was numbered with the transgressors. For He bore the sin of many, and made intercession for the transgressors." If you ever doubt the love Jesus has for mankind, you need only to read these verses. Our Lord and Savior left the majesty of heaven and came to earth fully aware of how

He would be received. He came for you and me. Praise be to God in heaven for His holy provision.

Go now to Isaiah 57:1-2. Is this a prophecy or is it a bit of heavenly wisdom? "The righteous perish, and no one ponders it in his heart; devout men are taken away, and no one understands that the righteous are taken away to be spared from evil. Those who walk uprightly enter into peace; they find rest as they lie in death." Have you ever felt that God called a particular person you know home to be with Him in order to spare them from future pain? This is a very intriguing verse. Could God be giving us a prophecy which matches what Jesus said in Revelation 3:10? This verse could apply to an individual or it can apply to a group. If it applies to a group, then this passage may be used to substantiate the rapture theory. This is the concept that the Christian believers of this world will be removed and brought to heaven prior to the tribulation period. Not all Christian denominations believe in this interpretation of eschatological events.

This is where biblical study becomes fun. Daily Bible study is not just a matter of learning verses so we become better educated in how God intends for us to live. Bible study should stimulate your creative thought processes. What a verse means to one person may be a little different from its meaning to someone else. Even more amazing, verses can reveal different bits of heavenly wisdom to the same person but at different periods in their lives. The Holy Spirit will guide you in the proper interpretation of verses if you will learn to stop when you encounter a difficult verse and pray for insight. Reading the Bible should not be like reading a mystery novel or a history textbook. It is meant to be engaging. By this I mean ask God what He wants you to learn from your study. Try to pray before you read the commentaries. It is invigorating and fulfilling when the Holy Spirit puts a progression of thoughts into your mind and the verse starts to have a clearer meaning to you. After reading the commentaries, it is rewarding to find that your thoughts are confirmed by men and women who are biblical scholars. God is so good.

Prophecies teach us about the character of the God we serve. Elohim is always faithful to His promises. For example, Genesis 17:16, 21 and 21:1-3 cover the prophecy God gave concerning a son for Abraham and Sarah. This was a very specific prophecy which God fulfilled. Despite their advanced age, God delivered on His promise. Look at Genesis 18:14 – nothing is too hard for God. Though we may lose our patience (as Sarah did), God is always faithful in His promises. This is one of the major lessons El Elyon is trying to teach us with His multitude of prophecies. <u>He will do what He says He will do</u>. If He promises to bless us, we can be assured of these blessings. When He promises His wrath if we rebel, we can be assured of His wrath. This should increase our trust in His word.

What we have to learn is that God's timetable and our time line are not necessarily in sync. This is where faith comes in. It is always about faith. <u>Prophecies help bolster our faith by God proving that He is steadfast to His promises</u>. El Shaddai also proves His sovereign dominion over man and nature with certain prophecies. As for man, just because some are not smart enough to recognize the fulfillment of these prophecies does not mean they did not happen. The skeptics will always try to find holes in God's predictions and ultimate fulfillments. This will be to their shame some day.

### *How Do We Know Jesus Is The Messiah*

How do we know that Jesus is God's Son? This is the question every person has to answer to their satisfaction prior to becoming a believer. The foundation for this belief can be found in Isaiah 53; Zechariah 9:9-11; John 3:14-21;

John 9:1-7, 30-33; John 14:10-11, Luke 4:16-21, Luke 5:24 and many other cherished Scriptures in both the Old and New Testaments. Please read John 1:1-18, "<u>In the beginning was the Word</u> (Jesus), and the Word was with God, and <u>the Word was God</u>. He was with God in the beginning. Through Him all things were made...The true light that gives light to every man was coming into the world. He was in the world, and though the world was made through Him, the world did not recognize Him. He came to that which was His own, but His own did not receive Him. Yet to all who received Him, to those who believed in His name, He gave the right to become children of God ...<u>The Word became flesh and made His dwelling among us</u>. We have seen His glory...For the law was given through Moses; grace and truth came through Jesus Christ. No one has ever seen God, but God the One and Only (Jesus), who is at the Father's side, has made Him known." In MacDonald's <u>Believer's Bible Commentary</u> he writes of these verses, "God has fully expressed Himself to mankind in the Person of the Lord Jesus. By coming into the world, Christ has perfectly revealed to us what God is like. By dying for us on the cross, He has told us how much God loves us. Thus Christ is God's living Word to man, the expression of God's thoughts" (p.1466). You either believe this as truth or you do not, but that does not stop this from being Ultimate Truth. Yes, despite modern man's "political correctness", there are moral absolutes and ultimate truths. These come from God. Political correctness comes from the dark and confusing forces warring against God Almighty. Be careful which side you listen to.

Jesus being simultaneously both fully God and fully human is a tremendous challenge to man's logical mind. Turn to Luke 1:26-35 to learn how God planned to bring Jesus into this world. Jesus was begot by the Holy Spirit and Mary in order to make this special condition possible. By His parentage we can see His special roots as being both

God and man. It is a matter of our faith in the truthfulness of the Holy Bible and Jesus' words that we accept this teaching as being true and trustworthy. <u>As we grow in our faith, it will mature to the point to where things which baffle modern man will nonetheless remain as valid in our unshakable faith</u>. As we grow older, we come to realize that not all that we see and do are explicable by modern intelligence. Much is beyond our understanding or technology to discover. That does not keep it from being real; it merely means we do not know the explanation for these things. In matters of faith, a steadfast resolve is our best asset against the assaults of Satan's temptations to destroy our personal relationship with God.

Incarnation is the theological construct covering this topic of Jesus being simultaneously both fully God and fully human. Much debate throughout church history has centered on exactly what is meant by Jesus being both Divine and human. The gospel of John gives the most balanced account of Jesus being both God and human (John 1:1-18, particularly the statements, "In the beginning was the Word", "the Word was God", and "The Word became flesh and made His dwelling among us."). Jesus being equally God and man is certainly one of the defining characteristics of Christianity. It is one of those about which unbelievers have such fun at trying to ridicule us. As I will say many times, in many ways – just because modern man does not understand something, does not make it any less real.

<u>The defense of Jesus being simultaneously fully God and fully man is crucial to our Christian doctrine</u>. It does not matter that it is hard to conceptualize or to explain. As humans, we have limited understanding and we need to admit to ourselves that there are things in this world which seem to defy our logic. I find it humorous that many of us will readily accept that God designed all of the heavens and the earth yet we question the incarnation. The complexity and vastness of our natural world testify to the existence of Intelligent

Design. This idea that God created the heavens and the earth makes perfect sense to us. The Holy Trinity designed all the fowl of the air, the fish of the seas, and the beasts of the fields. They placed the earth precisely where it is so that the sun will properly heat it and the moon will provide exactly the right gravitational pull so that we maintain our consistent orbital pattern. We accept the teachings that Jesus died for our sins and rose on the third day as triumphant over death and sin. We struggle though with His virgin birth and being fully God and fully human simultaneously.

Unbelievers challenge us and we become perplexed in how to explain in logical terms how these two things happened. We should not be disheartened when people disparage our beliefs in God. After all do we not reject their beliefs and explanations? Can they explain in perfectly logical terms how this earth was created? Can they offer a more plausible construction than a universal divine Being which interacts with our lives? Furthermore, who says something has to be logical in order to be factual? It was considered perfectly logical for thousands of years that the sun revolved around the earth. Modern men at the time prior to Copernicus certainly considered such a possibility as the earth revolving around the sun as ridiculous. These men were eventually proved wrong and so will be the case with those who scoff at Jesus being simultaneously fully God and fully man. I believe if the Holy Trinity can pull off all of the above instances of creation, then the Holy Trinity certainly is clever enough to achieve the perfect Incarnation for our Lord and Savior. Rather than trying to explain something which has never been before or repeated since, why do we not merely look to the Bible for what God and Jesus say about this topic?

Twice in the Bible God says He is pleased with His Son Jesus. In Matthew 3:17 after Jesus was baptized God spoke in an audible voice declaring His love for His Son. That verse pretty much sounds to me like Jesus is God's Son and God wants us to know Him as such. Again in Matthew 17:5 at the Transfiguration, God spoke in an audible voice. He declared His love for Jesus and that Jesus Christ is His Son. At the same time, the people traveling with and working around Jesus could see that He was fully man. He ate, slept, drank, became weary, wept, laughed, and even went fishing. He did as we humans do. He had the same bodily needs and functions as we have. He was not more God than human in some circumstances and more human than God in others. What Jesus did have was the clear voice of God the Father communicating directly with His spirit throughout His life. He took these communications and lived an extraordinarily obedient life. We have a Savior who leads by human example, not just Godly commands.

Jesus identified Himself as being the Son of Man (Matthew 8:20, 9:6, 13:37, 17:9, 26:64) and the Son of God (Luke 22:66-70; John 5:25-27, 10:30, 14:8-11). These verses help to establish our faith that Jesus is who He says He is. Jesus declares that He is both the Son of Man and the Son of God. He did not further clarify any of those statements by emphasizing that at certain times He was more God and at certain other times (or ways) He was more human. We cannot try to make it sound more logical by claiming that Jesus was physically human in His body but God in His spirit. Jesus' body could do things which mine cannot. No matter how many times I have tried, I cannot walk on water. Jesus' existence was not limited to being fully God only in His spirit since He could obviously do physical things we cannot. He had to be simultaneously fully God and fully human in order to do the things He did. If His spirit was not fully human as well then the temptations of Christ lose their value (Matthew 4:1-11). We all expect that God, being stronger than Satan, can certainly withstand his temptations.

If Jesus' spirit was totally God, then we lose our identity with that part of Him. Correspondingly, He loses His identification with us. Our struggles would not be His struggles. Our Lord faced everything we face, just as we face them. That is why He is so magnificent. Jesus was fully human and fully God when He fed the five loaves cited in Mark 6:38-44. He felt hunger just like everyone else that day. What He *did* was like no one else on that day. He was obviously like no other human because never before nor since has anyone performed the miracles which Jesus presented to the crowds. His great number of such miracles should prove to any open-minded person that Jesus is a full participant in the Holy Trinity. We know Jesus was fully human also by the physical way in which he died. His blood separated out into its component parts after He took His last breath on the cross (John 19:30-34). This same thing happens to us when we die.

At the crucifixion if Jesus was more God than man, then we have a problem identifying with Him. I can understand His suffering if He was both human and God at that time. I can appreciate the benevolent sacrifice of His human body at that time if He was equally God and human at that time. If He was more God than human, then that diminishes the pain and suffering Jesus did for me. I understand the human pain which would come from such a beating and crucifixion. I do not understand Divine pain. As such, I lose some of my identity with Christ if He was not equally human and God at the crucifixion.

If Jesus was more human than God during His ministry, then I have a problem with that as well. If He was more of a human than being our God, then how did He heal the sick, raise the dead, give the blind their sight, display dominion over evil spirits, and command a violent storm to calm itself? Furthermore, how can He offer forgiveness of our sins? This is where our Lord really drove the Pharisees nuts (Mark 2:1-

12). They declared that only God can do that. They were right, yet so wrong (because Jesus *is* God). If He was not equally God and man while on this earth, then He is a liar. He said in His own words in the above referenced verses that He is the Son of Man and the Son of God. He spoke often of Jehovah God as being His Father (Abba, Mark 14:36) – not just as our heavenly Father but His Father – meaning Jesus and God share in the same essence. Jesus either is or He is not both the Son of God and the Son of Man. We know that Jesus is absolutely not a liar. Never once was anyone able to justly accuse Him of any falsehoods. Jesus is who He says He is. He says He is both the Son of Man and the Son of God and I believe Him.

It is very important to the mission of Jesus that we know and accept Him as being simultaneously both fully God and fully human. His sacrifice at the crucifixion and His subsequent conquering of death and sin at the resurrection would be held in question if He is not who and what He says He is. As Paul puts it in 1 Corinthians 15:13-22, if what the Bible says is not true then we are promulgating a giant fabrication about God and we would be guilty of false teachings.

## *Our Evidence*

Our faith is not based solely on the quotes of God and Jesus claiming to be our divine Creator, Redeemer, and Sovereign Lord. <u>Faith is made certain through the fulfillment of biblical prophecies</u> (Hebrews 11:1). This is our evidence that God is who He says He is and He does what He says He will do. Without the fulfillment of these prophecies over thousands of years, Christianity would be much the same as the other world religions. Even with all the good evidence we have, most people will remain skeptical. This should not dissuade us. God knows His teachings seem strange to the average person.

For a more in-depth study of the specific prophecies relating to Jesus as the Messiah, I will be referencing William MacDonald's <u>Believer's Bible Commentary</u>, in the Supplements section entitled "Prophecies of the Messiah Fulfilled in Jesus Christ" (xviii – xxiii). MacDonald presents 44 prophecies from the Old Testament and relates each of these to the New Testament verses which reflect their fulfillment. Some of these notable prophecies are:

1. Isaiah 9:7 "Of the increase of His government and peace there will be no end, upon the throne of David and over His kingdom…" Luke 1:32 "He will be great, and will be called the Son of the Highest, and the Lord God will give Him the throne of His father David…"
2. Micah 5:2 "But you Bethlehem, Ephrathah, though you are little among the thousands of Judah, yet out of you shall come forth to Me the One to be ruler in Israel…" Luke 2:4- 7 "And Joseph also went up from Galilee, out of the city of Nazareth, into Judea, to the city of David, which is called Bethlehem, because he was of the house and lineage of David…and she brought forth her first-born Son…"
3. Isaiah 7:14 "Therefore the Lord Himself will give you a sign: Behold, the virgin shall conceive and bear a Son, and shall call His name Immanuel." Luke 1:26-31 "Now in the sixth month the angel Gabriel was sent by God to a city of Galilee named Nazareth, to a virgin betrothed to a man whose name was Joseph, of the house of David. The virgin's name was Mary…you will conceive in your womb and bring forth a Son, and shall call His name Jesus."
4. Isaiah 40:3-5 "The voice of one crying in the wilderness: 'Prepare the way of the Lord and make straight in the desert a highway for our God…" Luke 3:3-6 "And he went into all the region around the Jordan, preaching

a baptism of repentance for the remission of sins, as it is written in the book of the words of Isaiah..."

5. Malachi 3:1 "Behold, I send My messenger, and he will prepare the way before Me..." Luke 7:24 "When the messengers of John had departed, He began to speak to the multitudes concerning John: 'What did you go out into the wilderness to see?"

6. Psalm 78:2-4 "I will open my mouth in a parable..." Matthew 13:34 "All these things Jesus spoke to the multitude in parables..."

7. Isaiah 53:3 "He is despised and rejected by men, a man of sorrows and acquainted with grief..." John 1:11 "He came to His own, and His own did not receive Him."

8. Isaiah 53:1 "Who has believed our report? And to whom has the arm of the Lord been revealed? John 12:37 "But although He had done so many signs before them, they did not believe in Him, that the word of Isaiah the prophet might be fulfilled..."

9. Isaiah 53:5 "But He was wounded for our transgressions. He was bruised for our iniquities; the chastisement for our peace was upon Him, and by His stripes we are healed." Romans 5:6-8 "For when we were still without strength, in due time Christ died for the ungodly...But God demonstrates His own love toward us, in that while we were still sinners, Christ died for us."

10. Psalm 22:17-18 "I can count all my bones. They look and stare at me. They divide my garments among them, and for my clothing they cast lots." Matthew 27:35-36 "Then they crucified Him, and divided His garments, casting lots, that it might be fulfilled which was spoken by the prophet..."

11. Psalm 34:20 "He guarded all His bones; not one of them is broken." John 19:32-36 "But the soldiers came...when they came to Jesus and saw that He was already dead,

they did not break His legs…For these things were done that the Scripture should be fulfilled…"

12. Psalm 16:10 "you will not abandon me to the grave, nor will you let your Holy One see decay." Mark 16:6-7 "But he said to them, 'Do not be alarmed. You seek Jesus of Nazareth, who was crucified. He is risen! He is not here. See the place where they laid Him. But go and tell His disciples – and Peter – that He is going before you into Galilee; there you will see Him, as He said to you."

It is good that we review these prophecies periodically. We do not have a religion which is based solely on the wise teachings of dead prophets. We certainly do not have a religion based on myths. Historical evidence abounds to support the authenticity of the Bible and the prophecies therein. It then remains to each person whether they respond to the Holy Spirit drawing them close to Jehovah God or not. Some would remain skeptical even if God Himself from the heavens above announced each Easter in an audible voice that Jesus Christ is His Son and we would do well to place our faith in Him.

The decision to place your total faith in God Almighty is the greatest decision anyone will ever make. It determines where you will be for all of eternity. Be certain that you are right. Jesus teaches us in Revelation 3:10, "Since you have kept my command to endure patiently, I will also keep you from the hour of trial that is going to come upon the whole world to test those who live on the earth." Make no mistake, this world is a test. This verse is cherished by Christians because it is Jesus' indication that we will be raptured up with Him prior to the Great Tribulation. That is one experience I had just as soon miss.

## The Process of Sanctification

Sanctification is the process in salvation by which God conforms the believer's life and character to the life and character of Jesus Christ through the work of the Holy Spirit (Romans 8:29; 1 John 3:2). Jesus declared in His prayer to our heavenly Father recorded in John 17:14-19, "I have given them Your word and the world has hated them, for they are not of the world any more than I am of the world. My prayer is not that You take them out of the world but that You protect them from the evil one. They are not of the world, even as I am not of it. Sanctify them by the truth; Your word is truth. As You sent me into the world, I have sent them into the world. For them I sanctify myself, that they too may be truly sanctified." Paul taught the Corinthians in 2 Cor. 3:18, "And we…are being transformed into His likeness with ever-increasing glory, which comes from the Lord, who is the Spirit." This process of sanctification would be an impossible struggle if God required we do this of our own strength. The Good News is that we can count on God to help us during this process with all of life's challenges. He helps us with our fears, our setbacks, and our heartaches. Elohim works to sustain us when we fail and to strengthen us in our weaknesses (Psalms 34:14, 37:23-24, 55:22). We are to develop a Christ-like character, becoming more like Jesus and less like what the world has molded us into being. In the process, we become what God originally intended us to be.

With all of us, there will be many spikes, slumps, and flat-lines in the sanctification process. Some have a more consistent ascension up the graph than others. These are the people at whom I marvel. They have learned better than most of us how a truly surrendered life to Christ is by far the best life. Satan is constantly tempting us as believers so this process will either be stymied or abandoned. Some people never progress much in their spiritual walk with God. They are the same from one year to the next. When this happens, Satan wins. He did not stop that person from becoming a believer but he has cancelled that person's effectiveness as a witness. Unfortunately, some believers discontinue their relationship with God after a brief period of seeming to flourish. These two groups are the subject of Jesus' Parable of the Sower (Matthew 13:3-9).

If you have become unfruitful, then it is time to do a little spiritual pruning. Cut off the dead weight of your worldly habits and start to grow behaviors which will signify an active Christian life. Without the production of spiritual fruit, Satan takes home the prize. Satan uses guilt and frustration over missing the mark to discourage us and make us feel nothing we can do will please God completely. He knows it is impossible for man to ever be good enough within his own powers to be sinless over any period of time. The devil hopes this will make us feel unworthy and like failures. What we must remember when these feelings of despair hit us is that Jesus judged us "worthy" when He went to the cross for us. With that conviction firmly in your heart, do not allow any other powers of this world to make you feel unworthy or like a failure. Do not allow Satan to stunt your spiritual growth and render your life unproductive.

I think sometimes people confuse the sanctification process with salvation. Those who place a heavy emphasis on "works" seem to deal with salvation as though it is a life-long process. No one should expect that you become a "saint" automatically, but we do become redeemed sinners immediately. Salvation is immediate and God-given. Sanctification is a life-long, continuous process within us. Salvation is given to us by God through His grace and His desire to redeem us. We become sanctified by our free wills focusing on the character of Jesus Christ and allowing the Holy Spirit to guide us into being transformed into Jesus' likeness.

What is the grace of God? It is the unmerited favor of God that provides for our salvation (Eph. 2:8). Grace is God's redemptive love in action. It is unearned by us. It has nothing to do with us but everything to do with God. Jehovah God loves us and desires an eternal relationship with each of us. Grace is the instrument by which He makes it possible. It is because of this attribute of grace that God wired each of us to seek Him. He does not want only a special or chosen group to know Him. El Shaddai wants all of mankind to realize they are His creation and we should turn to Him with our praise and worship.

Sanctification is the process we participate in as repentant sinners to show our wholesome love for God. This love is what Martin Luther in his <u>Commentary on Romans</u> (p. 93) referred to as "caritas love". This is that special condition when you hold the object of your love in highest esteem. It is the apex of your ability to love. Luther goes on to say that "He who loves God merely for the sake of His gifts or the sake of any advantages, loves Him with the lowest form of love, which is with sinful desire. Such (earthly) love means to *use* God, but not to *delight* in God." We should approach God through a desire for a relationship with Him rather than what we want Him to do or not to do for us. As in Matthew 5:45, Jesus teaches us "…He causes His sun to rise on the evil and the good, and sends rain on the righteous and the unrighteous." As both Jesus and Martin Luther point out, both good and bad things happen to both good and evil people. This is part of God's wisdom. <u>If only good things happened to believers, then we would not believe out of faith but out of a desire for personal gain</u> (this is one of the many lessons in the book of Job). <u>We would then become manipulators of God</u>. He is much too wise for this. Our heavenly Father placed in each of us an innate longing to know Him and to worship Him (Romans 1:17-20, 2:13-15). God desires our love, but it must be on His terms. Sanctification is a life-long labor of genuine love and submissive obedience.

This love is not Hollywood's version of romantic love – an emotion of overwhelming feelings. This love which we should have for God involves both a *choice* and an *action*. You choose to love God according to His wishes, rules, and boundaries. It also involves acting on this love. This comes in the form of sharing your heart, your time, and your blessings with others. It is God-centered rather than being self-centered. The choice part is exercising your free will to believe in Him who created all things and His Son who is the Savior of mankind. The action component to godly love involves helping others and following God's commands.

In what ways can our lives demonstrate wholehearted love for God? This can be done by: (1) how we spend our time and our money, (2) how we set our priorities, (3) what we think and talk about, and (4) how we are a positive witness for God. Here is a penetrating question: *if what we do in God's name did not render a blessing for us, would we still do it*? Now we are getting at the heart of caritas love. We are to maintain our service to the Lord as an expression of our wholehearted love for Him and not as a way of manipulating blessings from our heavenly Creator. The nature of our love can be shown, for example, by the quality and quantity of our time and the offerings we render Him as expressions of our hearts. If we do these things as expressions of love rather than expectations of blessings, then were are in a righteous relationship with God. We are certainly allowed to recognize that His blessings flow to us as we honor Him with our love. The point is that blessings are one of the many ways in which God shows His love for us as we grow into the person God originally designed us to be.

Here is an interest morsel of historical insight. It was the writing of Martin Luther's <u>Commentary on Romans</u> which inspired Luther to break with the Catholic Church and its doctrines. He realized what Paul was teaching in the book of Romans was very different from what the traditional teachings were in the Catholic Church at that time. Paul teaches salvation by faith. The Catholic Church had a "works" centered approach to salvation. They also believed baptism was a requirement for salvation. This is not what Paul teaches in Romans. Faith and faith alone is the righteous vehicle for salvation. Martin Luther came to realize this as he was writing this commentary. Luther came to conclude that after faith secures our salvation, love is the basis for our relationship with God, not works or the payment of penances.

One of the many ways we show our mature love for God is by observing His sacraments. Baptism is one such sacrament. While baptism is important to Christians, it does not determine where you spend eternity. Baptism is a sacrament which *follows* our conversion. This is what Peter taught the crowd at Pentecost in Acts 2:38. "Repent and be baptized, every one of you, in the name of Jesus Christ for the forgiveness of your sins. And you will receive the gift of the Holy Spirit." As Peter points out, baptism comes after repentance. If you were too young to understand faith and repentance or you were insincere in your repentance, then your baptism was a false sacrament. It does not matter how many times you are immersed or who did the immersion, baptism does not beget salvation. What it does is it symbolizes our death to sin and rebirth into God's family. As such, it publicly confirms to the world our faith in Jesus as our Lord and Savior. Baptism does not save us; redemptive faith saves us.

People should neither accept what I say nor anyone else without confirming it with their own research of God's Holy Word. It is my hope that all people who feel the call from God will purchase a Bible which includes at the bottom of each page authoritative commentary to help explain and amplify these Scriptures to them. I reference authors from various denominations in this book, without regards to their church affiliation. I care more about their message than I do the letters on their church building. I am a Southern Baptist because I agree with the doctrines of this group. Regardless, all Christians should have one common goal in mind; therefore the sharing of ideas should be beneficial to us all. Hopefully our differences are in legitimate biblical interpretation and not in denominational pride and prejudice. Eternity is too long and the price for making a mistake is too great not for you to check out the facts for yourself. We should not rely solely on our church's doctrines as the only source for our convictions. If I am wrong in my understanding of the Scriptures which I am referencing, please forgive me. I may be guilty of ignorance but hopefully not of malice. Most of all though, I will be gratified if anything which I write motivates you to pick up your Bible and start reading.

Many of us feel that the Holy Spirit came over us in greater strength only after we started our daily Bible studies. Does this mean that the Holy Spirit was not with us prior to that? Absolutely not. What it means is that we never really experienced God in the fullness to which we were designed because we were not tapping into His power source, the Holy Spirit, in the best of all possible ways. The old line in <u>Star Wars</u> about "may the force be with you" is literally fulfilled via the Holy Spirit. This uniquely revealed aspect of the Triune God is our special, individually attached part of God. We do not serve a God who is millions of miles away. He is within us; guiding us, guarding us, praying for us, and reminding us of what we have learned. Where is the best source for us to learn of His lessons? The Holy Bible is God's way of reaching out to us; to grow us; to explain our role and purpose; to give us the lessons which will carry His family of believers into all eternity.

How do we acquire this divine Force? <u>Scripturally, I believe the Holy Spirit comes into our lives the moment God examines our hearts to see that our professions of faith are</u>

honest and true (Galatians 6:7-8 reaffirms that God searches our hearts; He cannot be fooled or mocked; and we will reap what we sow). What do I mean by "we will reap what we sow" in relation to salvation? If we sow with deceitful intentions, then we will reap a deceptive harvest. That deceptive harvest may be that we think we are saved when we are not (Matthew 13:24-30). Keep in mind, God examines your heart to see if your motives are pure. If you are wanting "fire insurance" only, with no real intentions of turning your life around, then you are using God for your own carnal desires. He is much too smart for this. God did not send His Son Jesus to die on the cross just to be mocked by half-hearted confessions of faith. Sometimes people make professions of faith in order to impress or manipulate others. Once again, they are sowing deception. If you cannot remember your original professing of faith, then do it again. It will not offend God. He will not say, "Hey, wait a minute. You've already done this. Don't take up my time again with this matter." No, He is always gracious to listen to whatever is on our hearts. He wants our honest communion. If we have doubts, go before Him and clear them up. It is better to be certain about this than to live in doubt.

Never become satisfied with where you are in the sanctification process. Press on. If you are experiencing failures, do not give up. Elohim loves it when we struggle for Him. We have God's assurance He will not give up on us (Isaiah 43:1-3). Jesus promises us in John 6:39-40, "And this is the will of Him who sent me, that I shall lose none of all that He has given me, but raise them up at the last day. For my Father's will is that everyone who looks to the Son and believes in Him shall have eternal life, and I will raise him up at the last day." If you are experiencing fulfillment, do not stop. It gets even better. The road to sanctification encompasses the full gamut of emotions. Living for becoming all that God designed you to be can be challenging, confusing, difficult, and very frustrating. It also will be vibrant, fulfilling, joyous, and yes, glorifying to our Lord Jesus. Jesus never stopped; neither should we.

## *A Transaction is Made*

It has been presented in our Sunday School class discussions that at the moment when salvation takes place, a spiritual transaction is made. This is a good analogy. We are all accustomed to transactional processes. All of us are familiar with giving our money in exchange for goods and services. Something like that happens when we profess our faith and give our allegiance to Christ Jesus. We give our faith; God gives His salvation. Both parties act. Both have to act in good-faith. If either is deceitful, then the transaction is void. We know that God is never deceitful (Isaiah 45:19). We also know people can be very deceitful. <u>For this spiritual transaction to move forward, we must be completely honest with God when we pray the sinner's prayer and repent of our sins.</u> Without the candid confession of our sins and a remorseful repentance away from them, there is no salvation. If a person is too young to understand sin and repentance yet they express the desire to invite Jesus into their hearts, then a responsible pastor should be enlisted to help them grow to the point to where their profession of faith is something which they fully understand. When this process *is* sincere and genuine on our part, the Holy Spirit comes to indwell us (John 14:15-18). The biblical account of this process is: (1) we are first drawn by God – John 6:44, 1 Corinthians 1:9; (2) saved by our belief in Jesus – John 3:16, 6:40; and (3) indwelt by the Holy Spirit – John 14:15-17, 16:7-8.

The New Testament is not the first mention of the Holy Spirit becoming entwined in our lives as we endeavor to be faithful to our Lord. In Ezekiel 36:26-27 God declares, "I will give you a new heart and put a new spirit in you; I will remove from you your heart of stone and give you a heart of flesh. And I will put my Spirit in you and move you to follow my decrees and be careful to keep my laws." Paul teaches us in Ephesians 1:13-14, "And you also were included in Christ when you heard the word of truth, the gospel of your salvation. Having believed, you were marked in Him with a seal, the promised Holy Spirit, who is a deposit guaranteeing our inheritance until the redemption of those who are God's possession – to the praise of His glory." The term "seal" is heavy in spiritual meaning. Paul is asserting by using the expression, "until the redemption", that this royal seal carries the assurance from God Almighty that *no force exists* which can over-power His claim on our lives. Neither Satan nor our own free wills are able to wrestle our spirits from the ownership which Jehovah Jireh places on a redeemed life. Our Lord will provide strength even when ours is weak. Paul assures us in 1 Corinthians 1:8, "He will keep you strong to the end, so that you will be blameless on the day of our Lord Jesus Christ." His protection is complete.

The King James Life Application Study Bible commentary says of these verses: "The Holy Spirit is God's seal that we belong to Him and His guarantee to us that He will do what He has promised. He is like a down payment, a deposit, a validating signature on the contract. The presence of the Holy Spirit in us demonstrates: (1) the genuineness of our faith, (2) proves that we are His children, and (3) secures eternal life for us. His power works in us transforming us now and is a taste of the total change we will experience in eternity" (page 2069). The presence of the Holy Spirit in our lives lets us know we have been accepted into God's Holy Kingdom for all eternity. If someone cannot attest with all honesty to the presence of the Holy Spirit in their life, then that person has not been received by God (much more detail is covered in chapter eight on how to know if the Holy Spirit is in you life). It will suffice to say for now that if the

Spirit has indwelt you with its transforming power, then you have all the assurance anyone can ever give you that you are part of God's Holy Kingdom. The Spirit of God is not a static power which is content on being relegated to a small corner of your soul. A perfectly amazing thing happens later to many of us as we mature in our daily walk with Jesus (through our Bible studies and prayers). The Holy Spirit is invited by our free wills to have an even greater abundance in our souls. Rather than remaining as a small, persistent voice to our conscience, He becomes the Commander of our inner spirit. A surrendered Christian heart has tremendous benefits!

The issue of transformation (leaving our carnal life and becoming spiritually guided) can be very confusing. Transformation follows a continuum. The speed of this transformation varies from person to person. As your transformation progresses, so does your spiritual maturity. If a person thinks they are saved but they cannot testify to any transformation occurring in their life, then they need to reassess their spiritual status. <u>If you were sincere when you asked Jesus to be your Lord and Savior, then the Holy Spirit immediately came into your life</u>. If the Holy Spirit indwells you, there should definitely be a change in your spiritual being. If you are the same person you were prior to your conversion, then that should signal that a problem exists within your sanctification process. It is impossible for you to remain the same person if the Holy Spirit has truly entered your life.

If a spiritual transformation has not taken place in your life, then you have not received eternal salvation. I know that is a hard statement but that is exactly as the Bible teaches. We are sealed by the Holy Spirit when saved. If you cannot see any difference in your behavior and thoughts after asking Jesus into your life, then you need to consult your minister. This spiritual transformation is such an important topic that chapter eight is devoted entirely to helping you determine if the Holy Spirit is actually present in your life. Unfortunately, what I am coming to realize is many who *think* they have eternal security actually have no salvation at all. I am referring to people who are sitting in the pews on Sunday morning. Certainly those who reject Jesus are not saved. Sadly, many who attend church and proclaim they are Christians have not complied in a sincerely genuine manner with the requirements of Jehovah God for eternal salvation. He is God. He gets to set the rules. Merely proclaiming Jesus to be God's Son is not sufficient. This is why we are spending so much time exploring the process of being certain of your salvation. By God's holy purpose, we are to be transformed. If no transformation occurs, or if it is only in appearance, then you need to review the Parable of the Soils (Matthew 13:3-9, 18-23) to determine which soil type you are. It is a pity that Satan has been so masterful in deceiving so many. Jesus is very persistent in His teachings to communicate to us through His many parables and lessons that a redeemed soul will be a productive soul (Matthew13:23, Matthew 7:16-23). I do not know how much clearer Christ can be on this point. Those who think all they have to do is to "ask Jesus into their hearts" are being greatly fooled. Salvation is not completely on our terms. Remember, it is a transaction between two parties. Casual acceptance of Jesus gives no one any security. A changed life is the evidence of your salvation.

### The Price for Rejection

Why do most people have such a reluctance to believe that God has a special place called hell for those who reject His Son? It is my impression that when the Holy Trinity originally conceived the idea of earth, they planned for this existence to be a test. This wisdom was revealed by Moses to the Israelites in Deuteronomy 13:1-3, "If a prophet, or one who foretells by dreams, appears among you and announces to you a miraculous sign or wonder, and if the sign or wonder of which he has spoken takes place, and he says, "Let us follow other gods" (gods you have not known) "and let us worship them," you must not listen to the words of that prophet or dreamer. The Lord your God is testing you to find out whether you love Him with all your heart and with all your soul." As Rick Warren states in his book, Purpose Driven Life, this world is a test (p. 42-44). He states, "Character is both developed and revealed by tests, and *all* of life is a test" (p.43). Why would God test us if He did not have a plan which depended on the results?

Sin did not surprise God the Father, God the Son, nor God the Holy Spirit. Our Triune God developed a plan for our salvation from a life of sin as they were laying the foundations for the world. Nothing we do catches God by surprise. If this is not true, then God would not rightly be considered omniscient (Job 9:4, 12:13, Isaiah 28:29). I believe God was disappointed in Adam and Eve for disobeying Him but He was not caught off guard by this. God allows Satan to roam the earth in order to test its inhabitants. This is by design.

One of the purposes of God's testing is to reveal to us at what level of faith we are functioning. This allows us to correct ourselves and to gain greater spiritual understanding (James 1:2-4). As a loving teacher, Elohim does not test us to fail us but to teach us and make us aware of where we need further work. The divine plan all along has been for those who live by faith to be highly rewarded. We trust in the heavenly Creators as our only source for salvation. Believers are made righteous by not demanding absolute proof. These are the people who listen to the still, quiet voice in their hearts, communing with their inner spirits. They are sensitive to the promptings of God and turn in obedience to a life of righteous service. Those who think of themselves only and who fail to recognize the existence of a supreme

God guiding their lives will be culled from future rewards. I feel this life is a testing ground for an even more important mission in a future existence – on the eternal earth.

God sent His prophets to help the people become better acquainted with His expectations for their lives. When the time would be right, the Holy Trinity planned that Jesus would come to this earth to further reveal God's kingdom to believers and God's wrath to unbelievers. It was to be through faith in His Son Jesus that redemption would be achieved. Redemption here means being bought from a life of sin. Sin was part of the original creation plan because God intended everyone to have a free will to make choices based on their own decisional powers rather than being instinctually driven like the beasts of the fields. <u>One of the essential messages of the Bible is that man has the free will to make his own choices and he will live by the consequences thereof.</u>

Two other essential messages of the Bible cover God's grace and His patience. God is infinitely gracious but His patience has a limit. Jehovah God is always willing to extend His grace to us, without restrictions to our race, nationality, gender, economical status, social class, or past sins. There are boundaries to His patience though. We are given until we take our last breath to place our faith in Jesus as our Lord and Savior. After that, there are no second chances. Why is this so hard for many of us to accept? In human terms, if I were God, I would certainly have a place like heaven to reward those who, despite public attitudes, developed a steadfast faith that I am who I say I am. Correspondingly I would have a place for those who rejected fellowship with me. If I were God and I had a son like Jesus, I would require certain allegiances to be placed with him. The earthly kings of old certainly required their citizens to pay homage to their sons. Why does it sound so mysterious to us that God would not do the same? Perhaps the reason is that El Olam (The

Everlasting God) will send you to hell *for all of eternity* for rejecting His Son Jesus.

That seems harsh until you envision it from our heavenly Father's perspective. Read history. The earthly kings could make your life a living hell on earth if you disobeyed them. If I were a king and I had sent my son to represent me, I would demand you treat him with respect and honor. If you chose to reject him, then I might reluctantly accept that decision. However, the problem for mankind is that the Holy Trinity is eternal. <u>Honoring your decision to reject communion with an everlasting God means you spend all of eternity outside of His presence</u>. If I were God, it stands to reason with me that your problem would be that you will be outside of my blessings for all eternity (1 Chronicles 28:9).

You would not simply cease to exist though at the time of your death. If my son died like Jesus died, you would be expected to recognize him for his sacrifice. A son who dies for the redemption of the world certainly merits praise. A son who never sinned certainly merits praise. If he did this sacrifice of his own free will out of love for me and mankind, I would require that all mankind give him proper homage. If they did not, they would be required to make a personal payment for rejecting him. Since we will all exist for eternity (that means forever), your blessing for having faith in him as my son would be forever. If you rejected him, thereby calling him a liar, your punishment would be forever.

Jesus teaches an excellent parable about this in Matthew 21:33-44. The lesson is that Israel rejected the prophets which God sent to them as His representatives. God went a step further and sent His Son. These same people not only rejected Him but they went so far as to kill His Son. The people in the crowd had the common sense to know that such rejection would not go unpunished. If Jesus were my son, I would demand exactly what our Father in heaven demands. All other religions would pay a heavy price for denying His sovereignty. No, at death, they would most assuredly not just cease to exist. Their sin in this case has extenuating circumstances. Since our beliefs are often passed on to our children (and to anyone else we might have influence), this lack of belief flows from them to their children as well. So, the sin would last for all generations. For that I would require an eternal payment.

### The Nature of Satan

Satan is neither omnipresent nor omnipotent. By no means is he equal to El Elyon (The Most High God) in attributes and power. Though it might sound unusual to nonbelievers, Satan is under God's dominion. People sometimes get the idea that God and Satan are fighting it out for sovereignty of this world and the stronger of the two will win. Nothing could be further from the truth. If you read the Bible in its entirety, you will find a number of references where it appears God recognizes that a majority of people will turn away from Him (is this not the lesson from the Parable of the Sower?). This world is not a test between God and Satan. It is our test. In a strange way Satan serves a purpose for us. He acts as the servant of God for trials and punishment (1 Chronicles 21:1, Job 1:6-12, 1 John 4:1, Revelation 2:10).

In the book of Job, Satan charges that people are only faithful to God because of the blessings which they receive from Him. This is where the righteousness of Job is called into question by Satan. Job 2:1-7 gives one of the earliest accounts of Satan accusing the faithful before God. It says, "On another day the angels came to present themselves before the Lord, and Satan also came with them to present himself before Him. And the Lord said to Satan, "Where have you come from?" Satan answered the Lord, "From roaming through the earth and going back and forth in it." Then the Lord said to Satan, "Have you considered my servant

Job? There is no one on earth like him; he is blameless and upright, a man who fears God and shuns evil. And he still maintains his integrity, though you incited me against him to ruin him without any reason." "Skin for skin!" Satan replied. "A man will give all he has for his own life. But stretch out your hand and strike his flesh and bones, and he will surely curse you to your face." The Lord said to Satan, "Very well, then, he is in your hands; but you must spare his life." So Satan went out from the presence of the Lord and afflicted Job with painful sores from the soles of his feet to the top of his head." Ultimately Job proves he is a man of integrity and righteousness. His faith in God out of a humble, pure, loving spirit reveals to us the type of relationship God desires all of us to have with Him. The testing we experience in this life should lead to our spiritual refinement and maturation (Jeremiah 9:7, 2 Corinthians 13:5, James 1:12).

At times, it seems like Satan is everywhere. All you have to do to get this impression is to listen to the evening news. Though it appears this way, this is not the case. It is Lucifer's legions of other demons which make it appear that he is omnipresent. They are the same demons which are cited so often in the Gospels where Jesus drove them out of variously afflicted people (Luke 4:33-35, 8:26-39). Demons (fallen angels) were very active during Jesus' ministry in order for Him to showcase God's ultimate power over Satan. These demons would attack a person's speech, sight, hearing, or mental condition. Jesus proves He had dominion over all mankind and nature by His miracles and healing ministry. While many today try to explain away these stories of demon possession as merely cases of mental illness, you can accept this teaching or not. If you do not, then you are calling Jesus a liar. I prefer to believe if the Bible says these unfortunate souls were demon possessed, then that is exactly what it was (Mark 1:23-27).

While not all-powerful, the enemy is strong and very clever. For the nonbelievers, Satan tries every masterful deception in his arsenal to keep them from seeking a meaningful and lasting relationship with God Almighty. He wants biblical teachings to appear as myths. Satan incites those who worship there own intelligence to denigrate the worship of God Almighty (Romans 1:18-23). He wants believers to appear as weak, unsophisticated souls who need a crutch to support them. God-centered living is to appear as a boring, hypocritical way of life for those who are too weak to grab life by the horns. Satan wants us to be certain of only what we can see and possess through our own efforts.

Please turn in your Bible to Revelation 12:10-12. Here John tells us that Satan's chief activity is being the accuser of the faithful before God (just as he did with Job). He loves to point out our failures to our heavenly Father. For believers, he uses guilt over past sins to try to separate us from God. Lucifer seeks to confuse us about God's true nature of forgiveness and the hope we have in God's grace. Verse 12 tells us "He is filled with fury, because he knows that his time is short." He is obviously pretty upset that he got cast out of heaven in the first place. Imagine having to leave heaven. Revenge is a terrible emotion to drive your soul. Since this is a war of good vs. evil, we need to know our enemy.

### *Repent or Perish*

Have you ever wondered how God's holy plan for our salvation came into being? Once the Holy Trinity saw that mankind was inclined toward sin, was there a meeting between the heavenly Father, Jesus, and the Holy Spirit so they could come up with a resolution for our sin problem? While it may appear that way to the casual reader of the Bible that is not what happened. Nothing man has ever done has come as a surprise to the Holy Trinity. The plan of salvation, through Jesus' sacrificial death, has been in place since the foundations of the world were laid (John 1:1-3, 10-14). This is not Plan B because of Adam's sin. It has been Plan A all along. For instance, God did not turn to Christ Jesus after mankind had to be punished with the Great Flood and they devised yet another plan for all future generations. No. This plan of redemption was masterfully crafted in *anticipation* of our sins, not as the result of our sins.

Dr. Henry Blackaby in Experiencing the Cross gives us the benefit of his wonderful insight into how this plan was devised. Blackaby explains, "The whole plan and purpose and implementation of our deliverance from sin is the work of the Father, coming straight from His heart" (page 20). Dr. Blackaby goes on to assert, "Always in Scripture, it's the Father who purposes and plans and initiates. He works through the Son to accomplish His work, then the Spirit takes what the Father has purposed and brings it into reality in the life of His people" (page 21). This is a magnificent picture of the Holy Trinity working together, each with their own distinctive personalities, yet working as a cohesive Deity to bring salvation to mankind.

As we read through the book of Deuteronomy we gain knowledge of the intricate details God revealed to Moses about the proper preparation and execution of the numerous sacrificial rules set forth by God which He wanted the Israelites to follow. As Blackaby explains on page 30, the whole sacrificial system was based on a blood sacrifice. This is not meant to convey that our God is bloodthirsty or anything such as that. To El Elyon, sin is serious business. By its very nature as a rebellious act, sin separates us from our Lord. God wanted His people to consider carefully the profound price of their sins. Unconfessed sins lead to death – both spiritual and physical. Jehovah God also wanted a way to point His children toward a very important future event which would take place in Jerusalem during a special Passover celebration.

On pages 28-29 Blackaby makes the following outstanding statement which should help us more fully experience the cross: "Simply asking God to forgive you is not what brings pardon for your sin. Nor is repentance, no matter how sincere...All the sorrow in the world can never bring forgiveness if we leave out the magnitude of what God had to do to be able to forgive us – yielding His Son to a bloody and absolute death...When Christ shed His blood, He poured out His very life to cover our sins, making a way for you and me to be made right with God." In doing so, Jesus gave us an avenue for a personal relationship with God Almighty. This is signified by the tearing of the curtain in the temple immediately upon Jesus' death on the cross (Matthew 27:50-51).

No longer was man separated from direct access to the Father. If you reject the blood of Christ, then any plea for forgiveness will be denied. If you accept Jesus as your Lord and Savior, then His blood covers yours sins and you are forgiven by the Father. This is Plan A. It has always been Plan A. There are no Plans B, C, or D for the Jews, Muslims, Hindus, Aborigines, and whatever. Jesus and only Jesus is the Way to salvation (John 14:6). Jesus said it; Blackaby explains it; I believe it.

Once the time was right in man's spiritual development, God's righteous plan moved rapidly toward fulfillment. As we read in the Gospels, Jesus proceeded resolutely toward His appointed mission. Our Savior's prayer in the Garden of Gethsemane (Matthew 26:36-39) reflects the myriad of emotions and the stress on our blessed Lord as He prepared for the ultimate fulfillment of the sacrificial system. What our sins cost Jesus, the Son of Man, was the horrendous reality of a very barbaric death. What our sins cost Jesus, the Son of God, as He was separated from the heavenly Host, is beyond our understanding. The Father made the most loving sacrifice which could ever be offered to His wayward children here on earth. Jehovah Jireh sent His beloved Son, who was without blemish, to be the supreme payment for our sin debt. Notice, God did not demand Jesus make this sacrifice. Christ made it for us! Jesus carried out the Father's plan. The Holy Spirit proclaims it to our inner spirits, so we will turn to God Almighty in our faith and obedience. All that is required is that we steadfastly accept God's Word that He did exactly what the Christian Bible says He did. We have to accept Jesus Christ as our redemptive Savior. We do not have to live perfect lives. We do not have to search for a perfect sacrifice to pay for our sin debt. No. God has done all of this for us. What we have to do is to believe with a heartfelt inner confidence that Jesus is our Savior and we dedicate our lives to seeking His will. In that sense, God has made it easy for us. This however is not a "works" theology. Our love drives our works; our faith seals our redemption. So, why do so many reject Him?

Jesus explains in the Parable of the Sower what Satan does with those who are not stalwartly accepting of His Holy Word. Matthew 13:19, "When anyone hears the message about the kingdom and does not understand it, the evil one comes and snatches away what was sown in his heart." This describes those who are like the first type of soil. The first soil was the path, where it was easy for the birds (Satan) to snatch up the seeds (the Good News of Christ). These are the people whose hearts have become heartened to the message of the Lord. The Great Deceiver finds them easy to manipulate because they have no belief at all in the Holy Trinity. In Matthew 13:20-22 we have the people who are like the rocky soil and the soil mixed with thrones. Both fall prey to various problems and persecution because their faith is both shallow and unstable. These are those who may have a casual acceptance of Christ as Lord and Savior.

Remember, faith has three basic components – belief, trust, and commitment (Chapter One – Components of Faith). The second and third groups of people described in this parable are those whose commitment is lacking any substantial strength. As such, their superficial faith is easily destroyed once it comes under attack. They have low levels of all three components, so it is easy for Satan's minions to confuse and deceive them. Only the fourth group – those who are fruitful – are the ones who will be received by our Lord when the final harvest is done (Matthew 13:30). Not until you are ready to make a steadfast, unwavering, genuine commitment in faith to Jesus as being the only true Lord and Savior of your life are you redeemed. Jesus did not leave the splendor of heaven for any half-hearted commitments by people who demand worldly proof of His divine celestial status. He did not leave the splendor of heaven to share your commitment with some other bogus gods of your own creation. He gave His life in order to redeem us out of a meaningless existence. The least we can do is to make Him the absolute center of our lives.

Does this seem harsh to you? Earlier in my life it seemed a little harsh but as I have grown in my appreciation for what Christ has brought into my life, it now makes perfect sense. Listen to what Jesus says about half-hearted commitment. Jesus teaches an excellent lesson about such unproductive lives where He highlights an unfruitful fig tree. In Luke 13:5-9 our Lord declares, "I tell you, no! But unless you repent, you too will all perish." Then He told this parable: "A man had a fig tree, planted in his vineyard, and he went to look for fruit on it, but did not find any. So he said to the man who took care of the vineyard, 'For three years now I've been coming to look for fruit on this fig tree and haven't found any. Cut it down! Why should it use up the soil?' " 'Sir,' the man replied, 'leave it alone for one more year, and I'll dig around it and fertilize it. If it bears fruit next year, fine! If not, then cut it down.'" How much clearer does God have to be? <u>Casual, nominal belief in Jesus as your Lord and Savior is not acceptable.</u> <u>CINO's (Christians In Name Only) will go the route of the unproductive fig tree.</u>

# Chapter Three Our Upside Down World

———∽⌘∽———

Note: read this chapter even if you do not want to. I know how most people are. We do not like to read what convicts us. We get comfortable in our ways. If that includes a few cherished sins, then we become reluctant to give them up. Like most, I have treated sin too casually through some parts of my life. It has cost me countless opportunities to serve my Lord and Savior. Until we more completely understand the wages of sin and the price Jesus paid at Calvary, we will not dedicate ourselves to living the righteous life God intends for each of us to live.

It does not take an overly perceptive person to realize our world is upside down. Why? Rebellion against God always turns things wrong side up. It is almost axiomatic that whatever the world tells us to do we should most often do the exact opposite. Whatever the world values, it is often the opposite of what God would have us value. The world would have you think that great intelligence is to be prized. How often do we find that those who are super intelligent to be sadly deficient in wisdom? Is it not amazing that often we find highly talented people to be lacking in patience with others? Often the economically fortunate lack any true sense of compassion. The great state of Mississippi is one of the poorest states in our nation. Did you know that Mississippians lead our nation in charitable giving when measured against household income? Often the truly gifted do not know the honor of hard work. Hard work is not something we should avoid. It builds character and perseverance. How in the world did we get so turned around?

The forces which wage war against what is good and holy delight in confusing people. Our Lord Jesus gives us some excellent spiritual jewels in the Sermon on the Mount (Matthew chapters 5-7). His wisdom in the Beatitudes (Matthew 5:3-12) is 180 degrees off from what the world would have us to think. Look at what He teaches us. We are to be poor in spirit. Most people shudder at being poor in anything. What Jesus wants us to be here is humble; to be reliant on God and not ourselves. He tells us to be meek. Often the world thinks "weak" when we hear the word "meek." Nothing could be further from the truth. Christians are not weak. The rest of the world may have you think that believers are weak and only looking for a spiritual crutch. We know better. Meekness to Jesus means obediently accepting God's guidance and vindication. To do this, you must have the power of self control. Meekness is best described as "power under control" or "gentle strength". To yield your free will to the will of the Holy Spirit is no small feat. <u>The Beatitudes capture the essence of the Christian life</u>. <u>They are also 180 degrees opposite of how the world would encourage you to live</u>. Christians seek harmony and contentment. Many nonbelievers live lives of quiet desperation. Some are not so quiet. Rebellion takes a heavy toll on you. Faith sustains you.

The world has not always been upside down. When God created our world, it was declared to be good (Genesis 1:31). The Garden of Eden is the intended life for all of us. Our heavenly Father created all the land and the seas for our enjoyment. We were to have dominion over all He created.

For this, we were to worship and praise Him. In exchange for the abundance which God created for Adam, God desired him to be obedient. Mankind's obedience would be one of the foremost measures of our sincere worship. Nevertheless, God did not design us to be spiritual robots. <u>God wants our worship and praise to come from our hearts</u>. <u>For it to be genuine love, Jehovah God had to design us with the ability to reject Him</u>. Have you ever thought about that? I have heard it said that if you love something you must set it free. Only in freedom is it capable to returning your love. Our Lord loves us enough to set us free. El Elyon gives each of us a free will. We are genetically wired to seek Him. We are not wired to blindly seek Him though. For man to have the kind of relationship with God which He created us for, it required God to put into place the ability to accept Him or to reject Him. As with good parents, sometimes you have to sit back and let the little birds fly on their own. It is a pity so many do not recognize the tender wisdom which God exercised in giving us free will. We take so much of what He has given us and never reflect on its origins.

### Are People Basically Good or Evil?

Of the four groups of people represented in the parable above, only one group has redemptive faith. This is why sin is so pervasive in our world. So many think they have faith but unfortunately they have not taken their initial acceptance of the message of Jesus Christ and grown it into a life trans-forming reality. Many are deceived into a false comfort that they have adequate faith. Is there hope for these people? Are we doomed from the very start of our lives? It is difficult to say if humans are, by nature, good or evil. Many books have been written about both sides of this topic. Probably the safe position to take is to say that little girls and boys seem to start out as neither good nor evil. Their family dynamics and their social environment therefore are the most prominent factors in influencing the quality of their subsequent character.

While it may appear safe to skirt the issue, I do not believe deep down in my soul that God created us in a spiritual void. It is my belief from studying the Scriptures that we all start out as being good (at least as infants). God called us that in Genesis 1:31, "God saw all that He had made, and it was very good." In Genesis 1:26 we learn that God said, "Let us make man in our image, in our likeness..." How can we be in His image and not start out as being good creatures? This can become a little confusing however when we reference Genesis 8:21 where God declares about man, "...every inclination of his heart is evil from childhood." Here God is bemoaning what appears to be a universal tendency in man to pursue his own self interests rather than the righteousness of the Lord. Nonetheless, this does not mean we are born evil. What we have is the inclination or tendency toward wayward behavior. This is a far cry from being labeled as evil from birth though.

I do not accept the collective guilt proposition either. Each will be held accountable for their own actions. Deuteronomy 24:16, "Fathers shall not be put to death for their children, nor children put to death for their fathers; each is to die for his own sin." God does not hold the son accountable for the sins of the father. This promise is also borne out in Ezekiel 18:20, "The soul who sins is the one who will die. The son will not share the guilt of the father, nor will the father share the guilt of the son. The righteousness of the righteous man will be credited to him, and the wickedness of the wicked will be charged against him." We will each answer for our own sins. All that we receive from our forefathers is the strong *tendency* to sin because we are living in a world which is characterized by sin.

Why some people over the centuries have thought babies are born spiritually corrupt is because of the fallen state of mankind in general. While this is true, what I believe is that as adults, we are extraordinarily first-rate teachers of sin. Children learn from their parents, siblings and friends – their good traits and their bad traits. I do not for a moment believe children are inherently evil or bad. How can you say a six month old infant is immoral? From whose perspective does this come? I do not think from God's perspective He considers them decadent. When you look at an infant, it is impossible to suppress the universal feeling that children are a blessing. How can you say something is a blessing, yet believe it is inherently sin soaked? Jesus teaches us over and over how the kingdom of heaven is made up of children with their unrestrained faith (Matthew 11:25, 18:3-4; 19:13-14). Children have a tendency toward sin because of the fallen nature of mankind. Civilization greatly facilitates that behavior to where it looks like we are born sinful.

We know that infants react depending on their particular environment and their own unique physiology. They each have their own distinct personalities. Some are more active than others. Some appear to be more contented than others. While there are differences, I think the core of each person's being is very similar. If this were not so, then for God to be righteous, He would need different rules for each of us. I believe we all start out as a good reflection of God. It is what happens while we are being nurtured by society which alters each of us. This I firmly believe – while in infancy, if a baby dies, I am certain God receives them immediately into His kingdom. It is only <u>after</u> we reach the "age of accountability" that we are to answer for our sinful actions. I will cover this concept of accountability much more thoroughly in the upcoming sections. Of this we can be sure, our heavenly Father is both a righteous and a loving God (John 14:21). Since we know this to be true, it is reasonable to draw the inference that He does not judge us as unrighteous until we can cognitively understand right from wrong. I feel this is true because it would take a callous heart to enact righteous standards on a person who is totally unaware of those expectations. God is righteous (Deuteronomy 4:7-8, Psalm 11:7, and Psalm 145:17); therefore how He judges is righteous. We as humans can see with our limited understanding how it is wrong in our criminal justice system to hold people accountable for crimes which they have no capacity to understand. Rest assured, God is without blame when it comes to His judgment.

## *What is Sin?*

Sin is missing the mark which Jehovah God has set for your life. There are two types of sins: sins of *commission* and sins of *omission*. Both of these types of sins involve not living up to God's will for our lives. Therefore, sin is anything which takes us away from living a righteous life with God. This concept of sin greatly expands the universe of behaviors which can be considered sinful. Transgressions are not just committing acts forbidden in the Ten Commandments (Exodus 20:1-17). These are acts which God wants us to avoid doing. There are also acts which God wants us to do. James 4:17, "Anyone, then, who knows the good he ought to do and doesn't do it, sins." These sins of omission occur anytime we fail to do good, such as: not being kind to one another, failing to take an elderly friend to the doctor because of your busy schedule, not helping the poor and oppressed, being reluctant to share God's Holy Word with a lost friend or relative, failing to give comfort to a friend over a loss, neglecting to care for the needs of small children and the elderly in our society, or not showing others God's love through us. We are to be His light to the world (Matthew 5:16). When we fail to do so, we sin. When we fail to act on the promptings of the Holy Spirit, we sin.

Sin is possible because God gave man a free will so he can choose to obey or to rebel. The Bible is very specific on what we must do whenever we realize we have sinned. Proverbs 28:13 "He who conceals his sins does not prosper, but whoever confesses and renounces them finds mercy." In Proverbs 16:6 the Bible goes on to teach, "Through love and faithfulness sin is atoned for; through the fear of the Lord a man avoids evil." The reward of forgiveness by God of our sins is represented by Psalm 32:1-2, "Blessed is he whose transgressions are forgiven, whose sins are covered. Blessed is the man whose sin the Lord does not count against him and in whose spirit is no deceit." We are blessed when we confess our sins to God Almighty. However, confession without repentance gets us nowhere.

Read Genesis 6:11-13. "Now the earth was corrupt in God's sight and was full of violence. God saw how corrupt the earth had become, for all the people on earth had corrupted their ways. So God said to Noah, 'I am going to put an end to all people, for the earth is filled with violence because of them. I am surely going to destroy both them and the earth.'" How did this corruption come into being? By mankind ignoring God's presence and guidance, sin had corrupted the world. Is God thereby admitting here that He made a mistake in creating the earth in the first place? No, it was not His mistake. Life is about freedom. Man had decided of his own free will to rebel against God, therefore it was not God's mistake but man's mistake. When bad things happen, there is a natural inclination to ask why God allowed these things to occur. I have asked this question many times myself. However, that is not the proper question to ask in most instances. Bad things most often reflect poor choices and the sinful nature in man, not the absence of God's love in our lives. I know this is a hard lesson for most. Far too many people want to blame everyone but themselves for the predicaments in which they find themselves. Certainly there are bad things which happen which are outside this statement. That is why this place is called earth, not heaven. More often than not though, bad things happen because of someone's bad choices.

God will not always explain to us all that we find perplexing, but He is always there with us, comforting and guiding us so that the challenges to our faith do not overwhelm us. Turn to Psalm 55:22, Isaiah 46:4, and 1 Peter 5:7 when your strength is drained. These verses reassure us of El Shaddai's loving protection during all of life's trials. Rather than blaming God, we should be like Joseph in Genesis 45:4-8. We should find how we can serve God through our suffering. Believers need to trust that Jehovah Jireh has a plan for our lives, if only we will seek Him.

I am firmly convinced that God allows bad things to happen to certain people in order to further His kingdom. When my mom died, she had crippling arthritis, Parkinson's disease, Alzheimer's, and had suffered from multiple strokes. She was no longer able to walk because her feet had curled inward. Mom's right thumb had to be amputated because it had curled into her hand due to arthritis. Never did she complain though. She never cried out that life had been unfair or bemoaned why would God allow her to suffer so much. Mom kept looking to heaven. She knew she could count on God. Through it all, her faith never wavered. I am firmly convinced God allowed her to suffer in order for her to be a witness to her sons and their wives, her grandchildren and other people. Mom had broad spiritual shoulders. God knew this. He used her strength to teach others how to remain faithful even in great pain and suffering. Praise God for believing in my mother! I know this sounds strange to praise God in light of someone's suffering but I believe Margaret Leonard was one of His unsung heroes of faith. She brought honor and glory to Him in her darkest moments. I praise God that I had the mother and father He so loving blessed me with. Before blaming God, stop and think – how has He blessed you? Then remember, above all else, <u>Jesus died on the cross for you</u>. <u>What more evidence do we need that God loves us</u>?

God promised Noah that never again will He destroy this earth by water. There *will* come a day in the future though when there will be an accounting of all sins. If you are an unbeliever, then on Judgment Day, you will give a total accounting of all the wrongs your life has produced. On the other hand, a believer's sins are completely and totally covered (removed) by Jesus' blood. They are accounted for by Jesus so perfectly that when God sees us, He sees us as cleansed children gathering before Him in praise and worship. Blessed be our Jesus, our Lord and Savior! Our heavenly Father always stands willing to forgive and restore us. Reference 1 John 1:8-9 "If we claim to be without sin, we deceive ourselves and the truth is not in us. If we confess our sins, He is faithful and just and will forgive us our sins and purify us from all unrighteousness."

Never ever let Satan break your fellowship with God because you feel guilty due to past sins in your life. After confession and forgiveness, God wants you looking forward. The problem is that Satan wants you constantly looking in your emotional rear-view mirror, being reminded of your failures. <u>We Christians are notorious for our guilt over forgiven sins</u>. We sincerely ask God for forgiveness of the transgression and we turn away from it. It is to stop at that point, right? What Satan delights in doing is to keep the memory of that sin and all the emotions which it caused alive in our minds. Satan may even enlist the help of family and friends in keeping the issue alive. The resulting guilt becomes a heavy burden. At some point the burden may become so great that we decide there is no use in trying to please God. We recognize we are not perfect nor will we ever be perfect. To try to live to the perfection which God demands is impossible. It is also extremely frustrating. The truth is these feelings are not biblical. This is where Satan is a master at deception. He has you frustrated and angry at God and yourself. The reality is that God has forgiven you long ago. The problem is that Satan has used guilt to make you not forgive yourself. He wins.

God is like a good parent in many ways. All of our children miss the mark we set for them at times but we still love them immensely. Their failures do not make us love them less. So it is with our heavenly Father. He is not overly demanding, super-critical, impossible to please, and continuously harboring grudges. As in the Beatitudes, Christians have a peacemaker (Matthew 5:9) in the form of Jesus Christ. Peacemakers restore relationships. They actively seek to bring back into harmony relationships which have been broken. Whenever we sin, Jesus actively defends us to the Father. In what better situation could we be? The Holy Spirit is our Paraclete (John 14:16) and Jesus is at the right hand of God being our Peacemaker (Hebrews 2:17-18; 8:1-2).

In the above scenario, Satan is only successful in alienating you from God due to guilt if you do not know the above quoted Scriptures (1 John 1:8-9 or any of the hundreds related to forgiveness). The caution here is that it requires more than mere casual knowledge of the Scriptures to fight against Satan. It is like faith. You have to *believe* so *firmly* in the promise and truthfulness of these Scriptures that no one can cause you to doubt their fidelity. In addition, newsflash, God knows we are not perfect! If we were capable of perfection, then He would have never sent Jesus as the atoning sacrifice for our sins. We should set as our *goal* to try to be obedient in all of God's commandments. In other words, we should try to be the best we can be. The beauty of God's provision is because He knows his children will slip at times, His grace comes in and makes right the damage we have done.

## *Accountability and Original Sin*

It appears we have a natural tendency toward disobedience to God's commands because of Adam's original sin (Genesis 3:1-19). This original sin has had far reaching consequences. The whole world fell because of man's sin. Eden is no more. What are we to glean from this biblical account of Adam and Eve's sin? We know that people are the products of both their heredity and the environment in which they live. Starting even at a very young age, the fallen state of the world has a tremendous influence on us. The question is whether this fallen state is the result of inherited sin or from learned behavior. As we mature, humans seem to have a strong tendency toward the sins of having a rebellious disbelief in God Almighty as He proclaims Himself to be in the Holy Bible, the rejection of His plan for their salvation, as well as a host personal sins such as pride, greed, sexual depravity, lust for power, jealousy, hostility, covetousness, idolatry, dishonoring God's name, deceit, lying, and other unsavory acts of disobedience (Exodus 20:1-17). This impulse to sin originates from where? Some have thought man to be inherently evil. If we are, in fact, genetically wired by God to sin, then we have an excuse. Here is what we know. God is pure and sinless (Psalm 18:25-26, Hebrews 7:25-26). As such, anything Elohim does to us or for us is both righteous and sinless. If God implanted in each of us some chromosome which activates sinning, then He would hardly be a righteous God if He held such actions against us. If this were the case, then how could this world be a fair test of our obedience to God's laws and commandments? If this were the case, when we sin, we would merely be acting as God designed us to act. God does not desire to condemn us though. He did not create us only to torment us with rules and laws which rage against our very nature. God is righteous in all He has ever done and all He will ever do.

We can be certain – we are never forced by our genetics or our environment to sin. <u>Our individual free wills determine the course of our behavior. This is why God can hold each responsible for their own actions.</u> We make our choices and we will be judged by them.

Read Genesis 3:1-24 and reflect on how we as modern men and women continue to follow the paths of Adam and Eve. God reacted in the only way He could to their rebellion. El Shaddai cannot allow sin to go unchecked. Our heavenly Father is first and foremost holy. <u>The New Unger's Bible Dictionary</u> states that "holiness is one of the essential attributes of the divine nature. It is, on the one hand, entire freedom from moral evil and, on the other, absolute moral perfection. The Scriptures lay great stress upon this attribute of God." God's holiness sets Him apart from all of creation. God's holiness requires that He not whimsically give us tests which we are doomed from the start to fail. That would be something which Satan would do. It would be unjust of God to design us with a genetic encoding for sin and then hold this sin nature against us for all eternity. His holiness requires Him not to be like an indulgent grandfather either who thinks we never do anything wrong. His holiness mandates He act as a righteous and pure God who demands respect and submission.

What I would like to propose now is what I call "The Onion Theory for the Tree of Good and Evil". To start, I would like to ask you, "If Adam and Eve had not eaten of the fruit from the tree of good and evil, would we all be living in the Garden of Eden right now?" Ponder this question as you read Genesis chapter 3. First of all, do you think the story of original sin is meant to be interpreted in a figurative sense or was it an actual story and to be interpreted in a literal fashion? I believe this account of original sin was an actual event which has tremendous symbolic meaning for all mankind. God is wise in selecting the stories of the Bible which He presents to us in order for us to know Him better. Although each story involved specific people, the basic truths in each biblical story have symbolic significance for all of us.

In studying the Bible, I believe it proper to first approach each passage as being literal in nature. The context of the surrounding verses will give you an excellent indication of whether the verses are to be interpreted as literal or whether they should be more properly taken as being figurative in nature. Next, review how the passage relates to other verses. This is another excellent tool for discovering the context of a specific passage. God does not present any of His truths only one time. Having a good concordance handy is an excellent way to study your Bible. Research the related references which most Bibles list in the margin of the page. These cross references will help you compare the message of that particular verse will other Scriptures which relate to that topic. It is a mistake to think that all verses in the Bible are literal. However, it is an even greater mistake to think that most verses hold only a figurative value. I believe the stories of the various events in the Bible are literal, not figurative. The reason they are relevant to us is that they illustrate the spiritual battles and conditions of all mankind. While literal, they are symbolic as well. Here in this story is an actual tree of good and evil and today there are symbolic trees of good and evil which each of us must face. There was also a large fish which swallowed Jonah and we still have symbolically large fish which swallow us today. <u>The Bible is not a collection of fables, myths, or just interesting stories. These are stories of actual events. Why they were chosen by the Holy Spirit is that they represent for all of us the spiritual condition of our souls. Times have changed but man's spiritual condition has not. The Bible presents the truths of God from the historical vantage point of specific people who faced what we continue to face.</u> This is why both the Old and the New Testaments should be studied by us. There are important lessons in each to teach us of God's character and how He wants us to live.

As you read chapter 3 of Genesis, you might wonder, "Is God callous for punishing all of mankind for the sin of just two people?" It seems unfair that mankind must continue to pay for the sins of Adam and Eve. The account of original sin produces spiritual dissonance in many of us because of this ostensible injustice. On the one hand, it makes God sound overly harsh and wrathful, being quick to blame and interminable in His anger. Yet, we know God to be loving and ready to forgive. Why did so much misery have to come to this world because of Adam and Eve's single act of disobedience? If God's wrath is passed on from generation to generation, what does all of this ultimately reveal about the true character of God?

The way I like to discover the truths which God has for me when I study is to read the verses, then reflect on what they are saying to me. Once I have an impression in my mind, I pray for God's guidance to other biblical verses which will substantiate this line of thought. Then I like to turn to the commentaries by men and women who are much more gifted in biblical wisdom than I am. With these, I get to see how my thoughts measure up to theirs. This is how I developed the Onion Theory for the biblical account of the tree of good and evil. <u>As we peel back the outer layers of this story, are there greater truths underlying this factual biblical story than merely the account of the first act of sinful disobedience?</u> As we look across the 66 books of the Bible we come to realize this is not simply the story of one sin by one man and one woman. This first act of disobedience makes known the core of our spiritual being and how it shapes our relationship with God Almighty in instances where our desires come into conflict with El Shaddai's will. <u>This was the original sin: Adam and Eve wanted what their hearts desired and they wanted it right then, regardless of how these cravings clashed</u>

with the commands of God. Basically, Adam and Eve put their desires ahead of being obedient to God. Unfortunately for mankind, this tendency toward sinful disobedience has gone from person to person, from generation to generation. Is this genetic or rather is it learned behavior which humans have mastered all too well?

If sin is genetically passed to us from our forefathers, then that means God has wired sin into our genetic code. That would indicate that Adam and Eve had sin already present in their biological makeup while in the Garden. This would indicate that the serpent did not so much tempt them as he merely activated the launch sequence. If that was the case, then God set them up for failure from the start. Elohim placed in them this rebellious trait which would separate them from Him. Doesn't sound like too smart of a design, does it? But we know that we are not at war against ourselves. As Jesus said, "A house divided against itself will fall" (Luke 11:17). We are at war against the forces of evil which roam freely through this world. Of this we can be certain – God is not trying to test us against our own nature. Our Lord is testing us against the principalities which seek to destroy our relationship with Him. Paul writes in Ephesians 6:12, "For our struggle is not against flesh and blood, but against the rulers, against the authorities, against the powers of this dark world and against the spiritual forces of evil in the heavenly realms." What our heavenly Father *is* trying to do is to refine us into being the people He originally designed us to be. For sure, Elohim does not cause us to sin. We *learn* to sin from others (including the agents of the great deceiver). If our Jehovah God had wired sin into our core fabric, then He would be guilty of predisposing us to sin. We know better than this though. God has gone to great lengths to help us champion our sin problem. He went so far as to send His only Son on a rescue mission to earth (John 3:16, 8:42). That does not sound like a God who would have us genetically transmitting our disobedience from one generation to the next, now does it?

Paul gives insight into our discussion of this idea of accountability for our sins in Romans 2:5-16. In verse 15 it states, "since they show that the requirements of the law are written on their hearts, their consciences also bearing witness, and their thoughts now accusing..." This suggests to me that our heavenly Father looks at the maturity of the individual when assessing their sin. I think this because of the role of their conscience as "bearing witness and their thoughts now accusing". Child psychologists are pretty unified that most children do not develop or are guided by a conscience until around age 8. They know what not to do in order to avoid punishment prior to that age for sure. To be more precise though, they do not generally have a well-defined conscience working *consistently* as a "guidance system" until about 8 years of age. Prior to this, they know what not to do but they do not always understand why. Their "thoughts are not accusing" yet. The point at which this developmental stage becomes active is dependent on the individual child. Of all the attributes of God, three of the most prominent are of Him being holy, loving, and righteous. How could a righteous God who is holy in all He does, hold a small child account-able for actions they do not understand? Even fallen man understands the role of maturity with regards to guilt and punishment. We are assured by Jesus and Paul in the New Testament that God clearly takes into account the status of the individual when considering judgment.

To further our understanding, go to Romans 5:12-21. Please pay particular attention to Romans 5:13 – until you are conscious of sin, you are not held accountable for sin. The law makes you conscious of sin when you reach an age to where you are conscious of right and wrong, even without the law (for the law has been written on all our hearts – Romans 2:13-15). The commentary in the NIVDSB for

Romans 5:12-21 states: "Adam chose to become like God rather than serving God. Adam thus separated the human race from God, creating a race serving itself rather than God. Through the first sin, each person became inclined toward sin. This does not mean sin is biologically transmitted from one generation to the next. Rather sin sits on the throne ruling the world. Each person follows the course set by Adam and encouraged by the sinful environment chooses to rebel against God." In other words, we are all responsible for our own sins. Since God has had a plan for our redemption all along, Adam did not spiritually destroy us (though his actions did condemn our world to being one where sin reigns). Adam did not singularly destroy us because each of us will commit the same disobedient acts toward God that Adam committed. As we peel back the onion, Adam basically represents each of us at the core level. We all have faced our own tree of good and evil and each of us behaved very much like what Adam did (we want what we want and we want it now, regardless of God's prohibitions). We are not therefore punished solely for Adam's original sin. God holds each of us accountable for our own sins, since each of us will sin (Romans 3:22-23). The NIVDSB commentary continues with this assurance about accountability: "God does not hold us accountable for our sinful actions until we are able spiritually and intellectually to be aware of and sense guilt for sins...Legal commands only increase the range of conscious sinning. All people are conscious of sin and guilt even without the laws. We may argue the how's of our relationship to Adams' sin. We cannot argue the fact we have sinned individually and must accept responsibility for our sin."

God chose to reveal the price for this disobedience through the story of Adam. When we peel back every layer of our spiritual onion, until we reach the core, we find every one of us has the same basic spiritual core. We are all destined to sin. Thankfully, God is righteous in how He deals with our sin problem. God does not play favorites; He does not make it easy for some to achieve righteousness and impossible for others. Moreover, was this problem not known by God as He was laying the foundations of this earth? If so, then we are <u>not</u> paying for Adam's sin but for our own sins. <u>Adam's sin simply represents what we all commit in our own various ways</u>. Since Adam and Eve, we find we have all been, at times, trying to be more like little gods rather than serving Jehovah God. <u>We have a tremendous tendency to sin when we approach life through the filter of our own selfish desires</u>. This does not mean we are evil by nature. All it denotes is that we have at our spiritual core, the same rebellious tendencies which Adam and Eve had. We want what we want and we want it now. Moreover, we really despise being told, "No." To us a prohibition is an invitation.

Did Adam's sin surprise God? Absolutely not. Our Triune God made a pathway for our salvation via faith, not works. It has always followed the same path. We are to have faith that God is who He says He is and that He does what He says He will do. El Shaddai provided this pathway from the very beginning of this world. Just as the story of Job teaches us of the battle between Satan and God, so this story teaches us that this world presents the same tests to all of us – and we all fail. God is disappointed in our failures, but He is not surprised.

This biblical story is the first of many which supports the basic tenet that we cannot gain salvation through works. All who have ever lived have sinned; therefore salvation has to come from some other source than ourselves. The point is that there was never meant to be a salvation through works. El Elyon designed this planet to be a test (Exodus 16:4, Deuteronomy 8:2, Job 7:17-18, Revelation 3:10). It has been a test since the very first man. God could have made us without these rebellious tendencies, but then this world would not be a test. Part of the test is of our obedience and what we will do when we have been disobedient (Judges 3:4-11). Will we hide, shift the blame, or even disavow our sins, or will we confess and repent of our sins? Here is the other part of the test – who will we turn to as our object of faith? When we turn to God to ask for His forgiveness of our sins, we are saying that we admit that we cannot ever achieve righteousness on our own powers. When we turn to God as the object of our worship and praise, we are saying we acknowledge that God is who He says He is and that He will do what He says He will do. Our only hope for salvation is through our faith in Jesus Christ as our Lord and Savior. He alone provides our pathway to salvation (John 3:16-18 and 14:6).

Why is it fair of God that mankind no longer gets to live in the Garden of Eden? When we study the entirety of the Bible, what we learn is that at the spiritual core of each of us, we are all basically the same. Our spirits lack the focus, the resolve, and the discipline to live a blameless life. Mankind has not changed much spiritually over our collective history. Each person encounters the same spiritual challenges (but perhaps in different ways) and usually makes the same mistakes. Some are more disciplined than others. Some make fewer mistakes. The reality is that we all fail, in varying measures, to remain completely obedient to God's will for our lives. Given this, each of us does things which eventually exclude us from a life in Eden. When we combine this story in Genesis with what Paul teaches us in Romans, it reveals God's ultimate righteousness: each is accountable for their own sins and each will be judged accordingly. Our only hope is in the saving blood of our Lord and Savior. Without Jesus, we are the same today as mankind was thousands of years ago. This is why God's removal of man from Eden was righteous. Each of us will fail in some way to live a totally obedient life. Whatever causes this failure of obedience will be our own personal version of the tree of good and evil. For that, we must take responsibility.

I repeatedly reference that we are accountable for our own sins. This is because, in our culture, we tend to want everyone else other than ourselves to be responsible for the bad things which happen in our lives. We are quick to take credit for our achievements and even quicker to play the blame game when things go wrong. Confession is dependent on you taking an honest assessment of your disobedience. Without such, you will never turn away in repentance from your sinful actions. Without truthful confession and genuine repentance, we will never be able to restore our relationship with God. Paradise will be lost forever.

So, once again I ask the question: If Adam and Eve had not eaten of the fruit from the tree of good and evil, would we all be living in the Garden of Eden right now? As we peel away the onion, the better question is: If they had not eaten of the fruit from the tree of good and evil, would they have been disobedient in some other fashion? The answer is yes. This is demonstrated by each of us who has followed them on this earth. We have proven that we cannot gain salvation through our good works. We all fail. Only through faith in God Almighty can any of us be rendered righteous. This is why we cannot blame Adam for our plight. He is us and we are Adam as it relates to the sin of disobedience.

Fortunately for mankind, God's holiness and grace shine through in this biblical story. Mankind being cast out of Eden reflects God's righteousness and His punishment for sin. God had to act decisively. As much as God loves us and desires communion with us, God has to remain righteous in His relationship with us. God fairly and justly warned them what not to do and the consequences thereof. We are so warned as well. God is holy because His actions are beyond reproach. He is holy because whatever He does, it is done with absolute moral purity. Whenever a Bible story seems to point to God being less than pure in His moral behavior, we must question our understanding. He is pure. Unfortunately, we are not able to understand all aspects of God's character or His ways, so at times we become confused. Our minds are not capable of judging God. Therefore, it is best we leave all judgment to Jehovah God and accept His judgments as righteously supreme. God's grace is revealed in this story of original sin because God did continue to care for Adam and Eve. He provided them with proper clothing (Genesis 3:21). God's grace shines in His providence of a pathway to righteousness. Though we sin, our heavenly Father continues to provide His grace in the form of eternal forgiveness if we place our faith in Him as El Elyon, the Most High God.

One final question is this – what was the magnitude of Adam and Eve's sin? Their original sin set into motion this tendency we have even to this day for being disobedient to God. It is most commonly referred to as our "sin nature." Cain learned to sin from his parents. These various acts of disobedience spread from person to person, from generation to generation. When you look at it from this perspective, you see why God had to cast them out of Eden. Elohim had to teach us from the very start that sin has consequences.

Even when we are forgiven, sin still carries negative consequences. Why? Because even forgiven sin damages our relationship with God – both with Him and with ourselves. This is not to say that a believer loses their salvation because of sin. No, it is that there are repercussions for sin – whether you are a believer or a nonbeliever. Salvation and damnation are the result of either accepting God or rejecting God as your sole object of praise and worship. Nonetheless, daily sins still are to be dealt with but they do not negate a believer's salvation. What makes the ramifications for daily sins so confusing is the timetable for their consequences varies greatly. This is where mankind's misunderstandings begin. <u>Since the negative consequences of our sins can be delayed</u>

at times, the problem is we start to think we can get away
with sin. We think, no big deal. Do it, then confess. This is
one of the consequences of sin. We draw the *wrong* conclusion and this leads us to further disobedience. Please stop to
ponder this statement. This is a very, very important teaching
for us to master. This is where man, from the beginning of
recorded history, has become confused. This misunderstanding of the nature of God has led people to make incorrect assumptions about how God interacts with us. A very
similar thing happens with our children. Punishment delayed
is often seen as no punishment at all. The children do not
stop to think how this affects the relationship they have with
their parents. As with good parents, God is wanting to give
us time to learn certain lessons without having to constantly
punish us to get us to do right.

The people of Zephaniah's time (640-608 BC) present
us with a typical situation related to the problem of God's
restraint and lack of immediate punishment. Many in Judah
had become rebellious. Jeremiah, Habakkuk and Nahum were
among the prophets who Elohim sent to restore their relationship to Him. Unfortunately, the people were not willing
to hear their godly messages. The Old Testament book of the
prophet Zephaniah holds a very important lesson for us even
today. In this story, God was giving Judah time to repent.
Judah had been warned when the Northern Kingdom fell in
722 BC. Hezekiah's reforms in 729-686 BC gave Judah an
opportune time to seek the Lord (2 Kings 18:1-7). Most assuredly, God did not act in haste to punish His people. Rather,
He urgently called them to repent and escape His judgment.
Turn to Zephaniah 1:12-15. The Jews of that time period
had become disrespectfully complacent. They felt God had
become too distant; that He no longer was concerned with
their behavior. To them the fear of Jehovah God had become
irrelevant. How wrong they were! They had watered-down
their worship of Yahweh to include certain popular worship

practices of the false gods Baal and Molech. Though our false gods have different names today, many who claim to be Christians are not much different from these Israelites. Look at these verses. God warns, "At that time I will search Jerusalem with lamps and punish those who are complacent, who are like wine left on its dregs, who think, 'The Lord will do nothing, either good or bad'" (Zephaniah 1:12-15).

A large number of the Israelites had become so complacent in their wickedness that they denied that God was active in their midst. Why did people back then not believe God would punish their sins? Why do people today still believe God will not punish their sins? The answer is Satan is very cleaver in confusing people. <u>Our society is full of victims but few of us look at ourselves as being on the receiving end of God's wrath</u>. Think about this carefully. It applies to believers and nonbelievers alike. We like to think that our misery is always someone else's fault, not our own. With most people, Elohim's punishment has been delayed so long that they no longer fear it. They misunderstand His patience (Romans 2:2-8). Most people do not think they will actually have to answer for each and every act of disobedience.

Furthermore, in our culture, many think they have the power and privilege to determine what *is* right and wrong. Today these confused people go so far as to consider moral values to be something which is up to the individual to determine. They are deceived into thinking there is no accountability. Moreover, they certainly do not realize that each of us is judged the moment we die – judgment is not some big event far off into the future. The moment you die, your spirit and soul are either relocated to heaven or to hell (much more about this will be discussed in chapter 9). The Day of Judgment in Revelation 20 is the final judgment. You can be certain of this – we do not go into some state of limbo at death. We do not simply cease to be.

It is amazing to me how correct the old adage is that "the more things change, the more they remain the same." How much of what is going on today closely resembles Judah during Zephaniah's ministry? Think about it. As an example, all this talk we have today of multiculturalism and celebrating diversity has turned our brains into spiritual mush! The Christian God desires unity not diversity in our understanding and worship of Him. While it is certainly appropriate for the different denominations to express their praise for God in their own chosen manner, we are all to submit to one unified set of beliefs, as stated in the Christian Bible. Having a choice between the denominations is a good thing. It allows people to consider the nuance differences between the various Christian denominations. People can then pick which one best represents how they interpret God's Word. The various denominations should have much more in common, with only a few interpretational differences separating us. None are to take worship practices and beliefs from other religions (and false religions) and incorporate them into their worship. This would be blending the doctrines of Christianity with other beliefs in order to possibly attract nonbelievers. We are absolutely not to do that. <u>We are not to pick and choose what of God's Word we like, delete what we do not agree with, and then further complicate things by adding beliefs from other groups to make our worship practices more appealing to the world at large</u>. These people are to become believers in Jesus Christ. There is no provision for some hyphenated brand of Christianity. God is very specific in this. Refer to Joshua 1:7, "Be strong and very courageous. Be careful to obey all the law my servant Moses gave you; do not turn from it to the right or to the left, that you may be successful wherever you go." People are not to add to or take away anything God has given us in the Holy Bible. We are not to become too lenient or too strict. We are to know our Bibles and follow God's Word. His Spirit inspired the writing of these 66 wonderful books and we would do well to personally know what is in these books.

Congregations who dilute their statements of doctrinal positions in order to make themselves feel better about their disobedience or to attract nonbelievers are going against God's commands. For that they will answer. Stop and ask yourself, "Where in Paul's writings do you find "diverse" ideas of worship which are radically different from what Peter and James presented in their letters?" These great heroes of faith sought to unify and bring into harmony the very specific commands of our Triune God. This blending of cultures to water-down Jehovah's teachings is exactly what was going on in Judah during Zephaniah's ministry. We are to be diverse in that Jehovah God appeals to all people. We are to be united in our core beliefs, as purposely given to us through the Holy Spirit. More precisely, <u>we are not to make God into what we want Him to be</u>. <u>We are to become what He wants us to be</u>! Elohim is the potter; we are the clay (Isaiah 29:16 and 64:8).

Many today mistake God's patience as Him being so distant that Elohim is no longer relevant. Now read Zephaniah 2:3. "Seek the Lord, all you humble of the land, you who do what He commands. Seek righteousness, seek humility; perhaps you will be sheltered on the day of the Lord's anger." What was the purpose of this message from God to the people of Judah? Zephaniah was to warn Judah of El Elyon's judgment in an effort to guide God's people into humbly turning back to the Father. Today God calls us from the worship of materialism, humanism, secularism, the worship of the earth, pleasure, and other false gods. Why is God so patient and merciful with us? The same reason He created us; He wants fellowship with us. God is patient. He is slow to anger. Elohim wants to give each of us a chance to realize our transgressions and come to Him in confession and repentance.

However, by being slow to anger, people of all ages have mistaken God's patience as a sign they do not have to worry about being held accountable for their sins (Romans 2:2-8). This is key to a proper understanding of our relationship with God. Adonai, our Lord and Master, holds us accountable for our actions – regardless of the time expanse between the disobedient act and His final judgment. If we would consider this more carefully, we would not have such a casual attitude towards what we consider everyday sins. This reflects how profoundly we underestimate the testing. Due to a dearth of maturity in spiritual discipline, most people want what they want and they want it now. With eternity in the balance, God gives us every opportunity to make Him the proper object of our faith. With our scarcity of spiritual maturity, man keeps placing his immediate desires ahead of refining his saving faith in God Almighty.

Now let us return to our original discussion point. Since each of us will act as Adam and Eve did, we too are not worthy of living in Eden. Be honest; look at your life. Look at the other Bible stories. Are theses stories not true of all of us? The Old Testament is still relevant today. Our lives are most often a microcosm of God's plight with the Israelites. We mistakenly think our sins are without consequences. We act as though God is too far away. Our society wants us to think God is no longer relevant. But God has a plan for those who *will* turn to Him in confession and repentance. Someday we will, as the redeemed children of God, return to Eden. What a day that will be. In the meantime, here's a sobering thought: what tendencies will you pass on to your children?

### The Nature of Sin

Dr. Henry Blackaby in his book Experiencing the Cross gives this insightful explanation of sin in the life of a believer. "Our sin nature is that controlling tendency that keeps drawing us away from God. But when we become a Christian, we die to sin as the dominating factor in our behavior. Being born again brings an immediate and totally changed attitude toward sin" (p.122). Notice, Dr. Blackaby is not saying that all sin in your life will be magically removed once you place your faith in Jesus Christ as your Lord and Savior. What he is saying is that our attitude towards sin should undergo a radical change. Sin is to be avoided, not excused. It must no longer be the governing factor in our behavior. Furthermore, we should not think we have reached a victory just because we are now sinning less. We should come to have the same disdain for sin that our heavenly Father has for it.

Still, we must deal with the reality of living in a fallen world. At times during the day, I am sure I commit sins which I am not even aware of them being sins. Our culture has watered-down our perception of right and wrong so much that you may be making inadvertent sins without your awareness. What can a sincere Christian do about our sin nature and the influence which this world exerts on us? First, we must demand of ourselves that sin is no longer to have a *dominating* power over our thoughts and actions. Blackaby addresses this by saying, "Does that mean we live a perfect life? Does it mean you're completely free from committing any sin? No, but it does mean a consistent pursuit of holiness and consistent growth in holiness. Though we still commit occasional sins, we no longer continue in sin; we no longer *remain* in sin" (Experiencing the Cross, p. 125-126). A genuinely sincere believer will no longer hold on to any cherished sins in their lives (Psalm 66:18). As Paul wrote in Romans 6:14, "For sin shall not be your master..." If sin still has a hold on your life, then either your salvation experience is invalid or, more likely, you need help from your pastor or spiritual friends to guide you in overcoming the grip of this sin. There is no shame in seeking help in becoming a better Christian. The shame is being the same person year after year and never making any progress in the sanctification process.

Our world's view of man's sin nature is 180 degrees off from what Scriptures teach us. Nonbelievers want to deny or minimize sin rather than rejecting it. They enable others rather than holding them accountable. Nonbelievers even try to reject the righteousness of God's judgment against sin. One of the ways nonbelievers try to trip up believers is by making God sound harsh and unreasonable in His stance on sin. They may ask "Do you mean that if a guy lived to be 20 years old and never committed but one sin, that he would go to hell for all eternity? What if all he did was to say a swear word. Would your God send him to hell for such a small thing?" What would be your answer? Most of us would say that God regards all sins as serious and this young man would be held responsible for swearing. Then they may use this to raise the question, "How can you worship a God who would send someone to hell for such a minor infraction?" What is happening here is that you would be falling for a sucker punch. This single sin is not so much the problem. What needs to be realized is that it indicates a much larger spiritual dilemma. The deeper personal crisis is not so much in the imaginary young man's predicament but rather it is manifested in the person asking the question.

To this world's determent, most people do not take sin seriously. They do not recognize it for what it actually reveals. Sin indicates the condition of a person's heart. In our world, absolutely no one can live to be 20 years old and not have a series of sins to be accounted for on Judgment Day. This is the superficial problem in the above scenario. More basic than the sin issue is that God examines where you place your faith. We are going to believe in something – that is how God Almighty wired us. Unfortunately many people mistakenly place their faith in other gods, such as wealth, status, the environment, science, government, man-made religions, entertainment, sports, and the list goes on and on. However, even if you have redemptive faith in God, you will still sin at times. We never escape totally from the clutches of our sin nature. If you do not have faith in Jehovah God, you will sin even more. The difference is where you have placed your faith. Our God is both a jealous God and a righteous God. He will not accept as righteous a life lived in goodness if it does not include Him as the one true God. If someone ignores (thereby rejecting) His offer of salvation, that is an open act of rebellion. As a righteous God, who is also eternal, rejection of His offer for the redemption of our soul carries an eternal price. The condemnation of a person's soul is for their rebellion against God, which is reflected in their sin nature. Therefore, sin is emblematic of where your faith is (or where it is not). John 3:16 does not promise eternal life if we never sin. God wants our faith and He sent His Son into this world to redeem us from our sin problem.

In addition to Paul's teachings on the subject of accountability and sin, Jesus presents the idea of individual responsibility in a number of passages. Luke 12:48 gives this revelation from Jesus, "But the one who does not know and does things deserving punishment will be beaten with few blows. From everyone who has been given much, much will be demanded; and from the one who has been entrusted with much, much more will be asked." By having the Holy Scriptures so readily available to us in our culture, we will be judged more harshly than people who have little or no access to God's Holy Word. We have been given much; so much will be demanded of us. Matthew 25:15-30 is Jesus' parable about the talents (money) and how each servant was held accountable for how he used his master's money to produce a dividend. The desired result was to hear, "Well done, good and faithful servant! You have been faithful with a few things; I will put you in charge of many things. Come and share your master's happiness." The unwise servant thought poorly of his master. He saw his master as a harsh, unethical person. His lack of trust led him to make a poor choice. He heard these words, "You wicked, lazy servant! So you knew that I harvest where I have not sown and gather where I have not scattered seed?" (This was not true of the master but because the servant was lazy, he did not take the time to know the truth.) "Well then, you should have put my money on deposit with the bankers, so that when I returned I would have received it back with interest. Take the talent from him and give it to the one who has the ten talents. For everyone who has will be given more, and he will have an abundance. Whoever does not have, even what he has will be taken from him. And throw that worthless servant outside, into the darkness, where there will be weeping and gnashing of teeth."

These teachings reveal a measure of *proportional responsibility* – being held accountable for how we respond to what we know of the message of God. For those who do not have the advantage of the Bible, they will be judged by what God has written in their hearts. The NIVDSB commentary for these verses states, "premeditated or high-handed sins have always been deserving of greater punishment than unwitting sins. The result of this principle is that there are to be degrees of punishment and reward". People who have at least a casual knowledge of Jesus will be held highly accountable for their lack of faith. They have been adequately exposed to the true nature of God, so He will be completely righteous and just in His judgment of them. My point here is that all three servants knew their master to one degree or another. With Americans, we have all been exposed to the truths in the Bible to one degree or another. Those who reject a saving faith in God will be justly punished. Those who respond with faith will be greatly blessed. Notice the money was taken from the unfaithful servant and given to the one who achieved the most with what was given to him. Does this mean that those believers who achieve greatly with what God has given them, will they be given greater rewards in heaven than the rest of us? I think so. Certainly Billy Graham deserves more than Glenn Leonard. God has told us our rewards will be given according to what we have done with His truths. Do not squander your time here on earth just storing up for yourselves treasures which are temporary. Store up future treasures in heaven as well. It seems to me someone else said this one time before. Who was that man?

We will conclude our present discussion concerning the nature of sin and personal accountability with Paul's teachings in Romans 2:5-16, "But because of your stubbornness and your unrepentant heart, you are storing up wrath against yourself for the day of God's wrath, when His righteous judgment will be revealed. God will give to each person according to what he has done. To those who by persistence in doing good seek glory, honor and immortality, He will give eternal life. But for those who are self-seeking and who reject the truth and follow evil, there will be wrath and anger. There will be trouble and distress for every human being who does evil: first for the Jew, then for the Gentile; but glory, honor and peace for everyone who does good: first for the Jew, then for the Gentile. For God does not show favoritism. All who sin apart from the law will also perish apart from the law, and all who sin under the law will be judged by the law. For it is not those who hear the law who are righteous in God's sight, but it is those who obey the law who will be declared righteous. (Indeed, when Gentiles, who do not have the law, do by nature things required by the law, they are a law for themselves, even though they do not have the law, since they show that the requirements of the law are written on their hearts, their consciences also bearing witness, and their thoughts now accusing, now even defending them.) This will take place on the day when God will judge men's secrets through Jesus Christ, as my gospel declares." Paul further explains in Romans 3:19, "Now we know that whatever the law says, it says to those who are under the law, so that every mouth may be silenced and the whole world held accountable to God." When we pray, we should ask God to help us desire in our hearts what He desires in His heart for our lives. That is when our sin nature will lessen and our righteousness will grow.

As Christians we know all these things, <u>so why do we continue to sin?</u> What is it about the nature of sin that allows it to have such a magnetic pull to us? The struggle is within us. <u>We want what we want and we want it now.</u> This is largely the answer. Our free will often leads us in one direction and Jesus leads us in another. That is because our free will is usually very self-centered. Jesus tries to get us to focus on kingdom things. Part of the problem is the element of time. Since God is so patient with us, giving us every opportunity to come to Him in genuine confession, He has been incorrectly labeled as being absent. Not only nonbelievers but many purported believers do not see God as being active in their lives. Though they may flippantly say 'praise God', most people do not give Him credit for the good things which happen to them. They see their achievements as being the direct result of their skills and intellect. They forget who gave them these skills and intellect. <u>Far too many people do not see the bad things which happen to them as being the consequences of their rebellion against God</u>. Put bluntly, most people no longer fear the holiness of God.

## *Our Lack of Fear of God's Holiness*

God gives the world a dramatic lesson early in His written word in how He holds us accountable for our sins. The story of Noah in Genesis 6:8-22 gives us also an excellent model of faith put into action. Noah built an ark of tremendous dimensions even though it had never rained. This took great faith. People back then scoffed at Noah because they did not fear God's judgment. Much like today, the people did not fear God's wrath. Throughout the ages, God's patience has been repeatedly misunderstood. Most think it means God no longer watches over us or cares to punish our disobedience. They are blinded by their sinful hearts. This leads to thinking Elohim is too distant to be concerned with them. As today, in Noah's time they came to feel that God's righteousness was irrelevant to them.

This lack of a proper respect for and fear of the holiness of God has led many to mistakenly think of God as being solely a loving creator. As I have said and will say many times, Yahweh is very much a loving God. However, above all attributes, El Elyon is holy. When a person develops the incorrect assumption that God is like a grandparent rather than the holy (and thereby righteous) God of the universe, this inclines them to minimizing sin in their lives. They lull themselves into thinking they can sin without any fear of correction, reprisal, or judgment. Our churches have gotten away from discussing how Christians are to hold God in proper reverence and fear. Due to this, many do not know how to balance the love of God with a proper fear of God. However, we *are* to fear God, in all senses of that phrase. Henry Blackaby echoed this sentiment when he wrote, "One of the great condemnations of our day may be that we have lost the fear of God." Blackaby goes on to point out the problems for which this condition is emblematic. "Those who perceive God as a benevolent and gentle grandfather will treat their sin superficially. They will worship halfheartedly. They will live life on their own terms rather that God's. But a reverent fear of holy God will dramatically affect the way a person lives." He concludes with, "A deep sense of awe is essential to knowing God" (Experiencing God Day – By – Day Devotional, page 154).

Moses teaches an excellent lesson about fearing the Lord. In Deuteronomy 10:12 -13 Moses proclaims, "And now, O Israel, what does the Lord your God ask of you but to fear the Lord your God, to walk in all His ways, to love Him, to serve the Lord your God with all your heart and with all your soul, and to observe the Lord's commands and decrees that I am giving you today for your own good." What did "fear the Lord" mean to Moses? Fear can be explained as holding God in the highest of reverential awe. This highest degree of reverential awe produces a willing obedience in our thoughts and actions. To fear the Lord is part of having a good relationship with Him. It also includes a good old healthy fear of God's wrath. Moses had seen God's wrath (Exodus chapters 7-12). He knew God's warning of punishment was no hollow threat. Moses knew to take God seriously. <u>As with Moses, we should have such a reverential awe that God is so holy, powerful and righteous that we dare not take Him lightly</u>.

The reason we are to fear the God who loves His creation is because, above all else, Elohim is holy. His holiness requires Him to treat all of us in a righteous manner – Jew, Christian, Muslim, Hindu, Buddhist, pagan, atheist, or whatever. God shows no favoritism (Romans 2:11). If we sin, that sin has to be propitiated. Regardless how much He loves each and every one of us, our sin debt has to be paid in full. For all of mankind, Jesus is the one and only atoning sacrifice (John 3:14-18, Romans 3:21-25). Without Jesus as your Lord and Savior, God's righteousness requires Him to hold you liable for your sins. Your sins therefore condemn you. The end result is – if you disregard Jesus, you will face God's judgment and wrath alone. That should put some healthy fear in your heart!

Even those who have Jesus as their Savior will still be judged. Ultimately, we will be judged righteous, yet even so, we will be held accountable for our thoughts and deeds.

These thoughts and deeds will determine the rewards we are to receive after the Day of Judgment (Matthew 6:19-21, Revelation 20:11-15 and 22:12). This is totally separate from the judgment of our eternal existence as in Revelation 20:11-15. A Christian is judged righteous when they accept Jesus Christ as their Lord and Savior. As we will discuss further in this book, your salvation is assured by the redemptive power of our Lord's royal blood at the cross. That judgment has already been decided. Do not be mistaken – we cannot lose our salvation. Jesus purchased that for you when He went to the cross. Our sin debt was paid in full. The theological point here is that God's righteousness requires Him not to act in a flippant manner towards sin. For even those who have Jesus as their Redeemer, we still must have the over-riding esteem for God Almighty that we fear treating Him lightly. God takes sin seriously and so should we. <u>We are not to claim to others that we have Jesus as our Savior yet have a casual disregard for our sinful thoughts and deeds</u>. This destroys our witness and misrepresents our Redeemer. If we claim to love Jesus, we must follow His commands (John 14:15, 21).

# Chapter Four A Right Side Up World

---

When you ask yourself how this world could be made right side up again, one of the first things which should come to your mind is that mankind needs to become more righteous. What is righteousness? <u>In its most basic form, righteousness is bringing yourself into harmony with God's will for your life</u>. To be in harmony with God, we also have to be in accord with mankind. Righteousness is not really tested if you withdraw from others and become a recluse. All of God's creation is important to Him. We are to cherish not only our relationship with our heavenly Father but with all that He has created.

Righteousness is defined by Dr. Merrill Unger as, "Purity of heart and rectitude of life; being and doing right" (<u>The New Unger's Bible Dictionary</u>, page 1081). A Christian is said to be righteous with God if they live in accordance to His commandments. The NIVDSB states, "To fulfill the will of God and to become righteous is to be actively involved in what God wishes accomplished in our world" (page 1415). Why is it so important that we be righteous? Is not having faith sufficient? It all depends on whether you want to do the minimum required to enter heaven's pearly gates or you want to be all that God originally designed you to be.

Imagine for a moment what this world would be like if mankind had maintained a righteous walk with God. Now imagine what your life would be like if all the people around you were concerned about living right with God. Go one step further. Imagine what your life would be like if you lived a righteous life. We cannot undo history. There is nothing we can do about this being a fallen world. One day it will be as our Lord promises us, but not right now. Additionally, we cannot force others to behave in an upright manner if they do not so desire. We cannot change history or others. What we can change is ourselves.

To effect a remarkable change in our lives, we must first try to understand the goal we are seeking. We do not have to fully understand moral rectitude before pursuing it. We can learn as we go. Is this not the process of sanctification? We discover how God wants us to think and act, and then we modify our thoughts and actions to reflect His desires. This is a daily process which will encompass our entire life. The first initial step in righteous is found in Romans 3:21-28. You might as well memorize this passage because I refer to it throughout this book. These verses teach us about God's righteousness and what is required for us to be righteous with God. *A righteous relationship with the God of Christianity is based solely on having a genuine, redemptive faith in our Triune God. This God graciously gives us forgiveness of our sins and eternal life as the result of our steadfast faith in Jesus as being the Son of God. Jesus, as a supreme act of love, sacrificed His atoning blood for the sins of man, thereby making the risen Christ Jesus our Savior and Redeemer.*

When we act in accordance with God's will, our righteousness will not likely win us many popularity contests. Most people will like you in that you are pleasant to be around. Nonetheless, you will not fit in with much of their activities. Your moral rectitude will make some feel awkward; others will consider you boring. Virtuous behavior is not something which this world at large will reward. That is fine. As Christians, we do not look to the world for its approval. Your church, your Sunday School class, and your minister will certainly appreciate this pursuit of righteousness. Your family and friends will be positively influenced by your steadfast quest for righteousness. Above all, you will be blessed; inwardly by both your own spirit and by the Holy Spirit.

What does the Bible teach us about the pursuit of righteousness? Solomon warns us by saying, "The path of the righteous is like the first gleam of dawn, shining ever brighter till the full light of day. But the way of the wicked is like deep darkness; they do not know what makes them stumble" (Proverbs 4:18-19). His father, David, tells us, "For surely, O Lord, you bless the righteous; you surround them with your favor as with a shield" (Psalm 5:12). David goes on to give us the best reason for pursuing righteousness in Psalm 34:15-19. "The eyes of the Lord are on the righteous and His ears are attentive to their cry; the face of the Lord is against those who do evil, to cut off the memory of them from the earth. The righteous cry out, and the Lord hears them; He delivers them from all their troubles. The Lord is close to the brokenhearted and saves those who are crushed in spirit. A righteous man may have many troubles, but the Lord delivers him from them all." God and only God can make this world right side up.

### *The Chain of Righteousness*

On our back porch we have our family swing. It is suspended from the ceiling by two eye hooks and a couple of eight foot chains. When I went to hang this swing, I had to go to the hardware store to purchase the chains. Knowing that my family's safety and enjoyment (along with my reputation) depended on the strength of these chains, I purchased two heavy-gauged steel chains. Suppose the hardware store had a "special" going on for a different chain. It was like the one I purchased but in the middle it had a couple of links which were made of thin plastic. Would I have been tempted to have saved a little money? Not at all. Having been raised in a rural setting, I know the value of a good strong chain. For years as a young man I had a chain which my grandfather gave me in the trunk of my car. Running into the ditch off a dirt road seemed to be a specialty of mine. I quickly learned that a chain is only as good as its weakest link. As my father taught me, it does not matter how strong all the other links in a chain are – if you substitute an inferior link or two in with the rest, the chain will fail.

A complex series of spiritual events interlocking much like the links of a chain work together to bring us into a righteous relationship with God Almighty. I like to think of this as the chain of righteousness. These links start with: (1) the conviction by the Holy Spirit (John 16:7-8) of our transgressions, which leads us to (2) the confession by us of specific sins (Leviticus 5:5, 1 John 1:6-9). We must be sufficiently sorrowful of these transgressions that this moves us to (3) genuine repentance (2 Kings 22:19, Luke 18:9-14, 22:56-62, Acts 2:37-38) which working together with (4) faith (Romans 1:17, 3:21-28) bring (5) forgiveness of our sins (Psalm 103:8-12, Matthew 6:14-15, 9:5-8, Luke 7:45-50). With this forgiveness from God this gives us (6) a restored relationship (Romans 5:8-11) with the Holy Trinity. All of these confessions are rendered (7) acceptable to Elohim (Hebrews 11:4) dependent on the (8) condition of our heart (1 Samuel 16:7, Proverbs 21:2, Jeremiah 17:9-10, Matthew 22:37-40). (9) Works follow which reveal the condition of our heart (Matthew 5:16, James 2:26, James 3:13). (10) It is by our righteous words and works that we are distinguished as belonging to Christ Jesus (Matthew 13:23, 16:27,

Luke 6:45, John 15:1-5). With most nominal believers, their hearts are not dedicated to repentance, so their faith, their attempts at righteousness, and whatever works they may perform are not acceptable to God. Think of the offering which Cain (Genesis 4:2-7, Hebrews 11:4) gave to God. It was not acceptable. Why? It seems his heart was not right with God. To be in a righteous relationship with Jehovah God our hearts need to be pure. A pure heart will support great faith (Psalm 24:4-6, Luke 1:26-38). As we know, it is by faith that we are judged righteous (Genesis 15:6, Romans 1:17).

Each of these links in the chain of righteousness will be discussed extensively in this book. How could it be a book about redemptive faith if we did not cover what is required of us to maintain a harmonious relationship with the Holy Trinity? This paradigm for righteousness should be embedded in our minds. It should guide our decisions. It should be written in our hearts. As with Abraham, we do not have to be perfect. However, we do have to have an ample supply of faith. Through our righteousness, we reveal our faith. And what does redemptive faith lead to? Listen to the words of our beloved Peter. In 1 Peter 1:7-9 he teaches, "These have come so that your faith—of greater worth than gold, which perishes even though refined by fire—may be proved genuine and may result in praise, glory and honor when Jesus Christ is revealed. Though you have not seen Him, you love Him; and even though you do not see Him now, you believe in Him and are filled with an inexpressible and glorious joy, for you are receiving the goal of your faith, the salvation of your souls." This is why we must study righteousness. The reward is heavenly.

In his wonderfully insightful book, <u>Mere Christianity</u>, C. S. Lewis talks about "Nice People or New Men" in chapter 10. Here Lewis covers the topic of sanctification. He asks, "If Christianity is true why are not all Christians obviously nicer than all non-Christians? If conversion to Christianity makes no improvement in a man's outward action – if he continues to be just as snobbish or spiteful or envious or ambitious as he was before – then I think we must suspect that his 'conversion' was largely imaginary. Fine feelings, new insights, greater interest in 'religion' mean nothing unless they make our actual behavior better" (p. 207). Lewis then warns us, "Christ told us to judge by results. A tree is known by its fruits. When we Christians behave badly, or fail to behave well, we are making Christianity unbeliev-able to the outside world" (p. 208). This is Lewis' way of saying that righteousness extends beyond our relationship with God. Since Christians represent Christ to the rest of the world, how else could it be?

### *Forgiveness*

Asking for forgiveness without turning away from those sins and back to a righteous relationship with God will not get you forgiveness. If you continue in sin, forgiveness will not be given by God. He demands obedience, not lip service (Isaiah 29:13). In 1 Samuel 15:22 Samuel admonishes King Saul, "Does the Lord delight in burnt offerings and sacrifices as much as in obeying the voice of the Lord? To obey is better than sacrifice..." Saul received this tongue lashing because he had not followed God's instructions in the war with the Amalekites. God's Word is not merely a set of desires or wishes by the heavenly Father. They are His commandments and He wants them obeyed.

Examples of God's wrath being turned aside can be found in the lives of King Rehoboam and King Hezekiah. King Hezekiah started his reign as a devout king. We learn in 2 Kings 18:5-6, "Hezekiah trusted in the Lord, the God of Israel. There was no one like him among all the kings of Judah, either before him or after him. He held fast to the

Lord and did not cease to follow Him; he kept the commands the Lord had given Moses." He had a heart for God and led his people accordingly. As with all people, along the way Hezekiah encountered temptations. In 2 Chronicles 32:24-26 we read of Hezekiah's sin, repentance, and subsequent forgiveness: "In those days Hezekiah became ill and was at the point of death. He prayed to the Lord, who answered him and gave him a miraculous sign. But Hezekiah's heart was proud and he did not respond to the kindness shown him; therefore the Lord's wrath was on him and on Judah and Jerusalem. Then Hezekiah repented of the pride of his heart, as did the people of Jerusalem; therefore the Lord's wrath did not come upon them during the days of Hezekiah." The lesson here is that God is slow to enact His wrath for He is graciously awaiting our repentance. If we will confess and repent, then God is quick to forgive. We serve an awesome God!

Turn to 2 Chronicles 12:5-12. Here we have King Rehoboam facing an invasion. "Then the prophet Shemaiah came to Rehoboam and to the leaders of Judah who had assembled in Jerusalem for fear of Shishak, and he said to them, "This is what the Lord says, 'You have abandoned me; therefore, I now abandon you to Shishak.'" The leaders of Israel and the king humbled themselves and said, "The Lord is just." When the Lord saw that they humbled themselves, this word of the Lord came to Shemaiah: "Since they have humbled themselves, I will not destroy them but will soon give them deliverance. My wrath will not be poured out on Jerusalem through Shishak. They will, however, become subject to him, so that they may learn the difference between serving me and serving the kings of other lands...Because Rehoboam humbled himself, the Lord's anger turned from him, and he was not totally destroyed. Indeed, there was some good in Judah."

Notice here that although God forgave Rehoboam, his sins carried a consequence. <u>Just because God promises to forgive us of our sins does not mean that we escape all consequences for these sins</u>. God always wants to bring us back into a righteous relationship with Him. Sometimes the only way to do that is for us to experience a little pain as the result of our disobedience. These consequences also help us to build up our defenses for future temptations. It is amazing how well I remember certain lessons which came from my failures. A wise person learns from the follies of others. That leaves the rest of us to learn from the school of hard knocks.

What are the main points these two passages about Rehoboam and Hezekiah teach us concerning forgiveness? If you will go to Matthew 5:3-12 Jesus gives us the character traits which He would like each of us to develop as being citizens of His Holy Kingdom. The Beatitudes teach us to be humble in our spirits and sorrowful over our sins. God does not take sin lightly and neither should we. Hezekiah was distraught over his sin and God saw in his heart his true remorse. God cannot be mocked. <u>To be forgiven, we must humbly approach God with a genuine confession and be resolute in our repentance</u>. Rehoboam became poor in spirit. In other words, he dropped his haughty pretense and became humble unto the Lord.

When we turn to God for strength and guidance rather than to ourselves and others, we are displaying the behavior which God wants us to have. The Holy Spirit is always searching our hearts; always convicting us and encouraging us to follow the commands of our heavenly Father. What else do the Beatitudes teach us? Yahweh wants us to be pure in heart, which means we should not have mixed motives. When we seek Him with sincerity, God honors us with His presence. By meekness God desires that we obediently accept His guidance and turn to Him for ultimate vindication (when others hurt us). We are to trust in His timetable for justice rather than taking matters into our own hands. This means we are to turn to our heavenly Father for strength rather than exerting our own control over situations. If we are to seek His mercy, then we must show compassion to others. God desires that we seek Him with all our hearts. El Shaddai does not want us to casually approach the truths which He has laid out for us. He wants us to have a real, burning passion for righteousness in our lives to where we deeply crave to live out the will of our Father. Whenever dissension arises (especially within the family of believers), we must actively seek to restore harmony. How can we be a light to the world if we are constantly fighting amongst ourselves? Being a peacemaker is a highly prized trait in the kingdom of God. We must also be tenacious in our faith. We are to expect persecution from this world. It purifies us and shows our true heart. At times, God can be mysterious in His ways but He is not mysterious in how He wants us to interact with Him and all His creation. If we will work to develop these traits, God will be quick to forgive us when we miss the mark.

Turn now to Psalm 103. Pay particular attention to verses 8-13, "The Lord is compassionate and gracious, slow to anger, abounding in love. He will not always accuse, nor will He harbor His anger forever; He does not treat us as our sins deserve or repay us according to our iniquities. For as high as the heavens are above the earth, so great is His love for those who fear Him; as far as the east is from the west, so far has He removed our transgressions from us. As a father has compassion on his children, so the Lord has compassion on those who fear Him;" God is not a God who desires to display His wrath. Our God is a God of love. His first choice in any situation with us is to be loving and merciful. How we embrace these truths as outlined in the Beatitudes determines how Jehovah God responds to us when we turn to Him in prayer.

## *Two Models for Forgiveness – God's and Ours*

When we search the Scriptures for lessons on forgiveness, we discover a remarkable truth. God has one set of rules governing the forgiveness we seek from Him and another set guiding how we should forgive others. For most of my life I have mistakenly thought we are to follow God's model when forgiving others. I am so thankful for a Sunday School class many years ago for pointing out to me the incorrectness of my thinking. Thank goodness I was in a class where we were encouraged to participate and ask questions. A whole new understanding was revealed to me. I had been following the wrong model for forgiving others and, in doing so, had not been as forgiving as I should have been. I had also allowed others to continue to negatively impact me because I was confused on what forgiveness mandates. In this section I want us to discover God's plan for forgiveness as it relates to us and to others.

The question is: Are we to model our forgiveness of others by the paradigm which God has for us? Not really. God requires we approach Him in humble confession and repentance. Only then will He forgive us. Even more so if you are a Christian should you ask for forgiveness. Our sins will not cost us our salvation but they definitely will tarnish our personal relationship with God Almighty. Here is the point – it is a very different matter when transgressions occur between two people. For one thing, when someone does something which would require your forgiveness, you can count on them having offended God as well. With that said though, man's forgiveness towards others takes a little different track. <u>We have to forgive even when the offending party does not ask for forgiveness</u>. Yes, you read this right! Even if they are glad they hurt us, we should still forgive them. This is a very hard lesson at times. It is much easier said than done. Nonetheless, it is what God wants us to do.

Why do we have to forgive others even when they do not ask to be forgiven? So we can maintain a righteous relationship with Jehovah Tsidkenu (The Lord Our Righteousness, Jeremiah 23:6). Enmity for others hampers our harmony with the Father. <u>For the sake of righteousness is why we forgive</u>.

In Matthew 6:14-15 Jesus teaches us, "For if you forgive men when they sin against you, your heavenly Father will also forgive you. But if you do not forgive men their sins, your Father will not forgive your sins." Notice that Jesus does not place as a requirement that the offending person must come to us asking for our forgiveness. We are to come to God asking for His forgiveness, but the same does not apply for us. The requirement for us is we must forgive if we desire to be forgiven.

Our love for God plays an indispensable role in forgiveness. We are to love Him *and* all His creation. What does Jesus teach us about love and forgiveness? Read Luke 7:36-47. Do yourself a favor. Stop reading this book and turn to this passage right now. Have you ever wept over the weight of your sins? Have you ever been so remorseful because you let our dear Jesus done with some habitual sin that you shed crocodile tears? This is my favorite lesson about the relationship between forgiveness and love. The remorseful woman in these verses should be dear to all our hearts. The weight of her sins caused her to mourn. She was pouring her heart out, like the perfume, with her tears falling on Jesus' feet. The sincerity of her emotions drove Jesus to acknowledge her confession and grant her forgiveness. Oh, that we all would approach the feet of the Master in such humility and love. The significance of this passage is that those who are forgiven much love much. The corollary to this is those who love much are forgiven much. Forgiveness by God should foster not only love but humility as well. <u>Humility gives us the *wisdom* to forgive others when they wrong us</u>.

Would you say Joseph displayed great wisdom in how he dealt with the approaching famine in Egypt (Genesis 41:25-57)? Did he show wisdom in how he reconciled with his brothers? Do you think God is trying to teach us that wisdom and forgiveness are linked? How are wisdom and forgiveness linked? Turn to Proverbs to learn the words of Solomon concerning human interactions. Proverbs 2:6-11, 11:2-3, 15:1-2, 20:22, and 28:13 showcase some of Solomon's insights. Solomon instructs us in Proverbs 19:11, "A man's wisdom gives him patience; it is to his glory to overlook an offense." A hot temper reveals pride and pride undermines wisdom. Of all the sins, pride seems to make forgiveness all the more difficult. This is why Jesus talks so much about humility. A humble heart embraces the teachings of forgiveness much more quickly than one full of self-pride.

To return to our original question: Is forgiveness given by God only when the offending party asks for forgiveness? Go to Deuteronomy 29:19-20. Moses reveals God's plan of wrath if someone tries to hide their sins. In Leviticus 16:20-22, Moses teaches the Israelites what must be done to atone for their sins. Go to Joshua 24:19-20, where Joshua warns of God's retribution if the Israelites turn to other gods. David tells us in Psalm 32:1-5 we need to confess our sins. "Blessed is he whose transgressions are forgiven, whose sins are covered. Blessed is the man whose sin the Lord does not count against him and in whose spirit is no deceit. When I kept silent, my bones wasted away through my groaning all day long. For day and night your hand was heavy upon me; my strength was sapped as in the heat of summer. Then I acknowledged my sin to you and did not cover up my iniquity. I said, "I will confess my transgressions to the Lord"— and you forgave the guilt of my sin." In 2 Chronicles 33:10-13 we learn God forgives when we sincerely ask for forgiveness. Each of these passages shows that God requires us to admit our sins to Him. We are to come in humble supplication. Nowhere is it mentioned that God automatically forgives the sinner. Here is what we know. As Christians, Jesus has paid our sin debt in full. On this we should all agree. I am not prepared to say though that since Jesus has paid my sin debt in full that I never have to seek the Lord's forgiveness ever again. While the matter of my salvation is secure, my righteousness *is* affected by my disobedience. A contrite heart and a confessing tongue are what God requires.

In Luke 17:3-4 Jesus teaches us about our responsibility in being forgiving unto others. Here Jesus tells us to forgive if someone repents, regardless of the number of times they sin against us. This is very similar to what we are taught about God forgiving us. The offending party is to approach us or God and confess their sins, right? We all know we must exonerate someone if they sincerely ask us to absolve them for some wrong they have committed against us. Matthew 6:14-15 and Mark 11:25 specify that we are to forgive others. Notice, this is not predicated on being *asked* to forgive. These passages do not stipulate that the person has to seek our absolution. In Luke 11:4 Jesus makes it clear we are to forgive everyone. "Forgive us our sins, for we also forgive *everyone* who sins against us." In Colossians 3:13 Paul instructs us to, "Bear with each other and forgive whatever grievances you may have against one another." In 1 John 4:20-21 this passage explains why we have to forgive even if not asked. John declares, "If anyone says, 'I love God,' yet hates his brother, he is a liar. For anyone who does not love his brother, whom he has seen, cannot love God, whom he has not seen. And He has given us this command: Whoever loves God must also love his brother." Bitterness separates us from the love God desires us to have in our hearts. This damages our relationship with each other and with Him, thereby causing us to miss the mark set for our lives by the Lord.

The Beatitudes clearly instruct us concerning what is expected of us by God. If you thirst for righteousness, are merciful, and seek to be a peacemaker, then being forgiving must be part of your character. From where does the strength to carry out these behaviors come? It can be appropriated via the fruits of the Spirit (Galatians 5:22-23). God does not require anything of us which He does not equip us to do. Paul reinforces this in 2 Timothy 3:16-17, "All Scripture is God-breathed and is useful for teaching, rebuking, correcting and training in righteousness, so that the man of God may be thoroughly equipped for every good work." Whatever the challenge, whatever the dilemma, you can find verses in the Bible which will guide you in the direction of God's will. If you are having a hard time forgiving others, you can start to learn God's instructions by turning to the concordance in the back of your Bible. This will launch you into many verses which relate to this subject. Then pray that the Holy Spirit will give you the self-control, gentleness, patience, kindness, and love to enable you to be more forgiving. When this is done, then joy and peace will come back in your relationships.

I want to be clear about a very important matter. Forgiveness does not mean Christians have to surrender their legal recourse when someone commits a crime against us. We can still seek justice against those who do us harm. To be righteous with God does not mean we are to be the world's doormat. If someone harms your family you should try to forgive in whatever measure you can. A peacemaker is not required to be an appeaser. My heart bleeds for families who experience the killing of one of its members by a vicious criminal. To have to sit in court and hear how someone savagely killed a loved one requires extraordinary strength. I would not want to walk up to those people and tell them they must forgive that person. However, that is what they are to do. Forgiveness like this though is a monumental task. If this happens, you should engage your minister and a professional counselor. Much time may be required for the process to be complete. Believers are perfectly right to seek society's justice against those who perpetrate crimes against us. Do not become confused on this. The victim's family should take the vengeance out of their hearts as much as possible. Whatever is left over, give it to God. Turn it over to the One who will avenge all wrongs. Honor His timetable and allow the vindication to be at His hands. He and only He can heal these wounds. I hope I never have to follow my own advice on this. May God have mercy on the poor souls who mourn over the loss of a loved one killed by an unrepentant sinner.

What about instances where there is no crime but someone has wronged you in a moral or an emotional manner? What God desires is that we do not allow the seeking of vengeance to destroy our walk with our Lord. <u>We are to trust in God's vindication, on His timetable, and in His manner</u>. We are called to forgive the person regardless of the conditions. However, forgiveness does not require that we have to be willing to go on vacation with the offending party or even to sit down with them over a meal (1 Corinthian 5:11, "But now I am writing you that you must not associate with anyone who calls himself a brother but is sexually immoral or greedy, an idolater or a slanderer, a drunkard or a swindler. With such a man do not even eat.").

<u>Forgiveness actually is very liberating</u>. We are not to wait until someone asks us for forgiveness. Do it immediately. This frees us from the unpleasant emotions of hostility, vengeance, anger, and hate. This is not only good for your spiritual nature; it is good for your mental and physical health as well. You will sleep better, digest your food better, and your face will look better as well. Bitterness puts stress on all aspects of your life. Forgiveness, on the other hand, frees you from all the aggravation of hurt feelings and the plotting of revenge. It purges you of enmity for your fellowman and reconciles you with God.

Why is such forgiveness so cathartic? It releases your soul from the antagonism which once held it captive. This is very therapeutic. The stress from negative emotions impacts all aspects of your health. Releasing this stress produces spiritual, emotional and physical healing. To no longer carry around any feelings of hostility toward yourself or others is very liberating. Release that stress. Forgive and go on with living. If you can reconcile with the offending person, that is the best of all possible resolutions. This is what Jesus calls for in Matthew 5:23-24. "Therefore, if you are offering your gift at the altar and there remember that your brother has something against you, leave your gift there in front of the altar. First go and be reconciled to your brother; then come and offer your gift."

What are we to do when we are unable to resolve our differences? For certain, we are not to be held captive by our own forgiveness. You are not required to allow someone who is continually combative and hurts you to have access to you. If reconciliation is not possible, then live life to the fullest, apart from that person. To be righteous in the eyes of God does not require us to disband human reasoning. As God requires us to turn away from our sinful behavior, we can require those who ask us for forgiveness to turn away from their harmful behavior. If they do not, we still have to forgive them, but we do not have to continue to associate with them. In Luke 10:8-11 and Acts 13:50-51 we have the biblical accounts of what to do when facing rejection. We are not to ask that fire be rained down on them (Luke 9:51-56). When the disciples shook the dust off their sandals, this symbolized their wish to separate themselves from those who rejected the message of Christ Jesus. What we are to do in these cases where we need to separate ourselves from the offending party is to trust God with the proper dispensation of justice. We are to pray that they learn from the situation. We should also pray that we grow in our reliance on the Lord for self-control and a forgiving heart. Truth is most altercations involve elements of improper behavior by both parties. They may be struggling to forgive you as well. You may still have hard feelings about a lingering hurt but as a mature Christian you are to place the offense in God's hands, to be dealt with on His schedule. Nothing anyone has ever done to me compares to what my sins cost Christ. He is our Redeemer; the least we can be is willing forgivers.

Dr. Stanley gives further amplification for this subject in his book, <u>Finding Peace</u>. Stanley writes, "There are also some people who take pleasure in making other people miserable. They see their ability to inflict pain on another person as a form of power or control. These people feel good only when others around them are feeling bad. They resent anybody who has genuine joy. Ultimately, these people are angry at themselves, but they rarely will admit that self-anger. Then again, conflict to some is the only life they have known. The possibility of peaceful coexistence is an unknown possibility!" (p. 179). It is terrible when family strife makes living together unbearable. If you have never been subjected to continuously being put down, discouraged, belittled, being the object of someone's constant anger, then you may not identify with Dr. Stanley's words. Marriage and family membership were never meant to be an emotional prison. People who treat others this way are in no way righteous with God.

If you have a family member who is characterized by this behavior, doing nothing is an option. Unfortunately, it probably will turn out to be the wrong option though. If these people will not change, then you may consider removing yourself from their presence before they destroy the rest of your family, your health, and possibly your sanity. Always keep the door open for reconciliation should they come to terms with their destructive behavior. Be patient; be loving. Give them as much time as possible. However, do not allow them to become destructive by their presence.

If remaining in their company starts to make you pull back from God because of the bitterness and hostility, then you must come to a decision. Sometimes family, friends, or acquaintances may push you to your breaking point. You may be considering taking some aggressive response if they cross you again. They may have pushed your buttons some often that you no longer feel comfortable calling upon God. Your thoughts of anger have become such that you know your intentions are not honorable to God. You may even start to pull away from God and distance yourself from your daily walk. How can God allow this to happen is what you start thinking. You may even begin to blame God for not correcting this situation. Please stop and reflect on what God teaches. Forgive them; then remove yourself from their presence. To walk away is far better than to act out in anger and violence. Walk away from them, not God. We are to fervently guard our close, personal relationship with our Triune God. Nothing should be allowed to come between our righteous walk with God (1 Corinthians 10:12-13).

In seeking peace, Dr. Stanley emphasizes, "We must always forgive" (Finding Peace, p. 163). Go to Col. 3:13, "If anyone has a complaint against another; even as Christ forgave you, so you also must do." Dr. Stanley goes on to say, "There is never any situation in which unforgiveness can be justified before God. Forgiveness does not mean we deny our injuries, dismiss our pain, or lay aside all claims to justice. It *does* mean that we must release that person from our judgment and let go of any bitterness or feelings of revenge. Should the other person decide to walk away from your relationship, you are not responsible for his action. Should the other person decide to continue to treat you with contempt, criticism, condemnation, or cruel behavior, you are not responsible for his behavior. Do all that you know to do to live in peace with others – with a pure, loving, patient, and forgiving heart – and you will have done what God requires of you" (p.163). Reread this statement. It has been so liberating for me. For too long I thought forgiveness meant I had to continue in a relationship with that person. If they did not change in their behavior, then I was essentially trapped by my own forgiveness. Dr. Stanley teaches that we are to always do what is required by God – to forgive them. We do not have to continue to allow them to mistreat us though. Remember the words of Paul in 1 Corinthians 15:33, "Do not be misled: 'Bad company corrupts good character.'"

## *What God Restores, He Restores Completely*

It is very important that we understand what it means to us to be restored by God. If we do not know what it conveys, we will not properly appreciate it. We will not react in the correct manner. Many of us have been restored by God, only to continue to act like our walk with Him is somehow defective. We can be our own worst enemy at times. Guilt can rob us of the joy of being restored. If someone makes you feel like you are not worthy of God's restitution, shame on them. Sometimes our own feelings get projected onto others. Perhaps it is your guilt or regret which makes you perceive they are trying to make you feel less than reinstated. Regardless, our heavenly Father has a wonderful plan for correcting our imperfections. Being restored to a righteous relationship with El Shaddai has tremendous healing powers.

Dr. Charles Stanley's words of encouragement for those in search of restoration are summed up in this quote. "True, you may still have to live with consequences related to the sin. But you are never required by God to live with guilt, shame, or regret. Accept that your past mistakes may have put you into the situation you are in, but quickly acknowledge the greater truth about your past mistakes – now forgiven by God – do not need to impact the decisions or choices you will make in the future. Remember always...What God forgives, He forgives completely. What God heals, He brings to wholeness. What God restores, He does so without any limitations placed upon a person's potential for sharing the gospel and being a witness of God's love, mercy, and grace" (Finding Peace, p. 108). These are not merely fanciful words spoken by a seasoned minister. These are wonderful words of truth. Look at Abraham, Moses, David, Peter, and Paul. Each of these great heroes of faith had major battles against sin. But when God restored each of these men, He restored them without any limitations placed upon their potential for sharing the gospel and being a witness of God's love, mercy and grace. Reflect on these words; meditate on their meaning in your life. These encouraging words minister to a hurting heart.

The pearl of wisdom here is that God is complete in His forgiveness. After being forgiven, we are open to whatever service God places in front of us. We are not relegated to a second-class status in our kingdom pursuits. If there are any lingering feelings of hurt and incrimination, then you need to look inward. Have you allowed yourself to receive the fullness of His forgiveness? What if Peter had given up after denying Christ? What if David had stopped writing psalms after his affair with Bathsheba and the killing of her husband? What if Paul, knowing he played a role in the stoning death of Stephen, had allowed self-incrimination to destroy his ministry? To our benefit, God used each of these men in mighty ways after bringing them back from their guilt and shame. Can He do the same for you? Only if you will let Him. Dr. Stanley tells us, "perhaps the most difficult part of forgiveness for many people is forgiving themselves" (Finding Peace, p. 106).

Never ever allow anyone to steal your joy (including yourself). This is what I tell myself and my family when things are not going our way. If someone says something hurtful to you and you get mad or offended, they have stolen your joy. If you plot revenge, they have stolen you joy. It is impossible to be happy and contented when pursuing acts of retribution. The lack of forgiveness will lead to conflict and disharmony. Chances are you will never enact all of the vengeful battle plans you have concocted in your mind. Who wins when this happens? Most of the time when we are hurt it is partly because we have allowed our pride to overextend itself. Humility goes a long way towards staving off hurt feelings. If you are struggling with self-doubt and incrimination over your sins, these two emotions can certainly diminish your relationship with God. They will make you feel like pulling away from your daily prayers and Bible study. Please do not allow this to happen. Every Christian should have a list of favorite Psalms to go to when their soul needs uplifting. Psalm 23, 25, 37, 103, and 143 are the ones which I turn to when my spirit needs a godly boost. The Lord has a wonderful plan for restoration if only you will avail yourself of it. Let go of your guilt and return to the joy which the Holy Spirit is so wanting you to experience.

By all means, we are definitely to take sin seriously. I am not advocating a flippant attitude toward sin (either ours or someone else's). I am not saying we should pursue spiritual joy by ignoring sin. There should be no joy in our sins. However, if someone hurts us, we do not have to minimize it by acting like it does not matter. This does not make us appear "more spiritual." On the other hand, if we have committed a sin, we should not minimize that either. A dismissive attitude towards sin will have consequences. If you have committed a sin, then react maturely. If so moved, mourn over it (Matthew 5:4). The weight of our sins *should* cause us to grieve. Realizing you have missed the mark which God has for you should be deeply troubling. Talk it over with someone you trust. If someone has sinned against you, then talk over what your Christian response should be.

It is great having friends and trusted advisors to help keep us balanced in our lives.

However, there is a time for talking and there is a time for burying. Some sins are such that we should speak with a trusted Christian advisor in order for us to gain a better understanding of all the ramifications of the event. When you gain this enlightenment, ask God to forgive you for the specific wrong you have committed. Pray that God will help you learn from this failure. Then, very importantly, forgive yourself. For many of us, this is the hardest part. After you have done all of this I suggest you do the following. Dig a mental grave. Take all the negative emotions – the hurt, guilt, shame, regret, anger, desire for vengeance, wounded pride, and any other emotions swirling around in your head – and put them into a coffin. Bury your negative feelings and all those unpleasant memories surrounding this event. Tap the dirt nice and tight on this grave. Do not erect a head-stone. Do not allow yourself or anyone else to go digging around this grave. <u>Once you have paid the price for your sin, stop paying</u>. What is the price? Sincerely asking God for His forgiveness of that specific act and then turning completely away from that transgression – this is the price which God demands. Anything after that is fodder for Satan to use to destroy your witness and your relationship with God Almighty. When God heals us from our sins, He heals us completely. When God forgives us, He forgives us completely. When He restores our relationship with Him, He restores it completely. Nothing else needs to be done. It is finished. Continue to remember the lessons of your sins but do not continue to relive the negative emotions surrounding these events. God does not ask that of us. Bury your failure; then get on with life.

As I reflect on my own life, no one has ever done anything so terrible to me that cannot be forgiven. Even more basic, no one has ever cost me what I cost my Lord and Savior. When

I go to the foot of the cross, it changes my whole perspective. When I meditate on what burden my sins placed on a totally innocent man, I feel ashamed of allowing my pride to rear its head. As I ponder the significance of our holy Jesus having to leave heaven to deliver me from my bondage to sin, what option do I have? I *must* forgive. What manner of man would I be if I did not? My Lord Jesus paid it all. The least I can do is to forgive and move on. Whether that means I have to forgive someone else or, more often than not, to forgive myself, that is what I must do. We serve a totally awesome God. <u>Our Lord Jesus takes us at our very worst and makes us whole</u>. He heals us with His gentle comfort and reassures us of our worth. When Christ restores us, there are no words of human encouragement which exceed His restitution. His essence permeates our total being. The only limitation to His restoration is when we have insufficient trust and faith that God does what He says He will do. Reread Psalm 103. Believe these words. They are faithful and true.

Here is <u>the wisdom of forgiveness</u> as related to when someone hurts you – it is not completely about the other person and you. You do not forgive because of the other person – <u>you forgive because you do not want anything (including your emotions) to separate you from God</u>. The other person may not care if you have forgiven them or not. They may not even ask for forgiveness. That is not the point. You may be in a situation where you are compelled to forgive in spite of the other person. Even if they have not asked for forgiveness, you are still to forgive them. Why? You do this so that you do not harbor any feelings of bitterness toward another person (Leviticus 19:17-18, Psalm 37:8-9, Romans 12:17-19, and James 1:19-20). <u>Trust God for the dispensation of His justice</u>. <u>Bitterness over past wrongs will fester and hinder your personal relationship with God</u>. This is so because you show in your continuing bitterness that you are not trusting God to properly handle the situation. <u>Forgive them not for their sake but for your sake</u>.

# Chapter Five Can Faith be Lost?

⸺᳁᳁᳁⸺

Hebrews 11:6 states, "And without faith it is impossible to please God, because anyone who comes to Him must believe that He exists and that He rewards those who earnestly seek Him." Notice the caveat in this passage. We must earnestly seek Him. This is added here so we will know that God demands a firm, steadfast faith. This closes the door on any casual, moderately interested mental acceptance of Jesus as your Lord and Savior. A belief which is resolute and steadfast is what I refer to as a core belief. The Bible references in Hebrews and 2 Peter where people "fall away" from their faith. How is it that some people can have faith, yet later renounce it? Can someone who once truly believed in Christ Jesus fall away from a saving conviction of Him?

When we say we believe such and such, what are we trying to convey? We most likely want the person we are talking with to consider our position on something as being worthy of their contemplation. The word "belief" has many components and forms. We have primary (core) beliefs, secondary, and tertiary beliefs. Each of these groups carries more significance with us than our daily thoughts and opinions. The three levels of beliefs vary in status according to our commitment in energy, emotions, and cognitive processes with them. Belief in a secular fashion is the psychological state in which an individual is convinced of the truth or validity of a proposition or premise (argument) without the ability to adequately prove their main contention for other people who may disagree (Wikipedia). Belief in spiritual terms is an acceptance that God's character traits and His words as revealed through the Holy Bible are authentic, trustworthy and merit our faith. Belief is one of the components of faith (faith includes belief, commitment, and trust; reference Chapter One). <u>We must have the belief that God is who He says He is; the trust that God does what He says He will do; and the commitment to pursue His holy will in our daily lives.</u> <u>These three components of faith are to be borne out in our righteous living.</u> <u>Anything less is not acceptable to our heavenly Father, our Lord Jesus, and our guiding Spirit.</u>

 I am reluctant to use politics as a discussion point for this lesson, but it contains the best example of a situation in my life where faith in something has been renounced. In reality, political beliefs often change as we get older. I am hesitant to admit it but I voted for Jimmy Carter for President. I was a young college student (need I say more?). I believed I saw something in Jimmy Carter as a person which would shape him into being an outstanding President. I trusted him because of his integrity and religious faith. I believed his scientific background, not being a Washington insider, and being the Governor of the State of Georgia would all make him a better President than Gerald Ford. I did not like how Ford handled neither the Watergate situation nor the way Ford was handling the Middle East. So I thought the country needed a change (boy was I in for a surprise). This was no small commitment on my behalf. My entire family was for President Ford. They did not ostracize me but I did break with my traditional voting pattern. Political views are important to my family but they are not what I would call a core belief system. My current attitude concerning politics is that I would never risk hurting a friendship over an argument about politics.

The less emotions a belief has associated with it, the easier it is to change. Since faith involves belief, it follows the same pattern. Our thoughts and attitudes combine with the emotions surrounding this mental framework to establish our beliefs. Intellectually accepted beliefs and casual beliefs are what you would call secondary and tertiary beliefs. Secondary and tertiary beliefs can change. Core beliefs remain with us. I slowly changed my belief in Carter when he proved to be completely inept as the highest executive in our government. When his failed economic policies caused my father to close his hardware store, I totally abandoned any belief I had in him as a forward thinking leader. Dad would buy a small item for $.50 and sell it for $.75. The problem was that on the next order this previously $.50 item now cost him $.68. A small business could not operate for long in this type of economic climate. For a host of reasons, Jimmy Carter, in my opinion, was the worst President of my lifetime (and has proven to be an even worse former President). As an aftermath, I fell away from my former belief that Carter represented a positive change for our country. I continued to believe he was a man of personal integrity but I no longer trusted in his abilities as a national leader, much less a world leader. I returned to my former political orientation as the result of this unpleasant national experience. The point is, certain beliefs change based on your life situation and experiences.

## *Our Core Beliefs*

Core beliefs help define you as a person. They reflect the very essence of your being. Examples of my core beliefs are such things as: my belief that my father and my mother (both deceased) loved me with all of their hearts; my belief that America is the greatest country to ever exist; my belief that Christianity offers the only path to eternal salvation; with a steadfast belief in Christ Jesus, I belief I can face all that life throws at me and with God's strength I will one day see the splendor of the eternal heaven; and I believe the Holy Spirit indwells me and guides me as I seek to know and follow the ways of God Almighty. Secondary and tertiary beliefs give your personality flavor and are important in shaping how you interact with others. My secondary and tertiary beliefs are such things as: I believe the Baptist doctrine most closely reflects my understanding of what God wants to convey in the Holy Bible; I believe less government is better; and I believe in taking personal responsibility for your choices and actions. If I were talking with a friend who thought Jimmy Carter was absolutely the best President ever, I would probably not even mention my opinion of him. My current belief about him is just not that important to me to risk an argument with a friend.

If my friend said he thought fundamental Christians are as big a source for world turmoil as radical Islamics that would trigger a much more animated response in me. I would want to know why they would make such a claim. I would want to know about specific instances which caused him to make such a statement. Then I would try to help that person to see that Christianity has become the favorite religion for the world press to malign. This might explain why they would have such a negative attitude toward something which I hold so dear. I would try to point out that everywhere Christianity becomes strong, freedom breaks out. It would be my desire to help that person understand that Jesus was constantly working to improve the position of women, children, the poor and the oppressed. Our Lord offers eternal hope through a personal relationship with each believer instead of a bunch of rituals which only make you feel good about being obedient. In other words, the emotions surrounding my core belief would motivate me to try to engage in whatever positive dialogue I could think of in order to change my friend's thoughts into a more favorable attitude toward something which I cherish. Nominal beliefs do not carry such a cherished status. They make for good conversation but they do not engender such a passionate defense which our core beliefs do. The one thing I admire about many in the Muslim world is they do seem to have a great passion for their beliefs. I respect this even though I do not agree with them.

The more central a particular belief is to defining your core values, the more resistant it is to being changed. These political beliefs of mine during the 70's were more than casual thoughts – they were beliefs (probably tertiary in status in this case). Through this entire period though, my core belief in Jesus as my Lord and Savior never changed. My belief that America is the greatest country in this world has never changed. My belief that the words in the Bible are holy and true has never changed. I must admit, my behavior has not always publicly confirmed these core beliefs because behaviors can reflect changing secondary and tertiary belief systems as well. Additionally, sometimes our core beliefs war against our selfish desires. Other times core beliefs are in conflict with newly developing secondary and tertiary beliefs. These psychic battles can cause noticeable fluctuations in our behavioral patterns. This is where I feel some of the confusion over the following biblical passages concerning people who appear to lose their faith can be traced. Where a person may give the impression that they have lost their faith may actually be the fluctuating dynamics of these secondary and tertiary beliefs which are not core to that person's being. These lesser beliefs vary as their life experiences change. It is for this reason that when someone becomes a Christian, it is imperative they progressively move forward in their sanctification process. Bible studies, Sunday School attendance, service in some area of the church, and developing a strong connection with a support group are vitally important in helping this person move their new found belief into a core belief.

Our faith in Jesus as our Lord and Savior is meant to be such a core belief (Hebrews 11:6, Psalm 51:10, Isaiah 26:3,). Peter says it very well in 1 Peter 5:8-10, "Be self-controlled and alert. Your enemy the devil prowls around like a roaring lion looking for someone to devour. Resist him, standing firm in the faith, because you know that your brothers throughout the world are undergoing the same kind of sufferings. And the God of all grace, who called you to His eternal glory in Christ, after you have suffered a little while, will Himself restore you and make you strong, firm and steadfast." Someone who "falls away" certainly is not standing strong, firm and steadfast. If you are *not* steadfast in being spiritually committed to God, then your belief is more fluid in nature. It is still a belief, just not a core belief. The point I trust I am making is that it is not altogether unusual for people to renounce some previously held secondary and tertiary beliefs. It is most unusual when someone "falls away" from a core belief though. You cannot read any of the Old Testament nor the New Testament without getting the impression that anything less than an authentic commitment to God is unacceptable (1 Samuel 7:3, Matthew 5:8).

Our redemptive faith is more accurately described as a core belief system. A core belief system denotes the presence of a network of multiple, related beliefs interwoven into a framework from which all draw support. It is obvious to me that anyone who "falls away" from a previously held spiritual belief in our Lord: (1) had not made that conviction a core belief; (2) had not trusted fully in God's plan for their salvation; and (3) had not genuinely committed to living their life seeking righteousness through faith in Christ Jesus. Without a real commitment to Christ Jesus as your one and only Lord and Savior, I believe you have no salvation. This commitment is given substance by the obedience of your heart to serving His kingdom. "Do not be deceived: God cannot be mocked. A man reaps what he sows...the one who sows to please the Spirit, from the Spirit will reap eternal life" (Galatians 6:7-8).

This discussion of faith and core belief systems should make it easier for us to consider the following question: since it is faith which opens us to God's salvation (Romans 3:21-28), can this faith ever be lost? Can someone who has accepted Christ at some point become so discouraged or hardened that they renounce their faith? This is what some Christian denominations believe. Eternal Security – "Once Saved Always Saved" – is a nice, clean, and emphatic doctrine which is dear to the hearts of many Christians. As we reflect over certain Scriptures though, there has been much debate among Christians over the absolute totality of this doctrine. We want to review whether these questions are over the interpretation of biblical truths, or are they reflecting beliefs which are not core beliefs of those who "fall away", or are these questions mostly about translational nuances of specific passages which have led to this confusion.

I want to use the discussions of eternal security primarily as an instrument to reveal an essential element of redemptive faith. Even if you do not totally accept eternal security as a doctrine, this element of redemptive faith which I am referencing is central to anyone's salvation. This book centers on genuine faith. It is in Satan's interest that you not question the authenticity of your faith. If you have a shallow or weak faith, he wants you to think that is sufficient. He wants anything which will keep you from having a strong, vital relationship with God Almighty. Why? Satan wants you to deceive yourself and others so that you do not become a life altering, effective witness for our Lord and Savior. I cannot say it enough. This world is a gigantic battleground for the forces of good and evil. In this book I will be using various discussion points like eternal security to highlight the integral role faith plays in our salvation. Since faith is so central to our salvation, we need to examine it from multiple angles to make sure that we "know that we know" that our redemption is for all eternity.

What we want to achieve with this discussion is an in-depth understanding of why we can believe so firmly in the security of our salvation. We will look at specific Scriptures which cause confusion to some, and we will also examine the Scriptures which very emphatically support this steadfastness of our faith.

In the KJVLASB commentary for Hebrews 11:6 it states, "God will not settle for your mere acknowledgment of His existence. He wants a personal, dynamic, life-transforming relationship with you. God assures us that all who honestly seek Him – who act in faith on the knowledge of God that they possess – will be rewarded". This goes for those who have never heard the Gospels (Romans 2:13-15) as well as for those of us who were raised in church. Be mindful, this is not a "works salvation" for either group. We will be judged by the faith which we have in whatever measure God has been revealed to us. We will all be held accountable for how we have responded in faith to God's message, either through nature or through the Holy Bible.

### *Who are These People Who renounce Their Faith*

The question we are researching here is: "Can someone reject Jesus *after* they have accepted Him as their Lord and Savior?" In 2 Timothy 2:11-13 Paul discusses this topic – "...For if we be dead with Him, we shall also live with Him...If we suffer, we shall also reign with Him: if we deny Him, He will also deny us: If we believe not, yet He abideth faithful: He cannot deny Himself." In the commentary of my KJVLASB, the writer states: "God is faithful to His children, and although we may suffer great hardships here, He promises that someday we will live eternally with Him...Don't turn away from God...Jesus will stay by our side even when we have endured so much that we seem to have no faith left. We may be faithless at times, but Jesus remains faithful to His promise to be with us always...Only one thing can break our communication with God – if we turn against Him and refuse His help." This turning against Him is precisely what worries some people about eternal security. Can it happen after you have accepted Christ as your Savior and cause your loss of eternal security, or are you no longer in a right relationship with Him but still His, or were you ever His?

The ultimate in rebellion is the rejection of your belief in God. The following 3 passages relate to people who have had at best perhaps a tertiary (or maybe as much as a secondary) belief in Jesus. Most likely they only had an intellectual acceptance of Christ. They obviously knew His teachings well enough to have been drawn to Him at least for a short period of time. It seems likely to me by how these verses flow that they did not go through any spiritual transformation while exploring the teachings of Christ. I do not get the unequivocal sense that the Holy Spirit ever indwelt them. I know it appears rather simplistic for me to assert that these people were simply not saved. How convenient. As we go through these passages, it can become rather tangled. Translations are challenging. Nuances might have been missed or enhanced by certain translators and commentators. I know all of this is possible with these and many other passages. I also know that sometimes simple is best. It is very hard to say the degree to which any of these people committed their souls to Christ. Only God knows a person's heart. This is why these 3 passages can cause so much debate. Words can be hard to translate and beliefs can be hard to correctly categorize if we do not have first hand knowledge of someone.

Please read Hebrews 6:4-6: "It is impossible for those who have once been enlightened, who have tasted the heavenly gift, who have shared in the Holy Spirit, who have tasted the goodness of the word of God and the powers of the coming age, if they fall away, to be brought back to repentance, because to their loss they are crucifying the Son of God all over again and subjecting Him to public disgrace." Does this not seem to describe someone who has renounced Christ as their Savior? The phrase "who has shared in the Holy Spirit" leaves lots of room for interpretation. Be cautious. It does not say they have accepted the Holy Spirit. It does not say the Holy Spirit has indwelt them. To have shared in the Spirit of God could mean they had knowledge of what the Holy Spirit does for a person but they have not been transformed by the Spirit. William MacDonald in his <u>Believer's Bible Commentary</u> on page 2174 supports this line of thinking. He counsels, "Before we jump to the conclusion that this necessarily implies conversion, we should remember that <u>the Holy Spirit carries on a preconversion ministry in men's lives…He convicts unbelievers of sin, of righteousness, and of judgment.</u>" In my own conversion, the Holy Spirit was very active in bringing my spirit into a proper awareness of the magnitude of my approaching decision. The Holy Spirit was tugging at my inner spirit to let go of any resistance and encouraging me to follow the promptings of my heart. Before He indwelt me, He had communion with my spirit.

Hebrews 6:4-5 are such intriguing verses. Frankly, they can be made to say whatever you want them to say. If you do not believe in eternal security, you can use these verses as proof that the people referenced here absolutely were believers. How else could it be said they had been "enlightened" or had "tasted the heavenly gift and the goodness of the word of God" if they were not genuine believers? Or maybe it is not actually saying this at all. This is why Bible study can be so invigorating. It challenges our investigatory skills. Think back to the time prior to your conversion. When you went to church, were there not times when you gained greater understanding (enlightenment) of the Lord. These experiences are how your belief system grew to the point where you finally accepted Christ Jesus as your Savior. Did you respond to the alter call the very first time you heard a sermon about Jesus? Not likely. There were probably times when you tasted of the goodness of the word of God prior to your conversion. Here is the point – these experiences are common among those who are investigating salvation as well as those of us who have accepted God's holy plan of salvation. If you are a nonbeliever, they are validating experiences and emotions which encourage you to further examine His holy words. If you are a believer, they add further confirmation to your growing belief system that God is who He says He is and that He does what He says He will do. The road to salvation is a journey. It is filled with all types of obstacles and challenges. If it were not so, then the Parable of the Sower and the Parable of the Weeds would not be so relevant. The conversion of our spirits out of darkness takes time. During this time, nonbelievers are gradually experiencing the same things we mature believers experience.

To further highlight the eternal dangers taught in these verses, Hebrews 6:6 relates to the sin of apostasy. William MacDonald in his commentary of this verse declares, "This signifies a deliberate, malicious spurning of Christ, not just a careless disregard of Him. It indicates a positive betrayal of Him..." (page 2174). What this boils down to is a rejection of the promptings of the Holy Spirit. <u>This is so final because without any response to the promptings of the Holy Spirit, one will never be led to confessing their sins</u>. Without the confession of sin, then no repentance will be made. Without repentance, then no forgiveness can ever be granted. No forgiveness means no salvation.

Apostasy is the turning away from the truths of God and embracing false teachings. This can only occur with someone who has spent time receiving at least a measure of knowledge about God. They may even have joined a church at one time. This is more than merely not believing after hearing a few sermons. It is not the same as being a backslider or being immature in your understanding of the Scriptures either. This is an act of someone's free will to reject God and turn to some other means to gain what they consider to be "truth". Perhaps the apostate considers the commandments too harsh or the Christian lifestyle too demanding. The hypocrisy of a believer may have turned this person totally away from church life. Perhaps God's Word labels as off limits something which that person really enjoys doing (like a cherished sin). False teachings most commonly have as their aim to justify some lifestyle which is contrary to God's Word and commandments. This is where apostasy is so dangerous. Our heavenly Father has one and only one plan for our salvation. There are no options B, C, D, and E. Only plan A – through faith in Jesus Christ as our Lord and Savior can someone be saved. The apostate rejects the terms for salvation which God has laid out for him and turns to seeking some other form of god as the object of their belief system. When people do this, they are playing with "fire"; even more so when they lead others astray. If you do not know God's Word, you are susceptible to teachings which will mislead you from God's truth. To be more precise, the apostatic person never nurtured their initial acceptance of Jesus into becoming a core belief system for guiding and defining their life. They are represented as the 3$^{rd}$ type of soil in Matthew 13:7 and 22.

These verses are very different from the backsliding ways of the prodigal son (Luke 15:11-32). Read John 17:12. Did Judas ever really accept Christ as his Savior, or was Judas greedily hoping to secure an elevated position in Christ's kingdom on earth by following Him? These Scriptures in

Hebrews seem to point to someone who has renounced Christ. They also seem to point to someone who originally had some measure of faith, regardless what that amount might have been. The question is – was it sufficient to be redemptive faith?

Now turn to Hebrews 10:26-29. "If we deliberately keep on sinning after we have received the knowledge of the truth, no sacrifice for sins is left, but only a fearful expectation of judgment and of raging fire that will consume the enemies of God. Anyone who rejected the law of Moses died without mercy on the testimony of two or three witnesses. How much more severely do you think a man deserves to be punished who has trampled the Son of God under foot, who has treated as an unholy thing the blood of the covenant that sanctified him, and who has insulted the Spirit of grace?" What do you think these verses reveal? Habitual sinning, meaning having cherished sin (Psalm 66:18) in your life, is a rejection of Jesus. Cherished sins signify a lack of commitment to transforming your life into being like Jesus. These are not the occasional daily sins which each of us fight to eliminate from our lives. These are habitual sins which continually cause you to miss the mark which God has set for your life. They are willful transgressions. By looking at the context of this passage, you can tell these are the sins which reveal a lack of authentic commitment to seeking God's righteousness. Hebrews is referencing a person who has heard the message of Christ but rejects it for his daily life. The soul who has genuinely received Christ as their Savior will not commit this mistake. Hebrews 10:39 instructs, "But we are not of those who shrink back and are destroyed, but of those who believe and are saved."

Let us now consider the third passage with deals with someone rejecting their belief in Christ Jesus. In 2 Peter 2:20-21 Peter declares, "If they have escaped the corruption of the world by knowing our Lord and Savior Jesus Christ and are again entangled in it and overcome, they are worse off at the end than they were at the beginning. It would have been better for them not to have known the way of righteousness, than to have known it and then to turn their backs on the sacred command that was passed on to them." In the NIVDSB on page 1610 the commentary for these verses teaches us, "The elect walk in an intimate fellowship with the God of election. He rescues the elect from the presence, penalty, and power of sin, while reserving the ungodly to the Day of Judgment for punishment. Election does not rob the elect of free will. We may be introduced to Christ and reject Him, as Israel repeatedly rejected God's prophets. To reject Christ leads to the most horrible condition a person can know." The key to this discussion is what does the phrase "knowing our Lord" mean in these verses? As we already have discovered, someone can know *of* Jesus without having a committed faith in Him as being their one and only Lord and Savior. If that person subsequently rejects Christ, then God has no other path of salvation available to that person. To "know of Christ" and then reject Him will carry a greater accounting when that person stands at the Great White Throne of Judgment than someone who had never before heard The Good News.

### *Translating the Bible is Challenging Work*

We owe much to the men and women who have labored so diligently to provide us with the best understanding they can convey of God's Holy Word. Ancient words present their own unique set of challenges. Words not only have meanings, they also have connotations. The same word can have subtle changes in meaning over time. This is where a study of the words "believe" and "faith" helps us. Christianity has many variations of the word "believe". Go to www. BlueLetterBible.org on-line and do the word search. The

Greek word "pistis" is a noun which means to have faith – its chief significance is a conviction respecting God and His Word and the believer's relationship to Him. The Greek word "pisteuo" is a verb and it means to be persuaded of; to place confidence in; to trust; a firm conviction – in this sense of the word, reliance upon, not mere credence. Other Greek words for faith are: elpis (hope, faith), and pistos (believing, true). Other Greek words for belief are: peith (persuade, have confidence) and pistis (assurance, fidelity). Each of these words has their own connotations which have to be derived from reading the entire original passage. As one can easily see, those of us who are not linguists have to rely on knowledgeable pastors and commentaries to help us in getting to the root of the meaning portrayed by the nuances of these words. The issue is we do not always know the exact meaning of certain words and so multiple views of these passages are possible. This is where we have to have confidence in our own church's doctrines to guide us. Within the Christian denominations which hold to eternal security, these passages in Hebrews 6:4-6 and 10:26-29, along with 2 Peter 2:20-21 denote people who do not have an abiding (or core) faith in Jesus. They are of a casual faith. Their problem is they have not made the resolution to decisively commit themselves in belief and trust to having Jesus as their Lord and Savior. As we know, Jesus is not one to accept that kind of faith.

There is nothing unusual about preachers and teachers asking believers to accept that words have multiple connotations. We see this all the time in our culture. Being a southern boy, I love fried chicken. I do not eat it often, but when I do I leave a plate of nothing but bones. I keep myself in reasonable shape, so this little indulgence is not too bad. I also say that I love my wife. Linda is one of those special people who, when they come into your life, they make all things better. She is always supportive and gracious. My wife's beauty radiates through her thoughtfulness and daily concern not only for me but for our two daughters as well. If Linda senses I have a preference for an activity, she will act as though it is her preference as well. She does not really care "what" we do as long as we do it together. Linda has been extremely encouraging to me in the writing of this book. She recognizes it takes a lot of my personal time but she feels it is something which is worth the effort. Our lives are in such harmony that it does not require much effort in order for us to have a good time at whatever we are doing. I love her dearly and I am so thankful she is my wife. Bottom-line, she has helped me to become a better man.

As to this discussion, are we to say that the use of the word "love" in both these examples is the same? Certainly not. If my physician told me that eating fried chicken will destroy my health to the point that I will probably die within 5 years, guess what? I will give up fried chicken in a heartbeat. Make no mistake, there is nothing which could be told to me that would make me give up my wife. I absolutely adore her. Linda has a way of making me feel like I'm 10 feet tall. She has a great sense of humor, which makes her a lot of fun to be around. I value her above all persons. My love is God first, Linda second, with family, friends, work, and hobbies following behind. The point is, please do not get hung up on the English translation to the Scriptures without first referencing what the Greek, Hebrew, and Aramaic words originally implied. Words can vary in meaning, depending on the context. <u>The Holy Spirit sought to reveal the truth of God as He guided the 40 writers of the 66 books of the Bible.</u> <u>His truth will be consistent throughout the Scriptures since it was the Spirit of God who was inspiring each person in his own style to present the specific messages God placed on his heart.</u>

How do we come to an academic understanding of the phrase "falling away" from God (as in Hebrews 6:4-6;

10:26-36, & 2 Peter 2:20)? First, we must recognize that translating the Bible is very difficult work. To verify this, pick up a King James Bible, then review the same Scriptures in another translation. Small differences in the translator's choice of words can shape the meaning of the verses in question. An excellent example of this can be found in the NIV translation of Matthew 5:22 where Jesus declares, "But I tell you that anyone who is angry with his brother will be subject to judgment. Again, anyone who says to his brother, 'Raca,' is answerable to the Sanhedrin. But anyone who says, 'You fool!' will be in danger of the fire of hell." We are all familiar with this verse. However, if you read this verse in the King James Bible, you will find an additional statement. The King James version includes the clause "without a cause" inset in between the words "brother" and "will be". To me, this adds an additional element of understanding for what Jesus is consistently conveying in other Scriptural passages about anger. Without this clause, it appears Jesus is a little inconsistent in His message. We can all think of times when our Lord got (justifiably) angry with people.

Here is the curious part. Why was this clause left out of the NIV? The NIV translators may have been using a different source of reference materials and ancient manuscripts than what William Tyndale used when he translated the King James Version. Whatever the case, I feel this clause more accurately reflects Jesus' intentions. Neither Jesus nor God Almighty tells us to never, ever become angry. Please reference Matthew 23:13-33. Here Jesus refers to the Pharisees as hypocrites, blind guides, blind fools, snakes, and a brood of vipers. These are hardly nice words. Were they defensible though? If you look at what had Jesus angry at the Pharisees, you will see the justification. Jesus was speaking harshly against the Pharisees because they were distorting the message of God and leading people astray. When someone harms our family, it is acceptable to become angry with them.

However, Jesus teaches us that this anger must never separate us from our righteous walk with the Father. If a person or a group negatively impacts another person's soul, this is very, very wrong and should engender righteous indignation on our behalf. The Pharisees were so steeped in religious legalism that they were obscuring the true message of God. This resulted in the further oppression of those who listened to them. This example points out that precise translations can be very challenging. Times have changed. Expressions carry different meanings from one time period to another. Ancient manuscripts and reference materials have subtle variances. Sometimes we may lose part of what is being presented via the particular translation.

The concept of "believe" in the above verses cited from Hebrews and 2 Peter is not what we commonly think of today as heartfelt knowledge. According to the commentaries which I have read (MacDonald's <u>Believer's Bible Commentary</u> and others), these Scriptures are referencing people who have more of a casual head knowledge of Christ than a deep-seated faith in Him as their Lord and Savior. The problem is that a literal interpretation of these Scriptures does point to someone of some amount of faith. I can see why certain denominations point to these Scriptures as evidence that eternal security does not exist in absolute form. The epiphany which manifests itself here is that anytime there appears to be a contradictory flow across Scriptures, we need to do the following: 1) look at the predominance of other related Scriptures surrounding those verses as opposed to a few Scriptures which may lead us in another direction; 2) we may want to consult knowledgeable friends, ministers, and commentaries which can help us in gaining the intended meaning of these verses; and 3) pray to the Holy Spirit that He will guide you in the proper interpretation of that passage. <u>The more knowledgeable we are of the Holy Scriptures, the</u>

more the Holy Spirit has to work with in us to bring the message to our understanding.

## *The Value of Tribulations*

Many may think that someone renouncing their belief in Christ is not so much a display of Satan's powers but rather the action of that person's free will. First, consider from where the temptation to renounce Jesus comes. Second, those who have genuinely surrendered their wills to Jesus are tempted even more so than nonbelievers by Satan (he loves nothing better than to destroy the witness of a believer). Third, a believer still has their free will; they just yield it to the will of the Father.

The major difference when faced with trials and tribulations is the actual presence of the Holy Spirit in the life of the believer. He is our active defense against Satan's beguiling ways. The Holy Spirit will make sure no person who is saved will ever be lost. This is assured us by Jesus in John 10:27-29, "My sheep listen to my voice; I know them, and they follow me. I give them eternal life, and they shall never perish; no one can snatch them out of my hand. My Father, who has given them to me, is greater than all; no one can snatch them out of my Father's hand." God's agent for this mission is the Holy Spirit. Be certain of this: whenever man is exercising his free will, the devil is right there trying to influence it. He hates God and wants to destroy anything which relates to God. Remember, he was in heaven but was cast out because of the rebellion. Satan has not stopped the fight though. He is determined to get as many souls in his camp as possible. He is cunning, but his adversary is Almighty. 1 John 4:4 states, "...the One in you is greater than the one who is in the world." Since Christ is omnipotent and it is His intention not to lose anyone who comes to Him in faith, then eternal security for genuine believers is absolute. We can also be certain that only through Jesus can we ever hope for eternal security (John 14:6, Acts 4:11-12). We are in His hands to stay.

Martin Luther in his Commentary on Romans, page 91, points out that "Tribulation does not make a person impatient, but proves that they are impatient. So everyone may learn from tribulation how his heart is constituted". He then references Acts 14:22 "We must through much tribulation enter into the kingdom of God." Luther then makes the following statement as he reviews Romans 5:3-4, "God accepts no one as righteous whom He has not first tried...as in Psalm 11:5: "The Lord trieth the righteous."...God tries us in this way, in order that we may know whether we really love God for His own sake. We thus read in Psalm 139:23-24: "Search me, O God, and know my heart: try me, and know my thoughts: and see if there be any wicked way in me, and lead me in the way everlasting."...If God would not try us by tribulation, it would be impossible for us to be saved." If Luther's interpretation is correct, then God may have used tribulation (testing) in the lives of these individuals who fall away to point out to them that they are not saved.

In the same vein, C. S. Lewis stresses for us Christians, "We begin to notice, besides our particular sinful acts, our sinfulness; begin to be alarmed not only about what we do, but about what we are. When I come to my evening prayers and try to reckon up the sins of the day, nine times out of ten the most obvious one is some sin against charity (love). And the excuse that immediately springs to my mind is that the provocation was so sudden and unexpected; I was caught off guard, I had not time to collect myself. Surely what a man does when he is taken off his guard is the best evidence for what sort of a man he is? The suddenness of the provocation does not make me an ill-tempered man; it only shows me what an ill-tempered man I am. It follows that the change which I most need to undergo is a change that my own direct, voluntary efforts cannot bring about. But

I cannot, by direct moral effect, give myself new motives. After the first few steps in the Christian life we realize that everything which really needs to be done in our souls can be done only by God. God looks at you as if you were a little Christ: Christ stands beside you to turn you into one" (Mere Christianity, p. 192-193). I am thankful for men like Luther and Lewis who help explain some of the mystery of why God allows certain circumstances to come into our lives. It is all about forging a closer relationship with God Almighty. Father truly does know best.

For certain, this discussion leaves me with some pretty sore toes – and deservedly so. I would at times like to blame God for when I speak or think improperly. If He loves me and wants the best for me He should be controlling situations around me better to where these bad things do not happen. Elohim knows how hard I am trying to change from being self-centered to being Christ-centered. It's His fault – except it is not. Why does He not give me a break? Actually, Jehovah Jireh is giving me a break. Without testing, how would I ever realize just how much I depend on the saving grace of God and the promptings of the Holy Spirit? This is where Christianity runs counter to the present American culture. *We are responsible* for our thoughts and deeds. It takes a very spiritually mature person to thank God for this testing. I do not think I am such at times. He still has a work to do with me. There is a lesson in here somewhere for parents as well (but then I would be stepping on toes).

The New Testament has a great lesson about tribulation in Luke 22:31-34, 54-62. This is where Jesus tells Peter that Satan is going to sift his faith. Peter was tested, experienced failure, but he repented and came back even stronger in his faith. Peter was mature in his faith; he just faltered during trial. Some may say this may have been as much a test of Peter's courage as his faith. Courage is affected by our determination and determination is a component of commitment, which is a component of faith. Either way, he did not have the resolve to carry forward with his promise of only a few hours earlier to Jesus. Judas was a whole different matter. Contrast what was different in each of their hearts. Luke 22:3-6, 47-48 & Matthew 27:3-5 relate the account of Judas in his betrayal. One was tested and made stronger in his faith. The other failed the test and let it destroy him. In these same verses (Luke 22:31-42) Jesus Himself was tested. Christ gives us the perfect example to follow when we are in tribulation.

Sin is taking action on our temptations (but not in merely being tempted). Job was tempted to sin against God by Satan but he resisted. Job questioned God but he never sinned against God. Questioning God is not sinful. That is a natural part of a growing, dynamic relationship. Acting out in anger or bitterness would have been sinful of Job. God allows Satan to tempt us in order that our faith is given a test, so it can be strengthened and refined (by having our weaknesses revealed). This is one of the ways of how God uses Satan (remember, God is in control). As we grow in our spiritual knowledge, it is amazing how God turns situations around (Romans 8:28 is forever with us). To us, the devil is completely evil. He is to be avoided at all costs. What Scripture is revealing here, as Martin Luther points out, is that the devil is actually rendering us a service. Only through his temptations can we know what needs improvement. With testing, our faith is either made stronger and more mature or it is weakened and reveals how shallow or even nonexistent our faith actually is. In a strange way, Satan is helping the faithful believers who take this sanctification process seriously to become more like Jesus. We are to resist these temptations by turning to God for strength and guidance. How do we do this? Follow Jesus' example - by prayer, meditation, and calling on His Holy Scriptures for strength and guidance (Luke 4:1-13).

As has been asserted numerous times in the Bible, God tests our inner spirit to see if we are earnest in this commitment to pursuing His kingdom. Paul proclaims in Galatians 5:22, "Do not be deceived: God cannot be mocked. A man reaps what he sows. The one who sows to please his sinful nature, from that nature will reap destruction; the one who sows to please the Spirit, from the Spirit will reap eternal life." If He finds you to be false in your statement of faith, then you are like those who Jesus derides in Matthew 7:15-23. "Watch out for false prophets. They come to you in sheep's clothing, but inwardly they are ferocious wolves. By their fruit you will recognize them. Do people pick grapes from thorn bushes, or figs from thistles? Likewise every good tree bears good fruit, but a bad tree bears bad fruit. A good tree cannot bear bad fruit, and a bad tree cannot bear good fruit. Every tree that does not bear good fruit is cut down and thrown into the fire. Thus, by their fruit you will recognize them. Not everyone who says to me, 'Lord, Lord,' will enter the kingdom of heaven, but only he who does the will of my Father who is in heaven. Many will say to me on that day, 'Lord, Lord, did we not prophesy (preach/teach) in your name and in your name drive out demons and perform many miracles?' Then I will tell them plainly, 'I never knew you. Away from me, you evildoers!'"

As the result of our limited insights, we have to accept each person's profession of faith on face value. Time will tell whether this proclamation is genuine or not. With God it is different. He searches our hearts immediately and knows the true nature of a person's heart. If after professing faith in Christ, you continue to live as of this world, then guess what? You were insincere in your proclamation of faith and God will not accept such disingenuous professions of faith. Go to Acts 5:1-11. Lying to God is costly. It certainly was for Ananias and Sapphira. God gave special insight to Peter in order to teach a very important lesson to the early church.

If you misrepresent your profession of faith, such will ultimately be your fate. An additional point I would like to make here is that once God has tested your spirit to determine its sincerity that does not mean the testing ends. There will be various times in your life when your commitment level will be running low. God will test you in order for you to become aware of this deficiency. The testing never stops because the refinement never stops. Becoming like Jesus is an arduous process. It is not fair; it is not easy. Rid yourself of these human emotions. To become like Jesus requires we function on a much higher plain of existence. Though the tribulations will be difficult, the rewards will be awesome.

It is for our life-long sanctification process why this testing and refinement must continue. Regardless of the circumstances of our spiritual status, testing is to help us to identify where we need work (either to accept the Lord or to grow our faith). In the case where one or more of the three components to faith are either lacking or weak, then the Holy Spirit has to help us discover this deficit. This is what Martin Luther was talking about concerning tribulation (testing). God will send tests our way in order to point out to us that one of the three basic components to faith needs work. If we have a good minister, Sunday School teacher, parent, or spiritual coach guiding us during this period, adjustments can be made. What happens too often is that most people think that once you have "walked down the aisle" and been baptized, all is finished. As Dr. Bailey Smith, an evangelist who spoke at our church, points out not all is well with some of these folks. This line of discussion is not meant to make you question your salvation, with the intention to make all of us doubtful. It does though recognize a very real problem in our churches. There are a certain number of church members who have never earnestly given their faith to the Lord. They walked "down the aisle" but they were not sincere in their profession of faith. Something was lacking. Dr. Smith wisely told our congregation, if you are in doubt of your conversion, pray to God to make you aware of any problems you might have. Our loving heavenly Father will not be troubled by this. He wants you to "know that you know" you are going to heaven. If there are doubts about whether you were sufficiently sincere or genuine, or resolutely committed, then pray the sinner's pray again. This is too important to leave to chance or a faulty memory.

The best way for you to know for sure that God has accepted your profession of faith will be discussed in great detail in Chapter Eight. We have already referred to it several times. The Holy Spirit is our authenticating seal (2 Corinthians 1:21-22; Ephesians 1:13-14). If you have the fruits of the Holy Spirit interwoven into your daily life, then your salvation is secured. If not, then make every effort necessary to better understand how His presence is made known in a redeemed person's life. If you cannot honestly see direct, observable, spiritual evidence of the Holy Spirit's activity in your life, then a person needs to critically review their spiritual status. Deceiving yourself about salvation carries too heavy of a price.

### *The Deceived Soul should be Our Real Target*

Rather than stressing over people who seem to reject our Lord, I fear there is a much greater issue which we are facing in the Christian church today. It is that of those who are deceived about their actual spiritual status. Not that the other group is unimportant; it is that the deceived are so wretchedly confused about God's eternal plan for our lives. This is where Satan's ruse has been so masterful. Being deceived about one's salvation seems to be much more pervasive than what I ever imagined. I have read numerous times the Bible verse where Christ warns us, "Enter through the narrow gate. For wide is the gate and broad is the road that leads to destruction, and many enter through it" (Matthew 7:13). It saddens me when I think about how gracious God has been to us and yet most people will reject His Son as their Savior. What blessings they are missing. Regrettably this applies to some who are sitting in the pews with us at church. There are three things which astound me about church congregations: (1) how few actually tithe, (2) how many do not pick up their Bibles except on Sunday mornings, and (3) how some have not honestly addressed the actual status of their souls.

Never has this last point been brought home more than it was by evangelist Dr. Bailey Smith's renowned sermon on the "Wheat and Tares" (Matthew 13:24-30, 36-43). Please turn to this parable and read the scenario. The obvious point to this parable is that Christians must live in a world along-side nonbelievers. Some will do us great harm. However, we must remain patient in waiting for God's timing before ultimate justice is brought on those who reject the message of the Good News.

There is a much deeper message though in this parable when you examine it further. Apparently there are many people who think they are saved, but they have not genuinely repented of their sins and been transformed by the Holy Spirit. These are those weeds which come to share the pews with us in our churches. Perhaps these are the ones who respond more to the social aspect of church life than to being dedicated to gaining a greater relationship with El Elyon (The Most High God). This is evident by how few times these people turn to His Scriptures to quench their hunger and thirst for His righteous (Matthew 5:6). There is absolutely nothing wrong with enjoying the fellowship of other Christian believers. I am just surprised by how few make it a daily habit of reading their Bibles and praying to the Lord. <u>I have always rather naively assumed that each person who made a public declaration of faith was being honest and sincere. Since we are taught not to "judge" others</u>

(Luke 6:37), I have never really thought much about how some people are sadly living confused lives concerning their spiritual status.

Some suggest that this parable does not apply to false believers. They claim it applies only to the world at large and not to false believers within the church. I find this humorous. Where do they think the church is? The Christian church is in this world but it is not to be "of" this world. The point of the parable is that Satan sowed deceptive seeds in the field where God has His wheat. Where is this field which God has His wheat if not the church? The reason I feel this applies to all believers and nonbelievers is additionally supported by the description of the weeds. The particular weed in this parable is thought to be the bearded darnel grass, which is found in that region of the world. If you are curious, go out to Google and do a search on darnel grass. It very closely resembles a stalk of wheat. In fact, it so closely resembles wheat that the two cannot be discerned apart until the wheat produces its ears of grain (the fruit of the plant, if you will). The darnel weed produces no such ear (therefore no fruit).

This analogy works very well with the other teachings of Christ on this topic. True believers will be discerned by the fruit they produce (Matthew 7:16-20 – "by their fruit you will recognize them"). The bearded darnel grass is a poisonous weed (tare) which entangles its roots in with the roots of the wheat plant. In this, the farmer showed great wisdom and this is why he did not want the workers to try pulling out the weeds. Where is this most applicable in Christianity? It clearly applies to the world at large since Christians live in the world alongside nonbelievers. We also know that Satan loves nothing better than sowing seeds of deception in God's church. From my understanding, I believe it applies anywhere there are believers, false believers, and nonbelievers associating with one another. These are the reasons why I think this parable should not exclude the church setting, but it should not be limited to the church either. I think the parable applies anywhere that Satan is operating.

Other biblical references clearly support Bailey's point – there are a surprising number of people who think they have a nice bow tied around their salvation, but they don't. Look at Matthew 7:21-23, "Not everyone who says to me, 'Lord, Lord,' will enter the kingdom of heaven…" Jesus warns us repeatedly of people taking the wrong road (Mat. 7:13-14), not producing acceptable fruit (Luke 6:43-44), and deceiving others about their spiritual status (Mat.7:15, 23:1-3). These are the obvious ones who have rejected God's offer of salvation. What is gaining more of my attention is how many there are within the church who have not correctly assessed their spiritual status. It has been there all along; I just have not paid much attention to it. Now that it has been brought to the top of my consciousness, I am seeing the warnings which Bailey was referencing (you may want to visit Bailey's website at www.baileysmith.org to get a more complete presentation of his thoughts on this parable).

If you stop to think about it, the apostle Paul (prior to his conversion) is an excellent example of this group of people who think they have their salvation all assured but do not. Back when he was Saul, he was an ardent Pharisee. Certainly Saul thought he was being righteous (Philippians 3:4-6) when he was persecuting the early Christians. Actually from the kingdom perspective, he was a wolf in sheep's clothing (Matthew 7:15). To the early Christians he was more like a wolf in wolves' clothing. In his mind though, Saul was doing the Lord's work. This is how incredibly deceptive Satan can be. Saul had to have a Damascus road experience before it all became clear to him. There are many who know they are the enemy of Christ. Regrettably, there are a great many others who think they are within the kingdom of God but they have been spiritually deceived. Saul was such.

As Paul progresses in his ministry, he becomes acutely aware of how misleading people can be. He warns his faithful believers in Ephesus to be on guard against deceivers of all kinds. In Acts 20:28-31 Paul encourages them, "Keep watch over yourselves and all the flock of which the Holy Spirit has made you overseers. Be shepherds of the church of God, which He bought with His own blood. I know that after I leave, savage wolves will come in among you and will not spare the flock. <u>Even from your own number men will arise and distort the truth in order to draw away disciples after them</u>. So be on your guard!" Wise counsel from our brother Paul. <u>Only when measured against the life of Jesus can we tell the wheat from the weeds</u>. Jesus sets the example for us in making our lives "fruit producing", thereby all will know the true condition of our hearts.

I wage war against weeds all spring, summer, and fall. I enjoy landscaping my home on the weekends. It gives me an excellent excuse to be outside and it allows me to see the results of my labor. When a person says they spend their weekends landscaping, you can bet they hate weeds. When I am at my best, my yard is a nice, well manicured lawn of fescue grass. My landscape areas are flourishing and are free from the unsightly and destructive influence of weeds. There is one little area however which causes me the most concern. The small strip of grass which separates my driveway from our neighbor's is a real battleground for weeds. For some unknown reason, each year patches of nutgrass infest this area. It is correctly named nutgrass because it drives me nuts. At first, this grass looks very much like fescue. The problem is that nutgrass grows about twice as fast as fescue. When you mow, it grows so quickly that you get some unsightly areas in your yard before it is time to mow again. I know those of you who do not like yard work probably think I need to "get a life." My wife and daughters think that as well. They will come home and there I am, on my hands and knees, pulling up the nutgrass. Why do I not just use weed controlling chemicals? I do at times but at other times of the year, it gets too hot, so the chemicals could harm my other grass. To me the problem is multi-fold. First, weeds use up needed nutrients in the soil. Second, they overtake the good grass. Third, they look bad. Fourth, they reflect on me as a gardener. My daughters laugh and say I take the role of being a good steward over what God has given me a little too seriously. Perhaps so.

Here is my challenge though with the nutgrass. My neighbor and I have to wait for both grasses to grow to a certain maturity. Otherwise we will accidentally pull up fescue instead of nutgrass. Both look very similar as young plants. Once there is sufficient growth, a trained eye can detect which one is nutgrass. It also has a little different feel to it as you are grasping the stalk. With patience, we remove the nutgrass, trying not to uproot the tiny blades of fescue. The more experience we have with this, the better we have become at controlling the weeds. When the weather cools down, we can then treat the lawn with the proper herbicide to kill the nutgrass but preserve the fescue. Is this not what Matthew 13:24-30 and 13:36-43 teaches about spiritual deception? This world is not any easy place for Christians (the wheat). The enemy is crafty in sowing seeds of deception (the weeds). The challenge is that it is not just the good guys who wear the white hats. For those of you who are much younger than my generation, on TV the bad guys in the Western shows always wore black hats and the really good guy (the hero) always wore a white hat. In real life, some bad guys wear black hats, but some of them wear white hats to fool us. Some wearing white hats think they are good guys but until they have a Damascus road experience, they are only deceiving themselves.

Remember David instructed Solomon that: "...the Lord searches every heart and understands every motive behind the thought." (1 Chronicles 28:9). This same wisdom is presented in Jeremiah 17:10, "I the Lord search the heart and examine the mind, to reward a man according to his conduct, according to what his deeds deserve." I am afraid most people (especially children) do not stop to think that God is searching their hearts to determine whether their professions of faith are genuine or not. With children under the age of 8, they seldom have developed a psychologically mature conscience. It is very important that young children get excellent spiritual counseling so that they are not confusing themselves. They have to understand repentance as well as moral judgment in order for them to resolutely make a genuine profession of faith. If they do not receive such counseling, they may find themselves to be like the seed sowed in rocky places (Matthew 13:5-6, 20-21). In this part of the parable there is insufficient soil for the plant to sustain life. When it comes to spirituality, we can deceive ourselves in so many ways. As humans, we get confused and we forget who sets the agenda. It is God, not us. Jehovah makes the rules; we are to follow. Sometimes we act as though God is like one of our pets – just sitting there waiting on us, ready to accept whatever attention we give Him. Do not be mistaken – this world will be judged on God's terms, so we should make every effort to be sure we fulfill them.

Perhaps we should more correctly refer to at least some these deceived believers as CINO's (Christians In Name Only). They want the label and all rights and privileges which go with the title, but they are not willing to stand firm in their beliefs. This sounds like most of our current crop of politicians, right? They talk the talk but they don't walk the walk. This is expressed in 2 John 6, "And this is love: that we walk in obedience to His commands." Christ our Lord in Matthew 7:1 teaches us, "Do not judge, or you to will be judged." Judging here means we should not make a pronouncement of eternal damnation on someone. That is reserved for God only. When Jesus tells us not to judge others He is not saying that we should not hold each other accountable for our unrighteous behaviors. The insincere always like to use the "do not judge" line anytime they are being held accountable for their inappropriate behaviors. Do not fall for this. Part of the brotherhood of Christ is that we are to help keep each other on track. Helping your brother or sister in Christ by paying attention to their character and walk is not judging. It is doing as Jesus, Paul, James, John, and Peter taught us to do. Furthermore, in the above chapter Jesus tells us in verses 15-23, "Watch out for false prophets. They come to you in sheep's clothing, but inwardly they are ferocious wolves. By their fruit you will recognize them...Every tree that does not bear good fruit is cut down and thrown into the fire. Thus, by their fruit you will recognize them..." From Jesus' mouth to our ears – we are not to judge the eternal condition a person may be destined for, but we are to inspect their fruit in order to know what kind of person they are.

In 2 Timothy 3:5 Paul teaches us about people with no genuine faith as, "having a form of godliness, but denying its power." The commentary on this verse in the KJV Life Application Bible further teaches us that "it may be difficult to distinguish them from true Christians at first, but their lives will give them away. The form or appearance of godliness includes going to church, knowing Christian doctrine, using Christian clichés, and following a community's Christian traditions. Such practices can make a person look good, but if their inner attitudes of belief, love, and worship are lacking, the outer appearance is meaningless. Paul warns us not to be deceived by people who only appear to be Christians." This is where hypocrisy has hurt our churches. The ones most often who are justly accused of hypocrisy probably fall into this group which Paul is warning us about. Paul gave much the same message to Titus warning him of false teachers and the detrimental effects they can have on a congregation. This was a problem back then and it still is a problem. In Titus 1:16 Paul states, "They claim to know God, but by their actions they deny Him. They are detestable, disobedient, and unfit for doing anything good." Our behaviors reveal our true beliefs.

With reference to Bailey Smith's penetrating message covering Matthew 13:24-30, we must consider the uncomfortable task of discerning our own spiritual status if we have any confusion over its beginnings. The significance of the Parable of the Weeds is as follows: 1) wheat and weeds were planted together (one by God, the other by the enemy); they both have the same experience of being planted and trying to survive alongside each other, 2) they progress together – they both look similar on the outside at first, and 3) they are processed together (harvested together at the time of judgment). The eternal significance is what happens to each at harvest time. <u>At the harvest, there will be no second chances</u>. If this can possibly apply to you (or a loved one), please take a spiritual inventory of your soul. Weeds are not only in the areas which are easily identified as being without the presence of our Lord. Both "wheat and weeds" can be sitting in the pews at churches all over our nation and the world.

Make no mistake – the devil wants you to believe you are saved and will not want you to doubt your salvation. Why? Satan wants you to be deceived so you will not be an effective witness for God. The deceived believer will not be fruitful. The CINO will possibly lead others away from Christ. This would work well in Satan's plan. As stated previously, this is not meant to make anyone needlessly doubt their salvation. What it is meant to do is to call you to taking a critical look at your spiritual status. Paul encourages us in 2 Corinthians 13:5, "Examine yourselves to see whether you are in the faith; test yourselves." If you are assured of your salvation, then praise God. If you are a little uncertain, then pray to God. One of the major tasks of the Holy Spirit is to convict us. Listen to His promptings. Please, please, do not allow your pride to get in the way of your eternal salvation.

Since we cannot see into the soul of another person, what are we to do? Are we to question the motives behind the fruit of our fellow worshippers? No, we should not try to ferret out deceived believers (as though conducting a Salem witch hunt). What we should do is to be honest if a person comes to us to ask our help in determining whether they have genuinely accepted Christ as their Savior. Help them to critically analyze if the presence of the Holy Spirit can be seen in their life. Dr. Smith warns us, "An unsaved person cannot grow in the Lord, but they can appear to others as doing so. The only way counterfeit money can be good is that it must look like the original." Church work and doing good deeds does not necessarily equate to true salvation. Through a redemptive faith in Jesus Christ as God's Son and your Lord and Savior, the Holy Word must be earnestly applied to one's life. Anything else is merely faking it. The true test is in the presence of the Holy Spirit, actively working to transform your life into being like Jesus Christ Himself.

There are a number of wonderfully related lessons to the Parable of the Wheat and Weeds. As Christians (wheat), we are to be patient in waiting for God's ultimate justice in dealing with nonbelievers (weeds). We are to withstand the persecutions targeting us, just as wheat has to withstand the weeds trying to choke it out. Believers are to stand firm and call on the Lord for our providence. We are not to be the instruments of vindication. God alone will handle that task, on His timetable and in His manner. We are not to ask God to speed up His timetable either. Why? Think about it. We were all weeds at one time! One of the overlooked ironies of this lesson is, as one of the men in my Sunday School class pointed out, wheat looks like weeds at times. Wheat has to become productive in order to distinguish itself from the weeds. Each day, weeds are being converted to wheat and the wheat stalks themselves are maturing. The Great Commission (Matthew 28:18-20) urges us to be active while patiently waiting for the Day of Judgment. So, what is our role? We are to be the vehicles of salvation. The world is to see God through us. Believers are at their very best when they can see a patch of weeds and then get active witnessing so that wheat takes root. Each new soul won is a soul who will spend all of eternity with us. What a victory!

Why did Jesus teach through the use of parables? Primarily, Jesus did not want to be known as just a miracle worker. He was a teacher as well as a healer and a redeemer to these people. He was concerned with their souls and their bodies. Jesus used parables for a specific reason. Jesus' revelations were reserved for those who would reach out to Him in faith. All others were without a clear comprehension of the ultimate message contained in the parable. To the unbelievers, they were interesting little stories but they did not carrying any particular meaning. Why did Jesus do this? This method of teaching allowed Jesus to give spiritual truths to those who were seeking Him, without giving his enemies any information with which they might try to trap Him. The Holy Trinity only wants those who earnestly seek a deep, personal relationship with the Triune God. For the seekers of God's truths, our heavenly Father has great plans. Believers will help Jesus rule forever (Rev. 1:6, 20:4). Do insights come to you as you read and pray over His Holy Scriptures? This is one of many ways which God allows people to know that we belong to Him. God is not in the habit of casting His holy wisdom to the swine (Matthew 7:6).

The parables of the Gospels have much to offer us. These parables contain great truths, but only those with ears to hear are to understand. It seems to me that the more we seek the truth of these parables, the more the Holy Spirit will reveal to us. Feast on each word. Let the Spirit guide you in your interpretation. The possible answer to the present question before us may be found in Luke 12:42-48. The unfaithful servant certainly bears a strong resemblance to the casual believer. These verses also corroborate Hebrews 10:26-30 and 2 Peter 2:20 concerning an unfaithful believer's punishment. One could easily argue the servant in Luke 12 was never really a servant with his heart set on his master. His punishment was great because he had knowledge of his master but no true submission. Much more will be expected of us who have heard the message of "The Good News". Those who turn away will be severely punished. The parable in Luke 12 focuses on obedient believers who are persons of action. Jesus does not seem to have much patience with supposed believers who like to listen to a good message, and then go on living in whatever manner they choose.

I have come to the realization, after searching the Scriptures, that these "deceived" souls are the ones with whom we should be more concerned and not so much someone possibly renouncing their belief in God. We need to step back and take a look at what it actually takes to be saved. We all want our friends and relatives to be with us in heaven. It is natural that we should think that because they attend church with us, they are saved. We need to stop and consider salvation from the biblical perspective though. God's perspective is much different from ours. We are usually all tied up with our emotions and what we think is fair. We need to always remember: He is the Creator, we are the created (Isaiah 64:8; Romans 9:21). These are His rules and He sets the criteria for salvation. May this be paramount in our minds: this world is not a backdrop to a popularity contest between God and Satan. If it were, and since God created everything, He could make the rules to favor Him. No, God is wanting only the very best – those who will accept His Word as holy and true based solely on heartfelt, genuine, steadfast, redemptive faith. We require no absolute proof. Our hearts attest to the evidence that He is who He says He is (the Great I Am!, Exodus 3:14). Only a few can accept this teaching. Far more never achieve genuine belief because their hearts are hardened and impure. God takes the best and leaves Satan the rest.

Only you and God will know what is in your heart. Unfortunately, some people have even deceived themselves. They think they are saved but upon examination of their motives by God, these people have not come to Him with the proper heart. The new challenge must be "how do we help people who think they are saved but are not find the correct status of their souls and turn to the Lord"? As Billy Graham said, "the church becomes the mission field". Hopefully this discussion along with Chapter Eight will help guide you through some of the spiritual foundations and characteristics which are prevalent in a genuinely surrendered life for Christ.

One final question is: "can a saved person commit blasphemy and thereby lose their salvation?" Some are hesitant to say that "once saved, always saved" because they see the possibility of this happening. They may fear it happening particularly in an immature Christian as the young believer starts to face life's challenges. These new converts have not become seasoned warriors against disappointment and disillusionment yet, so they are susceptible to Satan's tricks. The assurance I get from my studies of the Bible and various commentaries suggest that a Christian cannot commit this sin. The Holy Spirit's presence in your soul will work to prevent this from happening. The Spirit provides strength and support for a saved person's inner spirit when their faith becomes so weak that they might be tempted to commit blasphemy (more about this in the next chapter concerning when faith is weak).

Blasphemy is often defined as: to say bad things against God; to do actions that show disrespect to God; to attribute to the devil the work of God or vice versa. Isaiah 5:20 teaches,

"Woe to those who call evil good and good evil, who put darkness for light and light for darkness, who put bitter for sweet and sweet for bitter." Luke 11:14-20 and Mark 3:22-30 provide the classic examples of the Pharisees committing this sin. One note of reassurance is that if you are a saved person and you are convicted by the Holy Spirit to ask for forgiveness of any of your sins, then you can be certain Adonai (Our Lord and Master) will forgive you. The main point here is that since you are still sensitive to the convicting power of the Holy Spirit, you have <u>not</u> committed this sin.

Please read Matt 12:31-32 and Mark 3:28-29. The issue here is the denial and rejection of the Holy Spirit. The reason this sin is unforgivable is simply because the person committing it will never ask for forgiveness. If the Holy Spirit is totally walled out of a person's life, then no spiritual conviction occurs in their inner spirit to prompt them to confess and repent. Without confession and repentance, forgiveness is never granted. <u>If someone disregards the presence of the Holy Spirit, they have therefore rejected the only means available to them to approach God for forgiveness</u>. Conversely, if you feel the convicting power of the Holy Spirit at times working with your spirit to correct and refine you, then you have not committed the sin of blasphemy against the Holy Spirit. As believers we know that without faith in Jesus Christ it is impossible to gain salvation. Additionally, without the convicting power of the Holy Spirit working with your inner spirit prior to conversion, you will never respond to the message of Jesus. This is why it is the unforgivable sin. Paul phrases it well in 1 Corinthians 2:14, "The man without the Spirit does not accept the things that come from the Spirit of God, for they are foolishness to him, and he cannot understand them, because they are spiritually discerned." As long as the Holy Spirit is being allowed to commune with your spirit, you have a chance at recognizing your spiritual depravity and the need for Jesus in your life. If the presence of the Holy Spirit is completely shut off from your spirit, then you have eliminated any chance of ever seeking Christ as your Savior. All hope is then lost.

## *The Evidence for Eternal Security*

I think we have sufficiently established that salvation is not solely on our time table. As we have studied the topic of redemptive faith, there is significant biblical evidence that God examines the sinner's heart and motives to make sure they are pure in their intentions and resolute in their commitment (Matthew 5:3, 6, 8). This brings us to the question: when does God give us our eternal security? Is it possible that eternal security only occurs in the process of sanctification once our faith is so mature that it is unshakeable? I do not think God is testing us in that way. He knows it takes time to grow a strong, mature Christian. I do not believe the Lord wants to hold off in granting us eternal security by making us pass a series of tests. He is our loving heavenly Father and as such He wants us to have the guarantee of our salvation from the very beginning of this journey. I believe you are saved the moment you ask Jesus into your heart, provided God judges your faith as genuine.

The Old Testament certainly has many verses which relate to God's faithfulness to believers (Psalm 32:1-5; 33:4; 37:23-24; 55:22; 103:8-12; Joshua 1:1-9; Isaiah 25:1). These are wonderful verses which God gives us to encourage us to be steadfast in our seeking of His kingdom. He is forever faithful to us and we can hold to His promise to be forgiving when we turn to Him in our faith. One of my favorite quotes in the Bible is Joshua 1:5 where the Lord God promises Joshua "I will never leave you nor forsake you." That was neither a one-time promise nor a promise made only to one man. Our Father offers that same promise to all who turn to Him in faith. In Psalm 37:39-40 David teaches us of the security we have in the Lord. "The salvation of the righteous comes from the Lord; He is their stronghold in time of trouble. The Lord helps them and delivers them; He delivers them from the wicked and saves them, because they take refuge in Him." Please notice that David does not put any qualifying disclaimers with this holy promise. He does not say that we have to be totally absent of sin in order for the Lord to deliver us. He does not say we have to be leading perfect lives in order for the Lord God Almighty to remain as our stronghold. What these verses say to me is that once we place our faith in El Shaddai, He will remain forever faithful. I think David knew what he was talking about.

Let us turn our attention now to some of the verses which point to eternal security in the New Testament: John 5:24; 15:5-10; Luke 15:11-24; Romans 8:38-39; 1 John 2:17, 24-25 and 1 Peter 1:3-5. These are only a few of the many verses which point to eternal security. These passages are very emphatic in their promise. When God makes a promise, He keeps it. No one can say it any better than Jesus Himself. Consider John 6:37-40 where Jesus states His mission. "All that the Father gives me will come to me, and whoever comes to me I will never drive away. For I have come down from heaven not to do my will but to do the will of Him who sent me. And this is the will of Him who sent me, that I shall lose none of all that He has given me, but raise them up at the last day. For my Father's will is that everyone who looks to the Son and believes in Him shall have eternal life, and I will raise him up at the last day." This sounds to me like Jesus is promising to those of us who place our faith in Him that we will be His for all eternity. The only qualifier is that we "look to the Son and believe in Him". The process is straightforward – first we are drawn by the urgings God placed in our hearts to seek Him, then saved by our faith in Christ Jesus, and lastly we are indwelt by the Holy Spirit to guide, guard, and direct us in the paths of righteous.

We know that God is omnipotent, so if it is His will that Jesus "lose none of all that He has given", then I know of no force in this world or any other which can wrestle us from God's hands. Once saved, we have Jesus' oath that we are to never be without His providence. We will be kept by Jesus in this life and in heaven. Our Lord will then raise us up at the resurrection on the last day where we will receive new, resurrected bodies and will dwell on the new earth for all of eternity. You can treasure this promise. These are words from our Lord which should give us hope and reassurance when we feel life is harsh and the struggle is great.

In John 10:27-29 our Savior further declares, "My sheep listen to my voice; I know them, and they follow me. I give them eternal life, and they shall never perish; no one can snatch them out of my hand. My Father, who has given them to me, is greater than all; no one can snatch them out of my Father's hand." I do not think Jesus can be any more ardent than this. Eternal life starts the moment we place our earnest faith in Jesus as our Redeemer. When Jesus says "no one" I feel certain He is including Satan as well as the free will of the believer themselves. Jesus is promising us the mighty protection of our sovereign God over whom no one has supremacy. Once we are found to be worthy of the seal of the Holy Spirit, no force ever established can pry us away from our kinship with Christ. Paul teaches us in 1 Corinthians 1:8-9 this eternal promise, "He will keep you strong to the end, so that you will be blameless on the day of our Lord Jesus Christ. God, who has called you into fellowship with His Son Jesus Christ our Lord, is faithful." We are promised that God's Spirit will be strong for us, even when we are weak. Once again, I do not see any disclaimers with this promise. I trust the words of David and Paul. They were two men who intimately knew God. Their words carry weight with me. I absolutely trust the words of Jesus. A believer needs to be concerned about being a good student, or being a good employee, earning a living, paying their mortgage, paying their taxes, keeping their spouse and children out of harms way, but they should never waste any of their time worrying about losing their salvation. We can trust that God will do what He says He will do.

Some argue that you have to stay in obedience in order to maintain this security. Those who believe in eternal security do not hold to this interpretation. We believe that the atonement of Jesus' blood covers us completely for any misdeeds we happen to commit. We believe our salvation is not questioned (as assured us in these previous verses). Our actions (our sins) are not without a cost though. Sin keeps us from having a righteous relationship with our Triune God. That is a serious matter, but it does not cost you your salvation. We also believe that our future rewards in heaven are determined by our thoughts and deeds while here on earth (Matthew 6:19-24; Revelation 22:12). Sins can remove these rewards, so those who believe in eternal security certainly do not believe that "anything goes" once we are saved by the grace of God Almighty. As written in Matthew 16:27, "For the Son of Man is going to come in His Father's glory with His angels, and then He will reward each person according to what he has done." Does this not correspond to what Jesus told us throughout the Gospels? <u>Sin has consequences, but when our precious Savior went to the cross, the price for a believer's salvation was paid in full.</u>

This idea needs to be examined a little further. Some denominations accuse those of us who hold to eternal security that after accepting Christ as our Lord and Savior we can take on an attitude of "anything goes". This anything goes attitude is very different from being backslidden. One who is a backslider is someone who has accepted Christ as their Redeemer but has put aside their willingness to be obedient to God's commands (their commitment is weak). That person has started the transformation process known as sanctification but has allowed the world to tempt them, thus becoming derailed. This happens to most of us at one time or another. When you are backslidden, you are still saved but you have lost God's glory (the distinctive excellence of His attributes, as being present in the lives of obedient believers). This means people cannot tell the difference between you and the nonbelievers of the world. When we walk with God, we walk in His glory. These periods of testing either make us stronger in our faith or they lead to us spending lives wastefully short of God's desire for us. Dr. Henry Blackaby makes an excellent point when he admonishes us, "Perhaps you went through a time of rebellion against God in your past before choosing to obey Him, and now you might be tempted to think, *Well, God is still using me, even though I rebelled against Him before.* That may certainly be true, by the Lord's mercy and grace – but you'll never know what could have been! Because of the length of time it took you to get around to saying yes, there are great dimensions of God's activity you'll never know or experience" (Experiencing the Cross, p. 101).

By our rebellion, we pay a heavy price. There are Christians who appear to have such a rebellious inclination with respect to the authority of God. Some take this even a step further. They seem to think that because we speak of God as being the God of love, He must therefore be accepting of whatever they choose to do. The "anything goes" crowd are those who we have to question whether they ever started the transformation process or not (Revelation 2:14-16). The Nicolaitans in the church in Pergamum were such people. Jesus speaks very harshly of them in these verses. These are people who teach false doctrines and try to lead others astray. If rebellion has any place in your heart, do immediate surgery.

This begs the question: How can anyone read the stories of Jesus' life and not have them change their ways of behavior? The answer is – those who have not had a transforming experience with God. If someone is not markedly changed by the presence of the Holy Trinity in their lives and having Jesus as their Lord and Savior, then they are not saved. They are still in a state of spiritual death. This is why we have the term "born again". It is a dramatic change when the Holy Spirit starts leading us along the path to righteousness which our Jesus championed for us. We may stumble at times but at least we are to be making progress. <u>Be certain of this – being saved by our Lord is not merely a matter of us saying that we have asked Jesus into our hearts and that is the end of the story.</u> <u>We are to commit ourselves to being set apart.</u> Sanctification is the process by which we are transformed into becoming more like Christ and less like how this world would have us to be. Sanctification is not some mystical experience or a fleeting euphoric condition. It involves the very essence of a person's inner core belief system being changed to become God-focused. When this happens, the person is spiritually re-born. The degree of this change is determined by the strength of the person's spiritual commitment. <u>Since this transformation process is integral to our faith this makes Christianity more than a religion; it is a way of life.</u>

### Core Beliefs require Time to Develop

I trust this discussion about the various levels of beliefs a person may have has been helpful. Obviously not all beliefs carry the same status. Another interesting dimension about beliefs is the time element. Core beliefs take time to incubate. Ebullient feelings from emotional highs which lead to a quick acceptance of Jesus' message are most like the $2^{nd}$ type of soil in the Parable of the Sower. Such a mental framework would most accurately be characterized as a tertiary belief at best, but probably nothing more than a complex series of developing thoughts and attitudes. Even with the 3$^{rd}$ type of soil, it takes time to move newly established thoughts and attitudes into being tertiary and secondary beliefs. As with the 3$^{rd}$ type of soil, the weight and problems of this world will actively fight against your moving a nominal acceptance of Jesus into being a core belief system supporting redemptive faith.

Once again, this is why Sunday School, Vacation Bible School, youth retreats, mission trips, and such are so very important in moving the young Christian forward in the sanctification process. <u>A belief has to be nurtured. They are not instantaneous cognitive processes which immediately erect stalwart walls against Satan's attacks. Experiences and emotions have to build up around them to give them resolve and resiliency.</u> Resistances to assaults on these beliefs require time in order for your spiritual defense mechanisms to solidify. The more support we can give immature Christians to becoming mature witnesses, the better. This is borne out by the examples of the 2$^{nd}$ and 3$^{rd}$ types of soil. The sower's seeds did not flourish because these soils were not nurturing to them.

I spent my entire youth in the church setting. As a small child I had the advantage of hearing stories about Jesus. Even with this, my profession of faith developed over many months of talking with my parents seriously about what believing in Jesus meant. This is what I call an incubation period. I talked with my Sunday School teacher about this decision. My mother had our pastor to come to our home to visit with me. Mom and dad wanted me to be certain I was aware of just how important the acceptance of Jesus as my Lord and Savior actually was. With this incubatory period, my belief became more solidified. It moved from being an acceptance that Jesus was a real person whom I had heard about all of my life into becoming a core belief which would forever define my life once I professed publicly my faith in Christ Jesus.

To be clear, I am *not* saying that when you ask Jesus into your heart, that there is an extended amount of time where you are moving this belief from being a tertiary or secondary belief to a core belief. If that were the case, then salvation would not occur immediately. Here is where it can become complicated. Most of us believed that God is who He says He is prior to our actual conversion. We had even built the fundamentals of a trust in Him. What was lacking was a realistic commitment to seeking His kingdom as the only object of our worship and living a righteous lifestyle to reflect this decision. Many of us still had a little baggage of this world at the time of our conversion. Fortunately, all of the pieces to the puzzle were coming into place as we were learning more about what it means to declare our faith in Jesus as our Lord and Savior. The final step was to make *a genuine commitment* to the God of our faith.

A resolute commitment refers to our laser-focused, single-minded determination to worship and praise the Holy Trinity as the one and only true Godhead. No other gods are before us. No gods of money, power, status, enjoyment, and whatever else modern man may choose to have as the objects of their beliefs, trust, and commitment. This type of commitment does not happen automatically. Once again, think back to your own conversion. Commitment grew as you grew in the Lord. An authentic commitment does *not* mean you have to instantly become a saint, and if not, then it was not genuine. You commit to Jehovah as being your one and only God. In addition you commit to serving the Lord through your obedience. As we grow in our faith, we become more committed to living an increasingly more righteous lifestyle. Growth takes time. Conversely, time should produce growth. Has your faith grown over the last few years? What are the fruits of this burgeoning faith?

This is where Satan tries most vigorously to discourage us. If he cannot stop us from believing, he wants to at least stop our effectiveness in working for the kingdom. By being totally committed I do not mean we all are to become ministers. God needs Christian students, teachers, business-people, engineers, accountants, doctors, nurses, musicians, craftsmen, and even lawyers (perhaps I've gone a little too far on that one, but you get the picture). You commit to worshipping and praising only God the Father, God the Son, and God the Holy Spirit. You commit to growing in your service to His Holy Kingdom. You commit to becoming a better person – the person God originally created you to be.

Unfortunately many Christians remain lazy in their faith. They sit in the pews and watch others sing. They sit in the pews and let others lead in worship. They sit in their Sunday School rooms and let others plan trips to visit the lost, the sick and the hurting. The most activity some of these folks get is in criticizing someone else for not doing as they think they should do. Commitment is the action component to faith. Get active in your praise and worship of the Holy Trinity. It is the only way to be genuinely committed.

It should be obvious to you by now that where the wheels fall off the cart is when one or more of the three components to faith are lacking. The people we have been discussing concerning the three biblical passages in Hebrews and 2 Peter certainly appear not to have made any adequate commitments to augment their belief and trust. Perhaps their belief was shallow. They still probably had issues with putting their total trust in a God who they had never seen nor heard. It is hard to commit to anything in which you do not trust. <u>Where the time line for salvation works best is when the person has developed their belief, trust, and a measure of commitment over a period of time.</u> This interval of time has allowed them to sift through their doubts and hesitations. Once they are satisfied with the belief and trust components, then a commitment is ready to be made. This is when most of us meet with our pastor, Sunday School teacher, parents, friends, or trusted spiritual guide and we make the final decision. If all of this is in place, then when we pray the sinner's prayer, God *immediately* receives us into His kingdom. The Holy Spirit immediately indwells us and we start the lifelong process of sanctification.

The necessity of this incubation period is why we cannot debate a nonbeliever into becoming a Christian after only a few minutes of our eloquent recitation of biblical stories and truths. They have to see our beliefs in action in our daily lives over a period of time before our witness starts to be effective. God sends His Spirit to mellow their inner spirit to being receptive of our spiritual testimony (John 6:44). This may involve the lives of several Christians this person comes into contact with before their spirit is receptive to the calling of the Holy Spirit (Paul planted, Apollos watered... 1 Corinthians 3:6-11). Conversions take time; otherwise you have people who think they have established a new core belief but they have not given it an actual permanent status yet in their daily lives.

Trust in anything is developed over time. Test yourself. Think of the people and things in which you have placed your trust. How long have you interacted with them? What was your first interaction? Has this bond grown stronger over time? A good first impression is extremely important but trust is only visible after we have been engaged with a person over a reasonable period of time. You do not marry someone after one date (at least most of us don't). You do not place your spiritual faith in our God if you have only recently been introduced to Him either.

## *The Parable of the Sower and the Components of Faith*

The people who represent the 2nd type of soil (the rocky places) joyously accepted Christ but since there was no development of a belief system to support these newly acquired convictions, they "fell away" with the first signs of difficulty (Matthew 13:5-6, 20-21). Notice the terminology Christ uses in verses 20-21, "The one who received the seed that fell on rocky places is the man who hears the word and at once receives it with joy. But since he has not root, he lasts only a short time. When trouble or persecution comes because of the word, he quickly falls away." It takes time for our spiritual roots to sufficiently grow to where they have holding power. Once again, this is why Sunday School, vacation Bible school, youth camps, weekend retreats, and a host of other activities are so important in developing young Christians. Interacting daily with good spiritual friends is how we can best develop these spiritual roots.

This passage scores a direct hit on this group of so-called believers who "fall away" (as in Hebrews 6:4-6). To be more precise, these people in this parable never had any type of redemptive faith in our Lord Jesus. They believed only on the most superficial level (a fleeting moment of joyous emotions); their trust had not developed (no spiritual roots) since they had only received the message for a short time; and they had no commitment to God as being the sole object of their worship and praise (as evidenced by their quickly falling away when the first sign of trouble or persecution came). What they had were contagious, jubilant emotions which they received by hearing the message while in the presence of genuine, God-experiencing believers. This is why during vacation Bible school most churches are very careful in helping the children to sort through their excited emotions. These kids desire to be like their friends. They have to be counseled on what it actually means to accept

Christ as their Savior. These children are precious and their faith must be developed in a tender, loving manner. They are not meant to be a scorecard by which we measure our success. Children who jump into being like their friends and accepting Jesus will find their faith hollow as they grow older and face the harshness of this world. They will think they have salvation but all they really had was an emotional high over first starting to taste the goodness of the Lord.

This is where Satan wins. If he can confuse us into thinking we are saved when we are not, he wins. What I am saying is that Satan is at vacation Bible school, youth retreats, revivals, and all church sponsored events. His bands of hateful henchmen are waiting to pounce on these young believers and confuse them. This is where a responsible church works the hardest. The desire for these sincere emotions which encompass a Spirit-filled worship service drives these people to wanting to have this hope and joy in their lives. They can see the peace, the kindness, and the love which true believers share when we are worshipping our Lord. Certainly they want this. Everyone should. The problems come when their casual acceptance meets with the reality of the demands of living a Christian lifestyle. They may have cherished sins in their lives and find them difficult to give up. The same is true of genuine Christians. When we are converted, all of us have some cherished sins in our lives. The difference is we have committed our lives to living in a righteous accord with His kingdom. These nonbelievers never make that transition into a genuine faith. Commitment to the Christian way of life requires spiritual and physical discipline. This is where most fall away. Emotions are often one-time, short-lived experiences. Redemptive faith is a way of life. Do not confuse the two.

The people who represent the 3$^{rd}$ type of soil (the thorny places) had a little more incubation period but they did not commit strongly enough to their belief and trust in God as to make it a core belief system. These people may have had a nominal belief in God being who He says He is and a small measure of trust in His promises. They may be categorized as having had a tertiary belief in Christ Jesus. They had "received the knowledge of the truth" (Hebrews 10:26) and temporarily "escaped the corruption of the world by knowing our Lord" (2 Peter 2:20). Unfortunately, they found themselves "again entangled in it and overcome" (2 Peter 2:20). What they did not have was a sufficiently strong and resilient commitment to the Christian lifestyle which could fend off the attacks of a fallen world. They had no "staying power". Their spiritual roots had not yet strongly developed into a network of supporting structures to withstand the influences of a corrupted mankind.

These are the same folks who today claim they "tried Jesus before and it did not work for them." What they did was to get a sufficient knowledge of Christ as to know of His divine status and teachings. What they did not do was to commit to transforming their lives into a lifestyle which matched His. They may have tried for a short while to live the righteous life but when Satan's temptations came, they slowly returned to their previous attitudes and behavioral patterns. The Christian life is filled with tests and temptations. It is a journey which only a few will take (Matthew 7:13-14).

One thing is for certain: if you have surrendered your free will to God Almighty, then this problem will not be an issue for you. Unfortunately, most Christians do not completely surrender their free wills. Luke 8:43-48 is an excellent example of complete faith vs. curiosity (which describes many who seek Jesus). This is the story of the woman who had a long-term physical condition. Her faith was centered on Jesus. She was not merely curious about Him. She had the faith that as the Son of God, His gentle touch could heal her. Just seeing Jesus was not enough for her. Just hearing

Jesus speak was not enough for her. She had to reach out and touch Him. As for many today, going to church makes them feel good about themselves. Regrettably, with these folks, they do not "reach out and touch" Jesus (carnal love vs. caritas love).

The writer of Hebrews 4:2 teaches us that this is not a new phenomenon nor it is recognized by only a few. This verse says, "For we also have had the gospel preached to us, just as they did; but the message they heard was of no value to them, because those who heard did not combine it with faith." The KJVLASB commentary on this verse amplifies this by stating, "The Israelites of Moses' day illustrate a problem facing many who fill our churches today. They know a great deal about Christ, but they do not know Him personally – they don't mix their knowledge with faith. Let the Good News about Christ affect your life. Believe in Him and put into practice what you hear and read about Him." So, what do we do when we encounter such people? Do we ask them to leave because their faith is not what it should be? If they are trying to mislead others, they certainly need to be confronted and stopped. What is to happen most of the time is we are to befriend them, to pray for them, and to encourage them into growing their faith. <u>Remember, all of us were like these wayward people prior to getting our hearts focused on God</u>. We are no better. Each of us has had some loving Christian to remove the rocks and thorns from our soil. Thank God for your spiritual brothers and sisters who have nurtured your soul. God has loved you through them.

What is the challenge to us from this discussion? A growing, vibrant church must present programs which encourage young believers to grow in their newly established faith. This means: (1) to grow in their understanding of God through Bible study so as to increase this new belief with substantive knowledge, (2) to gain greater trust in His promises by learning how God interacted with the cast of characters in the Bible and experiencing how Jehovah God continues to interact with each of us in our daily lives, and (3) to commit to living a righteous lifestyle by engaging in acts of service as a sign of worship and praise. Youth retreats, youth mission trips, lock-ins, and such are all designed to help young people to develop the defenses for their faith so that when the enemy enters, they find a stalwart wall being built around that young soul. The same is true for adult converts. Faith is a journey.

It is my biblical understanding that once a person has made a genuine commitment to having Jesus as their true Lord and Savior, no power in this world or any other world can change that. In Romans 8:38-39 Paul says it best. "For I am convinced that neither death nor life, neither angels nor demons, neither the present nor the future, nor any powers, neither height nor depth, nor anything else in all creation, will be able to separate us from the love of God that is in Christ Jesus our Lord." This is a gloriously emphatic statement of hope and reassurance. Through Paul God gives us the promise that when we have Jesus as our Lord and Savior, we have eternal security.

If someone states they believe in Jesus as the Lord of their life but there have been no significant, positive changes in their life, then this person is deceiving themselves. If the Holy Spirit actually indwells you – you will be changed! Outside, observable changes in a person's life may impress your family and friends, but someone professing faith in Christ Jesus needs to keep in mind that God still searches their heart to know their motives and core beliefs. You may fool others; you may even fool yourself. <u>If you have not steadfastly placed your faith in Jesus Christ as your Lord and Savior to where it has become a defining, core belief system guiding your daily life, then you are deceiving yourself and facing a great disappointment when you take your last breath.</u>

# Chapter Six When Faith is Weak

⸺⸺∞⸺⸺

A re there times when our faith can be so low that it appears nonexistent? This seems to happen most often when we move Jesus to a far off corner in our hearts. Weakness in faith can happen to even the most fervent of believers though. You have not lived much if your faith has never wavered. It happens to us all. This is why Sunday School and corporate worship are so indispensable in the life of a Christian. They help to keep Jesus centered in our lives. Without organized worship and praise, the world will lure a Christian away from their commitment to our Lord. Having a spiritual support group is paramount in bolstering our faith when it becomes weak.

I like to think of salvation as "the 3 S's" meaning Submission, Surrender, & Servanthood. We must submit to Christ's authority, surrender our will to the will of the Holy Spirit, and enter into servanthood to God the Father. This is exactly as Jesus did while He was here on earth. Our Lord submitted to the Father's authority, surrendered His will to God's will and acted as God's servant to us. The Gospels are full of stories which substantiate this. Especially look at the accounts of Jesus in the Garden of Gethsemane (Matthew 26:36-44, Luke 22:39-44). Nowhere was the human side of Jesus so poignant. Nowhere was He faced with such a monumental challenge to His submission to the Father. Jesus paved the way for our submission, surrender and servanthood. If we will do these three things, then it is much easier to keep Christ in the center of our hearts. With Jesus at the center of your life, even when you are weak, He will be strong (1 Corinthians 1:8).

There are many biblical stories concerning when faith is weak. Turn, if you will, to Luke 15:11-24, the Parable of the Prodigal Son. This is an excellent parable concerning God's faithful love for us, even when we stray from our obedience. We are most likely to stray when our faith is frail. In this story, the young son did not feel his father was able to give him all the things he was desiring for his life. The son had allowed the attractions of this world to distract him. He wanted what he wanted and he wanted it now. Sound familiar? He wanted these things so bad that he was willing to betray his commitment as a son to his father. Notice – if the son had totally rejected his father, then he would have never returned (but this was not the case). It is not the case with true believers either who stray. In our weakness of faith, God will allow us to make mistakes. This is one of the ways we learn. As our sovereign God, He will not allow us to be destroyed though. When we return, God is always there! He waits patiently for us to come to our senses. As in the parable, it often takes great sorrow and tragedy to cause people to look to the only One who can truly help them.

### *How Much Faith do We Need*

How much faith is sufficient to judge us as righteous when we ask for God's salvation? I hesitate to use adjectives like "total" or "complete" since we all know that faith increases as we progress in our spiritual journey. Additionally, who can say they are totally or completely faithful? So how much belief, trust and commitment are necessary at the first of this journey? Does God have a criterion for the quantity of faith which a person must have in order for them to be judged righteous? If I have interpreted Scriptures correctly as relating to those who seem to renounce their faith, I say that He does. I think Hebrews 11:1 gives us insight into the right answer to this question – "Now faith is being *sure* of what we hope for and *certain* of what we do not see." <u>We have to have the measure of faith which allows us to be sure and certain of the existence and eminence of El Elyon, The Most High God. We have to have the measure of faith which allows us to be sure and certain that we can trust His plan for our salvation and that Yahweh is the one and only true God. We have to be sure and certain that Jesus Christ is His Son and that belief in Him redeems us and gives us eternal life.</u>

Faith vacillates at times. I have had periods in my life when my faith has been very strong. I have also had periods when it was weak. I have had challenges to my faith where I have grown as the result of that experience. I also have had certain tests where I have come out of them weakened. Such was the case when we learned that my first wife, Ida, had come down with cancer for a second time. Most families know all too well the disappointment and helplessness which this terrible disease brings on a family. Ida was a better person than I. She was much more caring and gracious than I was at 35. Ida worked as a speech pathologist helping stroke victims regain they ability to speak. As the cancer progressed, she went through a period where the brain tumor became inflamed as the result of the radiation treatment. This caused her not to be able to speak. What a sad irony. Mostly the tumors were throughout her abdominal area. It absolutely broke my heart to watch her struggle so valiantly with the pain and the resulting loss of hope after each new treatment protocol failed. Ida by nature had a cheerful heart. Cancer destroyed that. To watch all hope being drained from the one you love is devastating. I well remember asking God why such a kind, sweet person lay there in that hospital bed.

Why was it not some drug pusher or criminal? Why was it not someone who harmed others? Why was it not me? I should have been the one who was lying in that bed, not Ida.

She died at the young age of 35 from melanoma cancer. It was the absolute worst period of my life. I had no answers. No words comforted me. I would smile when people offered their words but on the inside I resented the shallowness of their encouragement. Never tell a grieving person that "God must have needed her home." I needed her. I needed her to be right here. After all, God has lots of other angels. We had no children; just two small dogs. Two weeks after Ida died, one of the dogs died as well. To my shame and guilt, I had allowed us as a family to drift away from regular church attendance. My commitment to worship and praise was low. For this I owe her the greatest of apologies. A man is to be the spiritual rock of the family. I was a pebble.

Cancer is such a vicious killer. It turns your world upside down. Cancer robs the patient of life and it can deprive the family of hope. Even though it has been over 20 years since Ida died, the memories and their related emotions are still very much alive. I have locked up and put away certain of the dark memories. That does not mean they no longer exist. It merely means I have resolved not to allow them to torment me any longer. It does a person no good to continually relive every episode in the death process. To watch a spouse suffer to death is something which stays with you forever. When she died, I became convinced that there is no use in praying over health matters – some are to recover, others are to die. I had not yet learned as Dr. Blackaby states, "Prayer isn't designed to get God to do our will; prayer is designed so that we can stand in His presence and know what His will is, and submit to it" (Experiencing the Cross, p. 164). This was definitely my lowest period of faith. While my faith was low, it was not nonexistent. As the months went by, I became very conflicted in my emotions of anger, loneliness, and despair. I hit "rock bottom" in my spirit. Nothing in life prepared me for the emotional and spiritual battle I was facing. I also hurt because I felt estranged from the God of my youth. Thankfully Adonai is both patient and kind.

One night I thought of ending all of the pain. When thoughts like these come to a hurting person's mind, it is not so much that they want to die as it is they want to kill the pain. This is when the precious Holy Spirit went into warp speed for me. He started flooding my mind with thoughts and images to dissuade me. I came to realize that night how such an action would dishonor Ida's memory. She would have been so disappointed in me if I had followed through with these destructive impulses. It would have caused her great sorrow as well. She loved me and would never have wanted such a moment of weakness to cost me my life. My thoughts turned next to my mother. My father had died 6 years prior of a heart attack. The grief over Ida added more hurt to her. If I followed through with my thoughts, the Holy Spirit allowed me to see how much this would hurt and dishonor my mother. She was too good of a mom for me to do that to her. I resolved myself to continue the fight.

When we fail to trust God for resolving a situation, what we are saying is that "God you failed to get me the results I wanted so now I'm taking charge." This is not the attitude a surrendered life should possess. Unfortunately, that had come to be my attitude. God did not answer my prayers as I had wanted so I needed someone to blame for all the pain I was experiencing. I felt from the start that I was to blame for much of my pain. None of us is the perfect spouse. I knew that but this realization did not lessen the guilt and regret which barraged me. Had I known my sweet wife would have lived to only be 35, I would have spent more time with her. I would have treated her better. I would have loved her more. I was tormented with so many regrets and so little absolution.

A few days later as I was driving to work one morning I did something which brought me back to a spiritual reality. I was so angry at God that morning that I lifted my fist at Him and shook it and cried out "God, I wish you would come down here so I can kick your ***." That shocked me. I thought. "Who am I to shake my fist at God Almighty and say such a thing?" This sent shivers through my soul. The Holy Spirit flew into action once again on my behalf. The Spirit was quick to convict me of needing to humble myself. This is the God whom I loved and revered. What had I done? As I cried, my heart began to mellow. I needed Jehovah Jireh so greatly. How could I be angry at the One force in this universe who could provide my soul the comfort it so badly needed?

I also came to realize that no one was to blame for some of the pain. Life is harsh at times. Biology goes awry. We live in a fallen world, so it should not shock us when bad things happen (even to good people). During this painful period, I had not yet become acquainted with Psalm 34:15-19. In this passage David reassures us by exclaiming, "The eyes of the Lord are on the righteous and His ears are attentive to their cry; the face of the Lord is against those who do evil, to cut off the memory of them from the earth. The righteous cry out, and the Lord hears them; He delivers them from all their troubles. The Lord is close to the brokenhearted and saves those who are crushed in spirit. A righteous man may have many troubles, but the Lord delivers him from them all." Our ultimate deliverance is through His salvation of our souls. The Lord also delivers us in each and every situation we face in daily life as well. How does Adonai do this? Go back to verse 4. It declares, "He delivered me from all my fears." This is key. When we experience difficult times, our Lord will bolster our spirits that He is right there with us.

Whatever we face, we will not be alone. How do we know this? Remember His promises: Joshua 1:5 – "I will never leave you nor forsake you" and Isaiah 41:10, "So do not fear, for I am with you; do not be dismayed, for I am your God. I will strengthen you and help you; I will uphold you with my righteous right hand." One of God's multiple attributes is He is a promise keeper. God does what He says He will do. <u>The relief from being absolutely alone in our trials is a tremendous deliverance</u>. Be certain of this – God does not deliver us around our troubles or over our troubles. Our Lord delivers us *through* our troubles. Remember Meshach, Shadrach, and Abednego in Daniel chapter 3. Our Lord did not take them out of that terrible situation. No, He was right there with them! He is right there, every step of the way with us as well. Elohim is our refuge, our fortress of strength. <u>Rest assured, no power on this earth can destroy one of His children</u>. <u>Though the deliverance may be painful, it will be sufficient</u>. His presence, in the form of the Holy Spirit, will become our strength and will empower our spirits to endure whatever we are facing. I know these words to be trustworthy and true. My life testifies to His promise of strength and deliverance.

Even when our faith is low, the Holy Spirit will pray for us with words we do not understand. We have Paul to thank for this magnificent insight. In Romans 8:26-27 Paul writes, "In the same way, the Spirit helps us in our weakness. We do not know what we ought to pray for, but the Spirit Himself intercedes for us with groans that words cannot express. And He who searches our hearts knows the mind of the Spirit, because the Spirit intercedes for the saints in accordance with God's will." God preserves your spirit, refines it, and then expects you to help comfort others as He has comforted you (2 Corinthians 1:3-5). Both Paul and David gave us many other brilliant verses which can produce spiritual healing.

My problem was that I did not turn to them. I was mad at God and it took a shocking offense to bring me back.

I was the one who had allowed my relationship with the heavenly Father to become distant, not God. My requests were prayed incorrectly. I did not pray that His will be done but that my will be done. God did heal Ida; just not in the way I wanted. Now I needed the Father to heal me. As I sought Him in my heartache, the anger turned to repentance. How could I have ever gotten so angry at my Lord? Thankfully El Shaddai has broad shoulders. He understands. <u>God never throws away a life just because it is broken</u>. Thankfully also my faith started to rebound and then, in time, surpassed what I had ever had before. From the ashes of my sorrows came a faith that has become unshakeable. "If the Lord delights in a man's way, He makes his steps firm; though he stumble, he will not fall, for the Lord upholds him with His hand (Psalm 37:23-24). Couple this with Isaiah 43:1-3 and you have set yourself a strong spiritual foundation. "Fear not, for I have redeemed you; I have summoned you by name; you are mine. When you pass through the waters, I will be with you; and when you pass through the rivers, they will not sweep over you. When you walk through the fire, you will not be burned; the flames will not set you ablaze. For I am the Lord, your God, the Holy One of Israel, your Savior." God is forever faithful to His children.

### *Conflicting Emotions erode Our Faithfulness*

As much as we would like to think we are logical and rational in our thinking, our emotions govern us much more than we realize. This is not necessarily a bad thing. The emotion of tenderness guides us to do acts of kindness. Compassion drives us to help others. Love is the emotion which Jesus wants us to cultivate the most. When the Bible references matters of the heart, it is meaning we are to check our level of love and all the other supporting emotions which urge us to respond to God and others as He would have us to do. The fruits of the Spirit are all positive emotions. These urges can help us to maintain a righteous relationship with God and man. The self-centered emotions are the ones which most often get us into trouble. Of those, pride is probably the worst of them all. When pride rears its ugly head, beliefs, trust, and commitment are greatly challenged.

Of the three basic components to faith (belief, trust, and commitment), whichever component is in conflict with our emotions is most often the culprit when our faith is weak. Any of the three can certainly influence the strength of our faith. Most often, after your belief in God has become a core belief system, it is trust and commitment which are most likely to waiver. Our faith is weak when our trust or commitment fluctuates because of issues with pride, doubt, insecurities, failures, disappointments, competing priorities, greed, sexual appetite, and any of the other influences of this world which war against a Christian. As in medical situations, it is important that we correctly identify the source of a problem in order to correct it. If all we are doing is treating the symptoms, then a cure will be difficult. This we do know, emotions vacillate. We also know the more disciplined and resolved we are, the less our negative emotions drive our behavior. <u>The process of becoming steadfast in our faith involves winning a lot of little skirmishes against being enticed to hang on to the things of this world as we strive to honor our commitment of surrendering our will to that of Jehovah God</u>. Without winning the little skirmishes, the big ones will be impossible.

The book of Isaiah has some wonderful passages which address the issue of when the beliefs of this world compete with our allegiance to the one true God. In Acts 19:23-28 Paul gives the New Testament account of a group of people with multiple gods and how this conflicted with Christianity.

The Athenians had gods for success, wealth, power, sexual pleasures, status, and many other aspects of their lives. They even had an altar for "the unknown god." This is not however a condition solely of those with multiple gods. Believers get enamored at times with these lesser gods as well. Our self-centered emotions drive us often in the opposite direction of what Yahweh desires. For our belief in God to be considered righteous, it has to involve the acceptance of our Triune God as the only true God. God says He is the one true God (Exodus 20:1-5, Isaiah 44:6-20). Once you have accepted the Christian God as the object of your faith, no claims for other gods are to be considered.

Christians go wrong in their beliefs when they allow their emotions to confuse them with false gods. Mind you, we do not call them gods, but how we behave towards them makes them into gods. The gods of sports, popular entertainment, pleasure seeking, financial security, status, power, and on and on masquerade as little gods to many. Do you know you have no other gods before our Lord? Ask yourself where you are spending your money and your time? Do you have more intricate knowledge of your hobbies than you do of the Word of God? How much money and time are you spending pursuing service for the kingdom of God? Do not allow your self-centered emotions to rage against your knowledge that Jehovah God will not tolerate your having lesser gods in your life. Until your belief in the Christian Godhead becomes a core belief system, it can be swayed by the allure of this world. Even then, this belief can be sidetracked by competing emotions and desires.

Are there other times when our emotions conflict with our faith? Could it be simply a matter of not being true to our commitment that God is our one and only God and we are to live a righteous life to reflect this commitment? Unfortunately, believers will sometimes move Jesus from the center of their hearts to a far off corner. They stop listening closely to the promptings of the Holy Spirit and start responding more to the attractions of their culture. Spiritual commitment is our pledge to Jehovah God that He is the object of our faith. As such, we promise to be steadfast in our service to His kingdom. In life, a lot of the time when we do not achieve what we are seeking, we write it off as we were not as committed as we needed to be. Is that the main reason why we at times seem to lack faith?

A strong case can be made that it is actually trust which is lacking. <u>The core of our trust is that we are certain in our confidence and reliance on His sovereign plan as the only source for our redemption</u>. From this we expand our trust in God for everything which concerns us (Psalm 55:22, Psalm 119:116, Matthew 7:7-8, 2 Corinthians 9:8). Believers are to trust in His promises. The faithful Christian will trust in God's commandments and teachings to help us to be righteous in our daily lives. We can rely on God's presence in our lives to guide, guard, and direct us. David gives us an excellent prayer of trust in Psalm 143:8-10, "Let the morning bring me word of your unfailing love, for I have put my trust in you. Show me the way I should go, for to you I lift up my soul. Rescue me from my enemies, O Lord, for I hide myself in you. Teach me to do your will, for you are my God; may your good Spirit lead me on level ground." In this prayer, David teaches us to put our total reliance in El Shaddai for all that we will face in our daily lives. As we grow in faith, our reliance increases in magnitude.

Since God is so prolific in His promises to us through the Holy Scriptures, it sounds better when we say we are low in commitment rather than admitting that our trust in God Almighty is faltering. This makes us feel less shameful in a way. To say that some action was just not a priority sounds better than saying we did not trust in God to help us with such and such. Unfortunately, it does not matter what makes us sound less spiritual – what matters is the truth. A diminution in trust often reveals itself through a low level of commitment, so it is easy to make commitment the first thing at which we point our spiritual fingers. As we reference the various biblical stories we are about to study you will see there certainly is a dynamic interplay between trust and commitment.

Basically, a lack of spiritual trust is made evident by us not relying on Jehovah Jireh but on ourselves for our needs. Abraham called God Jehovah Jireh (The Lord Will Provide) in Genesis 22:14 for a very good reason. The Lord provided for Abraham in this situation and He will provide for each of us as well. Since our faith tells us God is our trusted source for answering all of our needs, why do we allow our emotions to conflict with our faith? I think it is largely due to El Elyon (The Most High God) not immediately punishing us for our sins. Through His grace He waits patiently for us to repent. It is clear to me from the Scriptures that our loving heavenly Father would rather "welcome us back" than to "pour out His wrath on us".

David teaches us of God's patience and forgiveness in Psalm 103:8-14. "The Lord is compassionate and gracious, slow to anger, abounding in love. He will not always accuse, nor will He harbor His anger forever; He does not treat us as our sins deserve or repay us according to our iniquities. For as high as the heavens are above the earth, so great is His love for those who fear Him; as far as the east is from the west, so far has He removed our transgressions from us. As a father has compassion on his children, so the Lord has compassion on those who fear Him; for He knows how we are formed..." As you can tell by how many times I reference it, I treasure Psalm 103. Some people regrettably mistake this kindness from Yahweh though for a lack of accountability. We convince ourselves we can get away with our unacceptable behaviors since it appears God does not punish us immediately for our transgressions. Even if He did punish us, most would explain it away as being related to some other source. With some, it may be their intentions to deal with their sinfulness when they get older (perhaps right before they die). People allow themselves to be conflicted because, as a whole, we want what we want immediately when we want it. Most people do not take the long range, kingdom view as it relates to our daily living (Zechariah 1:1-6, Matthew 18:7-9).

A measure of our trust is revealed in our reliance on God's providence. We are to rely on God to be the ultimate source for our sustenance. This does not mean we do not work. What it means is that we give God the glory when we achieve success (or handle any of life's situations) because we recognize that it is only through His guidance and provision that we have the mental powers and skills to do the things we do. Moses tried to teach the Israelites about giving God the glory for their achievements in Deut. 8:17-18. "You may say to yourself, "My power and the strength of my hands have produced this wealth for me." But remember the Lord your God, for it is He who gives you the ability to produce wealth, and so confirms His covenant, which He swore to your forefathers, as it is today." It is God who gives us the skills to make money and provide for our families. In the Star Wars movie the saying "may the force be with you" reflects precisely what a Christian actually has who grows their faith regularly. As Luke Skywalker had to develop his skills, we still have to do our part as well. Fortunately for believers, we are plugged into an immense spiritual Source who wants only the best for us (Matthew 7:9-11, James 1:17). Listening to the Holy Spirit's guidance is the test. This is a skill which has to be developed through daily exercise and experience.

One of the components of trust is the certainty we feel in predicting an anticipated result. This can be good or bad in nature. If I stand in front of an oncoming train, I can predict a most unpleasant result – not for the train but for me. This anticipation of a resulting action should be a strong motivator shaping our behavior. God gives us many warnings against thinking He will not discipline us for our disobedience (Number 14:20-35). Yes, this is a quote from the book of Numbers – how many times do you see that? Do not disregard this amazing book simply because of its title. A different side of God's nature is revealed to us when He had to discipline His rebellious children in the desert. To know Him, we must know about *all* of His attributes. <u>Another measure of a low level of trust is revealed in our lack of fear that He *will* hold us accountable for our sins</u>. Many people do not in general fear that God will actually punish them for their wrong behaviors. Part of this is because most people do not interpret when bad things happen to them that this is the result of a sin for which God is correcting them.

In Numbers 20:8-12 it was a lack of trust in God which cost Moses his privilege of leading the Israelites into the Promised Land. The Lord tells Moses, "Take the staff, and you and your brother Aaron gather the assembly together. Speak to that rock before their eyes and it will pour out its water. You will bring water out of the rock for the community so they and their livestock can drink." So Moses and Aaron gathered the assembly together in front of the rock and Moses said to them, "Listen, you rebels, must we bring you water out of this rock?" Then Moses raised his arm and struck the rock twice with his staff. Water gushed out, and the community and their livestock drank. But the Lord said to Moses and Aaron, "Because you did not trust in me enough to honor me as holy in the sight of the Israelites, you will not bring this community into the land I give them." Moses allowed the emotions of anger and frustration to conflict with his commitment to be obedient to God. Moses momentarily was weak in his trust that God would punish him for not being entirely obedient. Had he feared God's wrath for disobedience a little more at that moment, Moses may not have committed this sin. <u>Believers are to trust God for His provisions and His righteous judgment</u>. By being a righteous and holy God, He cannot allow sinful actions to go without consequences. Though we are forgiven, we are not immune to His correction. Believers sometimes forget the stern nature of El Shaddai. Deuteronomy 8:5 teaches, "Know then in your heart that as a man disciplines his son, so the Lord your God disciplines you." Guess who wrote this passage? All of this is part of us trusting that God does what He says He will do.

Moses was punished because he was not completely obedient – he struck the rock rather than speaking to it and revealing God's providence. The striking of the rock was as though Moses himself magically brought forth the water. In this case, the emotion of anger toward the rebelliousness of the Israelites stirred Moses into disobedience. Was this action a lack of trust or a lack of commitment? It shows both when you analyze it closely. Moses was not obedient in following the Lord's command. This reveals a low level of commitment at that particular moment to following God's command in a righteous manner. If he had, then the glory would have gone to God for providing the water. This is why God got angry with Moses. A great lesson was lost. Had Moses trusted more in God's plan, then the water would have shown the Israelites that Jehovah Jireh will provide for them if only they would remain faithful. Moses' trust in following God's commands was low because he was dealing with strong, conflicting emotions. We know that Moses was a giant of faith, but at this moment his trust and commitment to God's plan to teach an important lesson were overshadowed by his resentment toward the constant complaining to which the Israelites subjected him. These conflicting emotions eroded his faithfulness.

In Matthew 6:28-31 Jesus teaches, "And why do you worry about clothes? See how the lilies of the field grow.

They do not labor or spin. Yet I tell you that not even Solomon in all his splendor was dressed like one of these. If that is how God clothes the grass of the field, which is here today and tomorrow is thrown into the fire, will He not much more clothe you, O you of little faith? So do not worry..." What does Jesus mean by the phrase, "O you of little faith"? I do not get the feeling Jesus is referencing a low level of commitment. Worry reflects a diminished level of trust. The NIV DSB commentary on this verse says, "Trust in the trustworthy, loving heavenly Father should replace worry, anxiety, and fear in our lives" (page 1180). Show me a Christian who is constantly worrying about situations and circumstances and I will show you a believer who has allowed their trust in God to be replaced by the worries of this world. This does not make them a bad person. Unfortunately for them they have lost their center of trust. These folks have come to feel that they must provide whatever solution is required because God seems far off or disinterested in them. When they repeatedly fail to achieve whatever results they desire, anxiety replaces their confident reliance on God. What did Jesus say about the 3rd type of soil? Nonbelievers allow a lack of trust to cost them their faith in God Almighty. Believers allow a lessening of trust to cost them some of the blessings which God has in store for those who walk in His ways.

Have I stepped on anyone's toes? I sure have mine. I was once a world class worrier. I use to worry about situations happening, but then they would not happen. This is when I got really smart. I would worry about things just so they would not happen. Pretty smart, right? Smart at least until you better understand the above passage. I finally came to realize that my trust in Jehovah Jireh being the Provider for what I *actually* need was being diminished by all this worrying about things which I thought I needed. Nothing has ever happened to me that God could not mend. Heartache, shame, disappointment, regret, guilt, marital failure, health issues – everything I have faced in life has been handled by my God. I am not the only one who God has championed. Read the Psalms. He loves being our champion. When I came to really accept that my God will guide, guard, and direct me in all my paths, I quit worrying. Worrying proved to be useless. Worse yet, it was an affront to my Lord.

To continue with Matthew, go to 8:23-26. This is the account of Jesus calming the storm. Once again Jesus rebukes his disciples for having little faith. Was this a lack of commitment to Jesus as being their Lord and Savior? No. What is happening in these verses is that a whole new dimension of the Son of God is being revealed to them. Jesus uses the storm to grow their belief in Him as the Son of God. The disciples also needed to increase in their trust that God will do what He says He will do. This is borne out by them worrying about their impending doom. They did not stop to think that Jesus would not fulfill His mission if their boat sank. If they had total trust in Jesus as being our Savior, then they would have realized God was going to deliver them in some manner. Jesus was not going to drown, thereby destroying His mission on earth. Jesus wants the disciples to grow in their trust that He will see them through all circumstances as He marches on in His earthly mission. Had I been with the disciples, I am certain I would have reacted exactly as they did. At that time, they were not as enlightened about Jesus' earthly mission as they were going to be in the near future. These men were of their time. They knew the perils of bad weather and boats. They allowed fear to grip them. Where their faith wavered was in the total package which Jesus brings on the scene. The disciples had a difficult time accepting that Jesus had dominion over all of creation. This is understandable since there never was before nor has there been anyone since who had such remarkable powers.

A different perspective is presented in Matthew 9:27-30. Here are two blind men who show remarkable trust that

Jesus can do the impossible. Remember, trust relates to God's providence. The remarkable truth in these verses is that while these men were physically blind, they could see what others failed to see. These men lay claim to the healing powers of Christ Jesus. How did they come to such faith? We do not know but probably the Holy Spirit was prompting them to step out in trust. For them, no other remedy was available. God uses these men to teach the followers that Jesus is concerned with all aspects of their being. Where the religious leaders of the day were consumed with rituals and rules, Christ shows compassion and concern. These men are the dramatic opposites of worriers. <u>Doubts about whether God will provide His blessings and support for our lives rob us of our faith</u>. Why do we have such doubts? Sometimes this happens because we are harboring feelings from unresolved sin as though we are unworthy of help. The lack of forgiving ourselves can also lead us not to expect Jesus' help. Most of the times it relates to God not answering our prayers the way we want them answered. We doubt El Elyon yet the irony is we are actually at fault for trying to manipulate Him. We can be some pretty messed up creatures at times.

The opposite of the blind men can be seen in Matthew 14:26-32. What happens here is almost comical. This is where Jesus walks on the water. Our Lord spooks the disciples by coming out to them while they are in a boat. Peter wants in the act but he waivers in his trust. He allows the worry of the stormy weather to make his trust weaken. Was his commitment low? Did he vacillate in his belief in Jesus? Neither. His trust that Jesus could be sovereign over nature is the culprit. Peter is doing fine as long as he has his eyes on Jesus. Comically, when he takes in the enormity of what he is doing, his trust that Jesus can pull this off fails him. Fear is the most powerful of all emotions for most people. The drive to preserve your life is the most basic. When trust conflicts with self-preservation, most of the time the drive for saving your life wins your attention. It is the truly remarkable person whose faith reigns over their fear. The men and women who have suffered persecution till death without losing faith are our real heroes (Matthew 5:11-12). What I enjoy though is how absolutely human Peter is in this story. He provides us with a great lesson. Whenever we have a mountaintop experience with God, Satan immediately moves in and tempts us with worldly concerns. Our trust that God will actually deliver us in an astonishing way is then tested. When we start doubting that God will do as He promises through Scriptures, our faith becomes weakened.

Let us return to the Parable of the Prodigal Son (Luke 15:11-32). How does this story relate to faith being weak? The younger son shows his lack of commitment to his father by wanting to leave the family's estate and to explore other, more exciting places. He represents the backslider in many of us. We want what we want when we want it. <u>Our selfish emotions war against what we hold as sacred</u>. <u>If this means rebelling against God, then most people typically place a greater priority on their emotional happiness than their godly obedience</u>. Many of us squander the energy of our youth on self-centered pursuits. We seem to think that getting right with God is only to be considered when we get older. Remember where the young man finally found employment – in a hog pen. For a Jewish man to work in such a setting reveals how utterly far he had fallen. What happened to him is what we might call "tough love" God style. He went from living life large to being envious of hog slop. As Dr. Doug Sager is fond of saying, "When you rebel against God, there is a hog pen out there waiting for you." There is nothing like hunger, poverty, shame, and humiliation to make us consider resetting our priorities. Backsliders face the shame of wasting much of their lives in frivolous pursuits. When they repent, they regret not doing more for the One who does so much.

Dr. Henry Blackaby presents us with a stern warning when he says, "A person who claims to be a Christian but deliberately holds on to a particular sin in his life is either totally quenching the Holy Spirit – which is an even worse sin – or has never known the experience of the Holy Spirit's conviction of sin, and isn't a believer at all" (Experiencing the Cross, p. 126-127). This is where the backslider is flirting with trouble. They have become indifferent to the convicting power of the Holy Spirit. When a believer starts such a pattern of ignoring the promptings of the Holy Spirit, then they are disconnecting with the one saving voice which is given them to keep them focused on being what God originally desired them to be. The best thing God can do for us at these times is to allow our lives to become completely miserable (as in the story of the prodigal son). Yes, we often forget the other side of the love dimension with God. Tough love is one of His tools in allowing us to feel the full brunt of our rebellious actions.

I think the best thing we parents can do for our children who stray is to pray to God that He makes them unhappy in all their new pursuits. If not, then they will continue to think they are prospering without God's hand in their lives. Success without God is the worst thing that can happen to us. As Solomon admonished in Proverbs 3:11-12, "My son, do not despise the Lord's discipline and do not resent His rebuke, because the Lord disciplines those He loves, as a father the son he delights in." As Christians, we should not enable rebellious believers by making excuses for them. More importantly, we should be cautious in rescuing those who God is chastening. Dr. Blackaby continues, "What happens if a Christian doesn't repent? Disaster. That person's heart grows hard, and God's Word loses its power and fruitfulness in his life."

So how can we make sure we are not slowly sliding into this precarious role? According to Blackaby, "You can always assess your relationship to God by your degree of responsiveness to His Word." As a word of encouragement, Blackaby adds, "When the Holy Spirit convicts a genuine believer of sin, that person can repent and be immediately restored to fellowship with God." Yes, Adonai, our Lord and Master, is a loving God – through the good times and the bad, always supremely wise in His interactions with us.

Now let us turn our attention to the other son in this parable. The older brother shows his lack of commitment to the welfare of the family by becoming jealous when the father gives a feast for his returning younger brother. Did the older brother not trust that the father would be fair with his inheritance? Do we ever show a lack of trust in our heavenly Father when we become jealous when it appears to us God is blessing others more than He is blessing us? The older brother represents the Pharisee in many of us when we act self-righteously. Paul and Peter had a number of altercations with the self-righteous Pharisees (Acts 15:1-11). The Pharisees seemed to be angry with the early Christians because it appeared to them God was willing to bring in the Gentiles to His kingdom even though they had not gone through all of the rituals of Jewish life. They felt the Gentiles were getting off easy. The Pharisees could not accept this idea of "grace" about which Paul and Peter preached. As with the older brother, they resented the welcoming arms of a loving Father who is far happier with a returning, repentant son than with the strict adherence to a set of rigid rules by a hard-hearted, self-righteous offspring. Envy and jealousy toward others whom we perceive as receiving unwarranted forgiveness can attack our faith. It shows we do not trust God's righteousness in dealing fairly with everyone. Both sons were low on faith both in God and their father; both violated the commandment to honor thy father. This is an excellent story about how the raging emotion of rebelliousness affects our faithful walk with God.

I am an animal lover, particularly dogs and horses. The best way to have a great relationship with a dog or a horse is for you to be calm and assertive. That way the animal can be calm and submissive. This is what the TV show on the National Geographic channel called "The Dog Whisperer" teaches and it really does work. Rebellious pets are not enjoyable for us. Whenever my horse refuses to proceed along a trail we are riding because something is amiss in his view, I do not kick or hit him. I check out whatever it is that is causing him concern. If it is because an old tractor is parked along the trail, then I nudge him to go forward. If that is not sufficient, then I spin him in a tight circle. This seems to clear his thinking and redirects his energy back to me. We then proceed around the obstacle and he sees everything is fine.

Rebellious believers are not enjoyable to our heavenly Father either. We correct our pets. He corrects us. Sometimes God has to spin me around in a tight circle as well. This redirects my energy back to Him. The proof that rebellious behavior is not pleasing to God is this: "Have you ever known a rebellious Christian who lived a contended life?" Neither have I. You will not get the spiritual gift of inner peace through contentment from the Holy Spirit working in your life if you maintain these little acts of rebellion as part of your behavioral pattern.

I have heard people joking about having a rebellious side. It is as if they secretly want to be bad but still be acceptable to good people. They may even think it makes them "alluring". This is ridiculous. Rebellion is not a characteristic which is in any way acceptable to the Christian lifestyle. Where in the Bible is there a story about a prominent person of faith being rebellious and that being acceptable to God? Think about Samson and Solomon. Samson is chronicled in the book of Judges (Judges 13:24 – 16:30). He had great physical strength, which at times exceeded his spiritual strength. As a gift from God, it was to be used in the service of God's people. Unfortunately, Samson became prideful of his great reputation as a mighty warrior. Into the story enters Delilah, a seductive creature of the opposite sex. Samson is tempted and he rebels against God's will for his life (Judges 16:4-21). We know the price he paid.

Solomon was a man of great wisdom (1 Kings 3:1-12). God gave him this gift and his father David told him what he must do to be a great king – to follow the Lord in all he does. God specifically warned Israel against making treaties with foreign governments (Exodus 34:12). Jehovah Jireh knew that with treaties for commerce, stability, and protection come requirements which would entice them away from His providence. This is exactly what happened to Solomon. He became prideful. He ignored God's command (in other words, he rebelled). He thought himself so enlightened that he could make treaties with neighboring countries and not suffer any ill consequences. With these treaties though came the sharing of religious beliefs. As Solomon took wives to seal the treaties, they brought their idol worship with them. These women did exactly what God warned against in Exodus 34:12. They ensnared him. We know the price he and all of Israel paid. After Solomon's death, the kingdom split, never to be reunited again.

It is amazing to me how many of these stories we have in the Bible which warn us of such dangers, yet we continue to make the same mistakes as the men and women of old. None of this surprises God however. He knows each generation is going to make their own mistakes. <u>Possibly the value these stories have for most people is that they show the consequences of unrighteous behavior and the willingness of God to accept us back in the family when we repent and return to Him.</u> It is the unusually wise person who can learn from the mistakes of others.

Both Samson and Solomon were men of God. Both had the issues of pride, power, status, and sexual appetites struggling against their faith. <u>Pride wars with our commitment to God because He alone is to be the sovereign power over our lives.</u> Just like it was with Satan as the fallen angel, pride is the enemy to a godly walk. Pride leads to rebellion. In no way are a person's little rebellious acts to be acceptable as something about which to make jokes. Celebrities and sports figures try to get away with this stuff all the time.

Submission to God does not mean we are being weak or cowardly. In fact, in Joshua 1:6 Elohim encourages Joshua to "be strong and courageous" as he is preparing to lead the Israelites into the Promised Land. Spiritual submission means we are showing that we have the power of our free will under restraint for and in service to God Almighty. Go to Matthew 5:5, "Blessed are the meek, for they will inherit the earth." What does meekness mean here? It is certainly not requiring men to act like "girly boys". Meekness here means obediently accepting God's guidance and relying on His righteous vindication. It implies gentle strength; power under control (whether it is will power or physical strength). Christian men do not have to act like sissies in order to show meekness. We are not weak because we choose to be meek. We are said to be meek when we choose to use our power under submission to God to do good rather than using our power to achieve selfish desires. The bit of the bridle is used to control my horse. He is a thousand pounds of beauty and strength. The bit does not change or diminish his strength in any way. It does allow me to guide him as we move along a path. He has learned that he can trust me as we go along to look out for places where gentle guidance is needed. This is much like what God desires of us. We are to remain the beautiful, powerful creatures which He designed. <u>Our trust in Jehovah Jireh allows us to follow His guidance. We are not diminished in any manner by submitting to our heavenly</u>

Father. It is just plain smart. He alone is omniscient. We can trust Him totally with our well being.

We need to realize there is a great deal of difference between an immature believer and a believer with a low level of faith. All of us start out as immature believers. With dedication to congregational worship, Bible study and prayer comes growth. With growth comes maturity. The immature are susceptible to more temptations of faith than seasoned believers, but they are, nonetheless, genuine believers. With spiritual discipline these trials will "refine" their faith. Spiritual maturity progresses at a rate which matches our dedication to serving God.

Low octane believers are those who are going through a spiritual valley. Psalm 23:4 is a wonderful encouragement when we find ourselves in such places. I think it is safe to say that all believers will have episodes of weak faith. We are human and the enemy is shrewd. Elijah provides us with a great example of a man with tremendous faith, yet after having a mountaintop experience with God, is left shaken by a vicious, evil queen (1 Kings 19:1-4). He trusted completely in God to provide the fire from heaven for the sacrifice. However he weakened when Jezebel turned the heat on him. Why do these episodes of weakness happen to us? This is so perhaps because during these times, we feel we cannot totally trust in God's providence, at least in a way which is preferential to us. With Elijah it happened when the emotion of fear overcame him. Notice what God did not do. Elohim did not strike him down. On the contrary, Jehovah Jireh sent an angel to minister to Elijah. Is it not funny that at the very times we feel God is far off, He is right there in so many forms and in so many ways trying to help support us and strengthen us?

People who are experiencing a weakened faith may have previously been disappointed possibly because God did not answer their prayers in the manner in which they desired. This is their fault though. How many times have we been taught to pray that our requests match up with the will of our Lord? Turn to Psalm 19:14, Matthew 6:9-10, and Matthew 26:39 to learn how we are to pray. It is summed up well in 1 John 5:14. "This is the confidence we have in approaching God: that if we ask anything according to His will, He hears us." If we follow this with Matthew 26:39, then we are assured of being righteous with God. The setting is the Garden of Gethsemane. "Going a little farther, He fell with His face to the ground and prayed, 'My Father, if it is possible, may this cup be taken from me. Yet not as I will, but as you will.'" Jesus is the Alpha and the Omega for submissive meekness in our prayers.

We know while modern man may be accepting of low levels of trust and commitment, Jesus has been very explicit with us on what is demanded. He demonstrated it all too well in the above passage. Believers with chronic low levels of faith keep the same beliefs and practices from year to year. They seem never to progress in their spiritual maturity. If you are dedicated to spiritual growth, new knowledge and insights into God's plan for your life will come to you. With that new knowledge should come greater avenues for service. As you serve our Lord Jesus, greater trust will develop. This is because as we serve we learn to depend on our Triune God for the results. Even with this, there will come times in our lives when all of us will experience doubt and weakness. This is where congregational worship, daily Bible study, and prayer will prove their worth to you. These practices will nourish a weak faith and replenish its strength. An honest dialogue with the heavenly Father will reassure you of His presence and His concern for every aspect of your life. How do you gain this reassurance? His urgings will be in your thoughts as you pray. The Holy Spirit will bring biblical verses to your memory. Things learned in praise and worship will start to flow into your consciousness. This is how the Holy Spirit guides us. Practice listening.

All of us will get tired at times. What we are to do is to be dedicated in our service and to trust God for how the work succeeds. Our trust will grow as we see the hand of our ever-present God in even the smallest of details in our daily lives. As this happens, then our commitment to Him as our only God and to the service of His kingdom will naturally increase in strength.

The reason I have such an easy time correcting my horse when we are riding on a trail is because he has learned over the years that he can trust me. Building up trust is critical for faithful obedience. Without trust, it is impossible to give any measure of commitment. In the last chapter we covered how beliefs have to be given time to develop into a core belief system. The other components to faith are extremely important once belief is established. They strongly influence our degree of obedience. When faith is weak, we can usually trace it back to either we are not trusting God's provision or we are not committed in our service to His kingdom. It is a tremendous challenge for people in our culture to surrender their will to that of the Father's. We treasure the idea of being self-reliant and self-sufficient. That is fine until you decide to ask Jesus to be your Savior. Then your reliance is to shift to the Holy Spirit for direction and guidance. <u>The problem of not surrendering our will to His is rooted in an absence of complete trust</u>.

Now I am going to step on a few toes. Are you ready? People who do not tithe are actually saying they do not trust that God will take care of their financial needs. Ouch. If they did, then they would feel perfectly comfortable giving a full tithe. A partial tithe is thus partial trust, which shows up in partial obedience. I know this sounds simplistic but it is just that simple. Those who do tithe learn a remarkable truth about trusting God with their finances – you cannot out give

God. Sure, He may not give you directly back in a financial manner dollar for dollar which you gave in tithe but what Jehovah Jireh does provide you will be exactly what you need. It may be greater wealth, but it also could be blessings related to your health, your children, your spouse, your profession, or a closer spiritual relationship with the Creator of the universe. To have a healthy, happy family which walks with God is probably the greatest blessing He can give any of us.

In conclusion, as parents we should be very wise in how we allow our emotions to spill over into our relationship with our children. They pick up on everything. If you are constantly hassled, discontented and fretful, guess what? They will be too. If all that matters to you is your personal happiness, they will quickly adopt this approach to life as well. Your little gods will become their gods. If not, they will at least learn they too can have other gods than Jehovah God. Where is it in the Sermon on the Mount that Jesus promises we will never have any disappointments? Where in the books of Paul, Peter, and John does it say only good things happen to those who believe in God? Our heavenly Father, the One who created the heavens and the earth, never promises us a carefree life. He does promise us eternal salvation – if. Yes, something is always required of us. That is a good thing. To live within yourself is not. Help your children to prepare to be a light to others. Be a good parent to your children. As our heavenly Father loves us enough to do the hard work of molding us into being good Christians, mold your children into being good adults. Help them to learn to shape their emotions into building up their faith, not eroding it.

### *Total Trust, Complete Commitment*

Now let us direct our attention to Matthew 4:1-11. This passage introduces us to total trust and complete commitment. The KJVLASB commentary on Matthew 4:1-11 states, "Jesus was able to resist all of Satan's temptations because He not only knew Scripture, He obeyed it. Ephesians 6:17 says that God's Word is a sword to use in spiritual combat. Knowing Bible verses is an important step in helping us resist Satan's attacks, but we must also obey the Bible. Note that Satan had memorized Scripture, but he failed to obey it. Knowing and obeying the Bible helps us follow God's desires rather than Satan's" (page 1558). The KJVLASB commentary associated with Luke 4:3 teaches, "Satan frequently raises questions about what God has said. He knows that once we begin to question God, it's far easier to get us to do what he wants. Times of questioning can help us sort out our beliefs and strengthen our faith, but they can also be dangerous. If you are dealing with doubt, realize that you are especially vulnerable to temptation. Even as you search for answers, protect yourself by meditating on the unshakable truths of God's Word" (page 1719). Remember the bumper sticker "Question Everything"? Pride in your intellect is a great hindrance to faith at times. Perhaps the sticker should have read, "Question Everything – except God".

Why did Jesus quote Scriptures to ward off the temptations of Satan? Why did He not just say as we would have said, "Get away from me Satan and stop tempting me." Our own words have meaning and they should carry weight if used properly. However, God's Word is all powerful and represents ultimate truth. Jesus is teaching us to use the most powerful weapon in our arsenal when dealing with the craftiness of Satan. God's Holy Word is our bastion of strength. <u>As we conquer temptations by using His Word, we gain in trust that God will provide for us.</u> As we gain in trust in small ways, this will lead to greater trust. <u>As our trust becomes firmly established in the promises that God will do what He says He will do, then our commitment to living a righteous life is strengthened.</u> There is great biblical truth to the old song, "Trust and obey, for there's no other way to be happy in Jesus but to trust and obey." When our faith is weak, we can depend on His Word to give us strength.

Weakness in faith is most often made evident by our lack of resolve or determination, which relates to our trust and commitment. In the same verses where Peter is to be sifted (Luke 22:31-42) Jesus Himself is tested. Christ gives us the perfect example to follow when we are in tribulation. What does He do? Jesus prays an honest prayer. Jesus is no delusional person who is seeking martyrdom in order to gain notoriety. He knows full well the agonizing pain which scourging and crucifixion will bring on His body. He also knows the separation from our heavenly Father which will be required as He takes on the sins of the world. Which do you think He is dreading more? Jesus prays very honestly that He wishes "this cup could be passed from Him." Then our Lord and Savior does what we are to always do. He finishes His prayer by stating, "not my will but Thy will be done." Perfect surrender; total trust; complete commitment.

Has the question ever arisen in your mind why David carried five small stones when he fought Goliath (1 Samuel 17:40)? At first glance, this shows a weakness of faith by man's standards – he did not trust God so he brought five stones. Actually the opposite is true. David trusted God; he just did not know if it was going to take more than one stone. As Henry and Richard Blackaby explain it in their book, Experiencing God Day-By-Day Devotional, page 278, "David was prepared for God to grant him victory with the first stone he hurled at the giant or the fifth. David was ready to accept God's victory, whether it came easily or with much effort." His faith was strong and his wisdom even stronger. Young David was not going to test God. Henry and Richard Blackaby go on to state, "The account of David and Goliath vividly pictures the source of the Christian's faith – not our own size, strength, or resources, but the power of almighty

God. If we focus on our opposition and problems, they will seem gigantic. But as we focus on God, we will see our situation in the proper perspective and be assured that all things are possible with God" (Phil. 4:13).

A dear friend in our church, Chuck Boyle, came down with cancer the second time. I remember very well the morning he stood up in our Sunday School class and thanked everyone for their prayers and concern. He said he wanted to live but most of all, he wanted to be with God. Chuck told us his spirit was well, just his body was wearing out. Then he said something which will always stick with me. He said, "I *will* be with God; it's just a matter of whether it is on this side of the grass or the other." What a remarkable statement of faith and contentment. Chuck was honest in what he personally wanted but regardless of the outcome, he had the assurance that his ultimate desire would be achieved. Walking in the will of God always brings remarkable strength. When you have this type of faith, you can see God in each and every situation. Each situation has its own value. Each gives you an opportunity to experience God in a little different way.

### *Who can We Trust*

We have one of my favorite biblical quotes framed and hung in our kitchen. A family kitchen is a wonderful gathering place. Some of our best times are spent in the kitchen preparing meals and discussing the events of the day. As with many homes, it is our practice to start our meals by saying grace. God has blessed my family super abundantly, so taking time out each day to thank Him is the least we can do. On the wall next to the table hangs the quote from Proverbs 3:5-6, "Trust in the Lord with all your heart and lean not on your own understanding; in all your ways acknowledge Him, and He will make your paths straight." Every once in a while

Linda will point to that verse when the daughters are stressed or worried about something. It is a masterful summary of our reliance on our heavenly Father. Our trust in Jehovah God is to be complete and all encompassing. Since the knowledge of this world will fail us at times, we must always be looking to God as our sovereign Lord. If we will remember to turn to the Father in all situations which confront us, He will graciously direct our paths. What a wonderful promise this verse makes to us!

Part of trusting someone involves developing an identity with that person. Have you ever thought about what it is with Jesus and His message that you identify? What draws you to a redemptive faith in Jesus Christ? Is it His message of faith, hope, joy, love, compassion, salvation, and forgiveness? What about His character traits? Which of these is most important to you? Jesus is described as a suffering servant, a kind and gentle teacher, a healer of the body and the soul, and someone who loved all of God's creation without limits or guidelines. Knowing what helps you identify with our Lord can help you to better understand what you need from Him in times of crises. This can then guide your Bible study when seeking strength from the Scriptures.

What does identification have to do with faith? As you know, trust is one of the components of faith. When we identify with someone or something, we are by nature drawn to them. Trust involves being able to predict how something will turn out (as in God will do what He says He will do). Identification allows us to predict a favorable outcome based on how we feel our own character would affect that outcome. If we feel an identity with someone and we feel confident we can predict their behavior, then we tend to place greater trust in that individual. Therefore, the more similar something is to us, the more we tend to trust in our ability to predict what will happen in certain circumstances.

Turn to Acts 8:26-40 and read about Philip and the Ethiopian. This man wanted to understand the message Isaiah was presenting. Not being a Jew, he was struggling with the text and what the Holy Spirit was laying on his heart. One of the problems here was that with the Mosaic Law he could never convert to Judaism since he was a eunuch. As this gentleman was reading in Isaiah, he had questions for Philip about the man who was to become the Messiah. Do you think as Philip explained to him the meaning of the verses in Isaiah which they were discussing that he came to identify with Jesus? Isaiah declared the Messiah would be the suffering servant of Israel rather than some great military leader (which was what the Jewish leaders were wanting). Since this man was a governmental official of Ethiopia, yet a eunuch, it is probably safe to say he suffered in some measure from being a eunuch. It could be he had been made a eunuch because people at that time thought castration would make men more docile and trustworthy. Perhaps Isaiah's description of Jesus moved his heart to looking to a Savoir who could understand his pain. The significance of this lesson is that God reaches out to *all* people through His Son Jesus. For the Ethiopian, he now had a Redeemer who was accepting of him just as he was.

What is it about Jesus and His message that builds your identification with Him? The more He reflects you and you reflect Him, the more trust you will have. Do you see why the sanctification process of being transformed into a likeness of Jesus is so indispensable to a genuine faith in our Triune God? To trust, we must be able to predict. To predict, we must understand. To understand Jesus, we must know Him.

There are others in our lives to whom we should be able to turn to when guidance and insight are needed. Ministers, teachers, family members, and spiritual friends are a great resource for a Christian to lean on when our faith needs bolstering. It is important that we know who to turn to in addition to God in times of need and confusion. What are the traits of genuine teachers of God's Word? Malachi 2:1-7 is a good starting point to consider such traits. Teachers and preachers are to: (1) honor God's Name with a reverential awe, (2) instruct the people in the ways of God, (3) turn people away from sin, (4) be God's messengers, and (5) walk in those ways themselves. Leaders such as Sunday School teachers, youth leaders, congregational ministries, deacons, and church ministers must be very careful to know God's truth, practice it, and teach it to those they lead. Such a ministry must be rendered to everyone impartially.

False teachers can be distinguished from these men and women by their lack of knowledge and respect for the true Word of God, by their manipulative practices, partiality, and their desire for status, wealth, and power. These people display a rather low level of commitment in faithfully living out God's plan for their lives. They appear to be more concerned about themselves and how they are perceived than they are the status of your soul (Luke 11:39-46). If their commitment is low, then what do you think you can conclude about their trust? False teachers generally have great issues with pride and adoration. Pride puffs a person up and makes them feel they have become self-reliant, independently resourceful, and inherently powerful (Psalm 10:2-6, Proverbs 16:18). Pride is the enemy to godly trust (Deut. 8: 11-14). Believers must learn to be critical listeners as well as being discerning of character as we move forward in the sanctification process.

### *Got Faith?*

Can we trust in our faith to get us to heaven? Please review John 6:39-40 and 10:27-30 again. We know Christ Jesus does not intend to lose any who are given to Him. This applies only to those who have yielded their souls in surrender to our Lord Jesus. This is not to be a conditional surrender or a partial surrender. Anything less than a forthright submission of your will to that of our Father's will leaves a person open to being deceived about their spiritual status. My pastor, Dr. Doug Sager, makes an excellent point concerning these verses. He asserts, "If Satan were strong enough to wrestle a Christian from Jesus' hands, then Satan would prove in these instances to be more powerful than Christ." We know though that the Holy Trinity is omnipotent (Genesis 17:1; Exodus 14:15-31; Joshua 3:13-14:24). To further increase our faith in this point, one of His many names by which we know Him is El Shaddai – Lord God Almighty. Dr. Sager declares, "It is impossible that Satan could ever be more powerful than Jesus. He cannot overwhelm Christ in any way." If you believe Satan can be that powerful, either you have greatly underestimated the actual power of our Lord Jesus, or your understanding of the assurance given us in being sealed by the Holy Spirit has become confused. Once we have made a sincere profession of our faith in Jesus Christ as our Lord and Savior, Jesus will be our strength even when we are weak. Is this not the promise which Paul gives us about our supreme source of strength, even when we are weak? It bears citing once again. 1 Corinthians 1:8-9, "He will keep you strong to the end, so that you will be blameless on the day of our Lord Jesus Christ. God, who has called you into fellowship with his Son Jesus Christ our Lord, is faithful."

This is why Christians can trust Jesus Christ in any situation they face. A deeper trust in Jesus is certainly needed when circumstances do not turn out the way we want (as in sickness, financial crises, family disputes, and the general storms of life). Why do some believers in difficult situations ask for God's help only after seeking help in other places? The answer may lie in their not being in the habit of praying everyday over everyday issues. They most likely do not remain in a dialogue with God throughout the day. Possibly they think they can handle it without troubling God – kind of like, we should only trouble God with the major issues. A contented Christian is one who has learned to keep a running dialogue with God throughout the day. God's blessings in their lives have proven to them He is to be trusted with any and everything.

When a Christian is being tempted, it appears to me that something like the following occurs. One of Satan's legions of demons is whispering in their ear to lure them away with an enticement to disobedience. Note, Satan and his demons do not inhabit believers but they still try to influence us. These forces are startlingly crafty in what they put in front of us to make us weak. Our free wills are then beguiled to act on these enticements (remember, demons cannot make a believer sin). This is why *we* are to be held accountable – we can be tempted but we cannot be forced. Please be mindful, demon possession only applies to nonbelievers. Once the Holy Spirit indwells you, all rights to your soul are reserved. However, keep in mind – this does not stop Satan from trying to derail you (especially your witness to others).

In Hebrews 1:14 the author questions us, "Are not all angels ministering spirits sent to serve those who will inherit salvation?" Absolutely this is one of the many functions which God has for His angelic army. From the above passage we are assured that God sends to believers His angels to minister to us. With the protection of a ministering angel and the indwelling Holy Spirit, you should be able to withstand the temptation of Satan's minions (1 Corinthians 10:13). When you fail to have sufficient resistance, then confess and repent. God is not some all-consuming deity who is rigid and harsh like in Greek mythology. Yahweh does not demand that we be perfect. What He demands is a contrite heart (Isaiah 57:15, 66:2) seeking a righteous relationship with Him. Hebrews 2:18 gives us further assurance.

"Because He (Jesus) himself suffered when He was tempted, He is able to help those who are being tempted." Remember, the Holy Spirit is Jesus' agent with us, to help us to do the work which Christ desires us to do. Couple this with the presence of ministering angels and we should begin to see just how much Jesus values us.

What is our mission as the result of this discussion? Mature believers are to be a light unto the young in faith as well as those who are confused in their faith. We are to love them as others have loved us. Paul gives us the model for this ministering spirit in 2 Corinthians 1:3-5. "Praise be to the God and Father of our Lord Jesus Christ, the Father of compassion and the God of all comfort, who comforts us in all our troubles, so that we can comfort those in any trouble with the comfort we ourselves have received from God. For just as the sufferings of Christ flow over into our lives, so also through Christ our comfort overflows." How do you show others compassion and love? First, by putting a smile on your face. Ask them questions about their life. Listen. Show a real interest in them. Where they are happy, share with them that even greater happiness can be found in a daily relationship with God. Where they are hurting, comfort them as you have been comforted so they can know they can always count on the strength and mercies of the Lord. The most effective way of doing this is by letting them know how God makes a real difference in your life. We are never to be self-righteous. Genuine Christian love goes a long way in combating the perception of self-righteousness. So, the first thing we must do is to look at ourselves. Get our hearts ready to show to others what God has done in our lives. Mature believers are to live out His teachings in our daily lives. Who else will model this behavior if we don't? We should always be thankful to the people who have helped us along in our walk with God. None of us start or end this journey on our own. I am so thankful for a Christian home and the loving churches where I have been a member. Without their patience and kindness, I would never have developed the resolve in my redemptive faith which I have now. May God bless all of those who have been with me on my journey.

# Chapter Seven The Sadly Deceived

⸺◦≈◦⸺

Can a true believer renounce their faith or go so far as to commit blasphemy against the Holy Spirit? The more I read, the less I think either is possible for a genuine Christian. The nagging problem is the casual Christian. The obvious question is: how can anyone be a casual Christian? I think this is precisely the point – you can't. Jesus said you are either for Him or against Him (Mark 9:40). He offered no middle ground, nor did He minimize the cost of following Him (Matthew 8:19-22). It is hard to read the Gospels of Jesus' life to think that He would accept anything other than a complete and total acceptance of His Holiness. Anything less and you are risking the same judgment which Christ spoke of when addressing the Church of Laodicea (Rev 3:14-16).

If you do not believe that a Christian can renounce their faith and thereby destroy their eternal security, then you are even less likely to believe a Christian could commit blasphemy against the Holy Spirit. What scriptural verses are there which support this position? Are they the same ones we use to support eternal security? It seems impossible to me that any believer, after having received the Holy Spirit, would ever commit this unpardonable sin. To deny the Spirit after experiencing its wondrous presence seems unlikely, even for a new believer.

Refer to Luke 12:10. In my <u>KJV Life Application Study Bible</u> the commentary states: "The unforgivable sin involves deliberate and ongoing rejection of the Holy Spirit's work and thus God Himself. A person who has committed this sin has shut himself off from God so thoroughly that he is unaware of any sin at all. A person who fears having committed it shows, by his very concern, that he has not sinned in this way." How does this compare to your understanding of the unforgivable sin? Jesus proclaims in Matthew 12:31-32, "And so I tell you, every sin and blasphemy will be forgiven men, but the blasphemy against the Spirit will not be forgiven. Anyone who speaks a word against the Son of Man will be forgiven, but anyone who speaks against the Holy Spirit will not be forgiven, either in this age or in the age to come." With reference to Matthew 12:31-32, the KJVLASB commentary states: "Blasphemy against the Holy Ghost is denying that the Holy Spirit convicts us of sin. <u>Because a person can be saved only through the Holy Spirit's work, to refuse to repent or even to acknowledge our sin is to refuse God's forgiveness...Jesus said they can't be forgiven – not because their sin is worse than any other, but because they will never ask for forgiveness</u>. Whoever rejects the prompting of the Holy Spirit removes himself from the only force that can lead him to repentance and restoration to God."

After much study, I think we need to be more concerned about someone thinking they are saved when they are not than worrying about losing our eternal security. While other denominations may debate this doctrine, eternal security is substantiated by many scriptural verses. When you weigh the total evidence, there are an overwhelming number of verses which give us hope that once God has put a claim on your life, it can never be broken, either by the believer or by anything else.

Sometimes the obvious answer is the right answer. Our culture gets so caught up in "spinning" everything. We seem to enjoy making things which normally our fathers would have called black or white, we seem to delight in making them gray. Perhaps this helps us not to feel responsible or guilty. Regardless, sometimes the simplest answer is not only the obvious answer but it is the right answer. Therefore, there appears to be strong scriptural support to believe the obvious – perhaps those who fall away from their belief in Christ were not genuinely saved from the start. The idea of them "falling away" is more metaphorical than actual. To fall away from something, you have to have been there. These folks never did really belief in Christ. They were never really there. They may have pretended to others that they were believers. They may have even pretended with themselves. The reality is that pretending is just that – pretending.

As we have seen through our study of eternal security, if the Holy Spirit indwells a person's spirit, He does not relinquish this position. The Holy Spirit puts a bear hug on your spirit, never to let go. You may fall in the mud and get stained from your own failures, but the Holy Spirit is right there with you. Wherever you go, He goes. Someone who "falls away" is only described as such for figurative purposes. Jesus takes title to your being when you become a genuine believer in Him as your Lord and Savior. He sends the Holy Spirit to secure possession of what He holds title. Not even the person themselves through their free will can ever dissolve this relationship. I say this not because you can't; it is because you will not. The Holy Spirit will marshal His forces to convict you before you go too far. He will help you to never wall Him out of your life. David provides the believer with this promise from God: "Though he stumble, he will not fall, for the Lord upholds him with His hand" (Psalm 37:24). If someone has fallen away, they have only done so in their own imagination. My understanding from

Scripture is that their soul never made any transaction with our Lord in order to seal the deal in the first place.

Jesus' teachings about the narrow road (Matthew 7:14) and the rich young man (Matthew 19:24) certainly support that few are willing to do whatever is necessary for eternal life. Also Paul's and James' writings that "works" must follow salvation as a natural result of our love for God may point to people who incorrectly claim to be saved but do nothing. This "do nothing" response reflects their lack of a "change of heart". C. S. Lewis made an excellent analogy about works and salvation in his book, Mere Christianity. "Christians have often disputed as to whether what leads the Christian home is good actions, or faith in Christ. I have no right really to speak on such a difficult question, but it does seem to me like asking which blade in a pair of scissors is most necessary" (page 148). The bottom-line is: a genuine profession of faith is not merely a matter of words (which make us feel better) and then Jesus is to accept whatever behavior we care to give. Being a sincere Christian requires genuine belief, complete trust, and a steadfast commitment. Once these are given, we never have to worry about the eternal destination of our souls. The acts of our daily lives will bear witness to the true condition of our hearts. Even when we sin, we are still His. Even when we doubt, we are still His. He owns our hearts. We are His and He is ours.

The Holy Spirit is always associated with acts of obedience and service in genuine conversions (Matthew 7:16-21 – it is not enough to believe; we must become "doers" by doing God's will). While works are not required of salvation (Romans 3:28), they are a natural outpouring of our love and gratitude to God for His grace. In Deut. 10:12-13 Moses stated, "And now, O Israel, what does the Lord your God ask of you but to fear the Lord your God, to walk in all His ways, to love Him, to serve the Lord your God with all your heart and all your soul, and to observe the Lord's commands and decrees that I am giving you today for your own good?" <u>Both the Old and New Testaments emphasize that a righteous relationship with God involves active service and obedience</u>. <u>If one is not active in faith and obedience, then this "do nothing" reality reveals one's true heart</u>. Only a heart that is genuinely dedicated to the Lord God Almighty will be able to claim His promise of eternal security. Do yourself a favor and now read Psalm 103 and Romans 3:21-28. These are some of the most reassuring verses for me in the entire Bible concerning the security we have in His salvation. I praise God for David and Paul and for their words. These two men certainly exemplify Matthew 5:8, as each revealed a pure heart unabashedly in love with God Almighty.

### Genuine Believers and CINO's

It is time to pull the mask off those who are deceived as well as those who live by deception. What are their traits? What does Jesus tell us which helps us to know who these people are? Are there various types of Christians In Name Only? To start, CINO's are very different from those of us who have been prodigal sons (who have faith but were back-sliders at one point). The differences are:

a. Prodigal sons have remorse and feel guilty. Even when backslidden, the Holy Spirit is still at work, prompting you to confess your sins and repent. One of the best things we can do for a backslider is to pray that the Holy Spirit makes them miserable in their plight. *It is remarkable how often misery is used by the Lord to bring us back to Him.*

b. Prodigal sons sooner or later return to their faith. Rebellion has a price. If a person has truly tasted the Holy Spirit, they will eventually return. They may be a little bloody and soiled, but God is there to give them a fresh robe and welcome them back (Luke 15:20-24). You cannot live apart from your faith for long. If you can, then your faith was not what you thought it to be.

c. Prodigal sons often become stronger in their faith and gain a greater understanding of God's love, patience, mercy, and forgiveness. However, this is not to encourage people to backslide. Certainly it can increase your faith but for a heavy price. Sin has consequences. The scars will not be things of which you will be proud to display.

There are 3 basic types of CINO's:

1. Those who *think* they are Christians but in actuality they have not made Christianity one of their core belief systems. Perhaps they have doubts about the evidence that God is who He says He is; thereby their belief is not solid. These doubts may be the result of worldly ideas infiltrating their less than stalwart religious beliefs. Remember, we are to be in this world but not of this world. Conflicting beliefs, which are so prevalent in our culture, tend to compel a person to water-down any staunchly held religious positions. Sadly for these folks, they do not seem to grasp it that Jesus did not die a horrendous death from crucifixion just so people can sit on the fence and play both sides. Jesus rebukes the church in Laodicea for being lukewarm – neither hot nor cold (Revelation 3:16). Our spiritual beliefs are to make us fervent supporters of Christ. Steadfastness in our faith is to be our hallmark.

Another possibility is that these CINO's have never put unwavering trust in God's promises, so they hold back in living the righteous lifestyle. Some may think God is too far removed to be relied on for their daily needs. Others may feel they have to take matters into their own hands or else life will deal them a tremendous blow. This shows they like having the ultimate power in their own hands rather than trusting in a divine power which is not under their control (and beyond their understanding). Chronic worrying about things is another indication they are uncomfortable with turning their concerns over to God, then trusting in His providence. They may feel He has let them down on numerous occasions. Of course these pretenders would never actually say this, but their actions reveal their hearts. If this is the case, then these deceived individuals may also have a hard time in resolutely believing in the promises of God. These Godly promises all sound good but there is this lingering doubt they have which the world keeps reinforcing. If this is the case, Elohim is not your God. If you dig a little deeper, something else has become your center for trust. Worse yet, you may not have absolute trust in anything. What a sad existence.

Perhaps these CINO's do not understand the earnest commitment required to be accepted by God as a true believer. They may not even realize it is a two way transaction. The KJVLASB commentary for Revelation 12:12 covers why God allows Satan to be evil. "God allows Satan to work evil and bring temptation so that those who pretend to be Christ's followers will be weeded out from His true believers." Unfortunately, this places these pretenders in the ranks of the deceived. They will never spend the time to personally investigate the knowledge which is available to those of us who accept Christ as our Savior. This knowledge is very important because Christianity is not just a heartfelt conviction. You have to "know that you know" God is who He says He is and He does what He says He will do. We are all going to be tempted. Without a strong intellectual assessment and knowledge of the foundations of our beliefs, Satan will be able to entice you away with his cleverly crafted schemes. As much as it may amaze our detractors, Christians are smart people. We have a hunger and thirst for the knowledge and wisdom our Lord offers us. The best way to gain this knowledge is to attend church regularly and read the Bible. There are other ways, but I cannot imagine someone being serious about developing a new belief system in something without being eager to learn about it. This is the first test. Do you have a hunger for the things of Christ (Matthew 5:6)? If you are not willing to invest time in the pursuit of your faith, then your faith is not faith but rather a fleeting interest.

2. <u>Those who think they are Christians but *deny* the dedicated commitment required to be known legitimately as a child of God</u>. We are to live righteously, not just say the words or worse, to lower our standards of behavior so it fits our immoral activities. Paul teaches us in Galatians 3:26-27 that we must clothe ourselves with Christ. This certainly does not convey a casual commitment. Continuing in Galatians 6:3-4, Paul warns, "If anyone thinks he is something when he is nothing, he deceives himself. Each one should test his own actions." Paul is referring to people who are presenting themselves to be Christians, yet they continue in their sinful nature. We are to be careful with these folks for they may tempt us with their actions. Jesus refers to this in Revelation 2:20-23 where He warns the Thyatira church against false teachers. These false doctrines will dilute their beliefs and corrupt their resolve. This will lead them into a willingness to accept immoral behavior as being moral. This happens because without a steadfast belief system, these people are often more desirous of acceptance by man, more so than living righteously for God. Even for

good Christians, we must be careful with what we allow to float around in our minds. These false doctrines will infiltrate our thoughts and have us pursuing worldly pleasures while acting like we are following Christ as our Lord and holy Redeemer.

The reality for these deceived people is they are actually spiritual underachievers who desire greatly to set their own lower standards for admission into God's heavenly realm – it does not work that way though. They are underachievers both in faith and actions. They "somewhat" want to be Christians, but, more importantly, they want it on their terms. These are the ones who like to "contemplate" God. They have their own version of God. Let me guess – it is one where they do not have to do anything but rather all they have to do is to "feel the love". These deceived souls construct their own version of God so that He fits conveniently into their schedules and does not require things from them which they do not want to give. Much like a pet, their version of God is always waiting for them to give Him whatever attention they choose at that particular moment.

These are the CINO's who like to talk about what they believe but they have absolutely no biblical substantiation for such pronouncements. Their faith is based on what they would like for Christianity to be. These thoughts are not based on what Jesus actually reveals in the Gospels about what our beliefs are to be. How terribly inconvenient going to church must be (especially every Sunday) for these folks? As for as acts of service, that is for the pastors to do. This bit about tithing is for those who have more money than they. God certainly does not mean 10% of your gross pay, not with childcare, high taxes, ipods, designer jeans, and stylish cars (and oh my gosh, what about those credit card bills – they just never seem to end). Many of these folks seem to think they can deal with becoming righteous once they get older and life settles down a bit. What they want is a God of convenience, not holiness. If a friend or a sermon does not get their attention in time, they are headed for a great surprise when God starts reading the names from the book of life (Revelation 3:1-5). They will not be in there.

3 Those who want *others* to think they are Christians but they know they are not genuine believers because they are not willing: (1) to make faith in Christ a core belief, (2) to place an unwavering trust in the promises of Jesus, or (3) they are not willing to make the necessary commitment to living the Christian life. Jesus paints a portrait of these folks in Matthew 23:3, 13-33. They do not practice what they preach. Worse yet, they mislead others who are sincere in their pursuit of righteousness. According to our Lord, the price for their deception will be an eternity in hell. Paul sums it up well in Galatians 6:7-8. Those who sow to please their sinful nature will reap destruction.

This group of CINO's is the most destructive of all. These are the people who are usually seeking to exert power over us and/or to separate us from our money. Whatever the case, their intentions are to manipulate and to deceive. They are the ones who cause the world to think our churches are filled with hypocrites. Such men as these where the church leaders who perpetrated the ungodly holy wars of the Middle Ages. These wars were not fought to bring people to Christ. They were fought to bring revenue to Rome. Rather than being clothed in Christ, they hide themselves under the mantle of religion. The modern day version of this crowd wants the perception of righteousness in order to disguise their unholy hearts. They deceptively interlace beliefs and practices which are not biblically supported with slogans which rally unsuspecting believers. False doctrines will be found to be their friends. They depend on their skills of communication and persuasion to entice the undereducated believers into their schemes. These are the ones who Jesus, Paul, Peter, and John had the harshest of words to describe their plight (Matthew 3:13-33, Matthew 15:7-9, 1Timothy 1:3-11, 2 Timothy 4:3-4, Titus 1:9-16, 2 Peter 2:1-21, and 1 John 4:1-6).

Deceivers in this group do the most harm to the church. They take advantage of our trust, our desire to believe the best in others, our obedience to Christ in trying to bring His message to others, our willingness to forgive, and our hesitancy to be judgmental. These folks know our beliefs and tendencies. They use this knowledge to exploit us. For a con artist to be successful, he must blend in. He must know the right words. He must be perceived as being a trustworthy fellow. Woe is the day they stand before the Lord and give an accounting for the souls they have misled. Woe is the person who has used the name of our Lord and Savior to deceive others with their willful lies.

Once again, this discussion is not meant to make people *doubt* their salvation. It *is* meant to scare the heck out of people who are not *certain* of their salvation. Many think they are saved but they are not. These are not my words but the words of our Lord and Savior. Turn once again to Matthew 7:13-23. Jesus warns us, "Enter through the narrow gate. For wide is the gate and broad is the road that leads to destruction, and many enter through it. But small is the gate and narrow the road that leads to life, and only a few find it." Jesus continues with further words of admonition. "Watch out for false prophets. They come to you in sheep's clothing, but inwardly they are ferocious wolves. By their fruit you will recognize them. Do people pick grapes from thornbushes, or figs from thistles? Likewise every good tree bears good fruit, but a bad tree bears bad fruit. A good tree cannot bear bad fruit, and a bad tree cannot bear good fruit. Every tree that does not bear good fruit is cut down and thrown into the fire. Thus, by their fruit you will recognize them. Not everyone who says to me, 'Lord, Lord,' will enter the kingdom of heaven, but only he who does the will of my Father who is in heaven. Many will say to me on that day, 'Lord, Lord, did we not prophesy (teach) in your name, and in your name drive out demons and perform many miracles?' Then I will tell them plainly, 'I never knew you. Away from me, you evildoers!'" From Jesus' mouth to our ears, let us hear and understand His words of warning.

### *Soft Sermons*

In many churches so much gets said about the loving side of God that they neglect His other attributes of holiness, righteousness, law giver, tester of our souls, refiner of our spirits, judge of our thoughts and deeds, and our sovereign God who will not be mocked nor deceived. We must desire sermons which are a more balanced presentation of the totality of God's ways. If not, then we will fall prey to these disingenuous deceivers who promote false doctrines and practices. Solomon shares his wisdom with us in Proverbs 9:8-9. "Do not rebuke a mocker or he will hate you; rebuke a wise man and he will love you. Instruct a wise man and he will be wiser still; teach a righteous man and he will add to his learning." Christians should demand total instruction from their pastors and teachers – not just the things which are pleasing to the ears. Do they think we are merely a bunch of mockers?

Soft, cotton candy style sermons devoid of any conviction are largely to blame for this scarcity of spiritual breadth. These sermons are designed to be pleasing to the ears of the hearers. They make you "feel good" about taking time out from your busy Sunday morning to attend church. Sermons are supposed to educate us about how to walk in righteousness with God. If you are doing that, then you will feel good about yourself. If not, then they are to convict you of your unrighteousness and motivate you to repent. The sermons are to be God-centered, not self-centered. These ministers speak in soft, bed-time style voices which are to be soothing to the ears. Give me a preacher like Jesus, Paul, Peter, and John who used the full range of their voices to exhort us. Go to Acts Chapter 7 and read about Stephen in front of the Sanhedrin. Do you think he was speaking in a cotton candy, bed-time story voice? Absolutely not! This man gave his voice over to the Holy Spirit. As such, truth was ringing out in all its power! Praise God for ministers who will deliver stirring sermons designed to bring us back to God rather than to make us feel like we have just watched an episode of Mr. Rogers. Give me a minister whose voice rings of passion. Stephen did not get the Jewish leaders feeling like they had been cut to the bone by talking about Jesus as being a "loving" man of God. Jesus was the Messiah, in all the totality of its meaning. Christ Jesus was Stephen's redeemer. From these verses we imagine Stephen's voice carrying the trumpeting sound of victory, not appeasement.

Some preachers who seem to be more concerned with popularity than with accurate doctrine will have us thinking God is only in the business of love. They may be wanting our contributions so much that they become reluctant to tell the complete story. They must worry they will offend us if they seem stern at times. These pastors want our laughter and feelings of encouragement. Their version of God is that of the grand ole guy who loves all His creation, no matter what we do. The truth is He does love all of creation. Nevertheless, He also will righteously hold each accountable for all of eternity for our beliefs and behaviors.

These ministers will have you thinking if you will trust in God, He will make everything right. Paul trusted. Peter trusted. Both led lives which required tremendous sacrifices. However, in the end, they met the martyr's death. God made everything right with their souls but powerful men gave them endless persecution for their beliefs. The ministers who neglect the battles we face and the judgment of God for those who reject Him do their congregations an injustice. When is the last time these good times ministers preached on the price of sinning? Do their worshippers believe in hell as the eternal consequence of unrepented sin? Have these ministers led them to think the good ones of us go to heaven but the bad ones merely cease to exist? We would not want anyone to "feel" uncomfortable now, would we? When have they firmly warned their congregations of God's holiness requiring Him to hold us accountable not only for our deeds but for our thoughts as well? This does not happen in these churches because they do not want to step on anyone's toes. When have they delivered a sermon which warns of false doctrines, little alone of a place called hell?

A pastor who does not step on a few toes regularly is playing to the crowd. They cause us to miss the point of worship altogether. Christians during worship are to be focusing on a crowd of One (the one God in the form of three Persons) and not on themselves. El Shaddai and that Son of His named Jesus, along with the ubiquitous Holy Spirit are to be the objects of our worship. We are to be worshipping God Almighty, not getting a feel good makeover. The truth is the truth and it should be preached. If it convicts us of our unrighteousness, then we are the better for it. Not every Sunday has to be this way, but they cannot all be about love, blue skies, and positive thinking. The music lifts us to praise and the sermons are to help us orient our lives to God. <u>Living a righteous life is extremely difficult.</u> <u>Pastors and Sunday School teachers are to prepare us for the spiritual battles</u>

we will be facing. As in any warfare, this means instruction for any and every situation which we will encounter. It is also important that we know whether we are being tempted by Satan or disciplined by God. Solomon provides the following insight in Proverbs 3:11-12. "My son, do not despise the Lord's discipline and do not resent His rebuke, because the Lord disciplines those He loves, as a father the son he delights in." If you are unclear as to whether you are being tempted or disciplined, consult your pastor. Of course, you could pray that the Holy Spirit will guide you in your spiritual discovery – but then that would be too simple.

Getting your toes stepped on is one of the greatest values of attending church regularly. Our pastors and teachers help to hold us accountable. They are to help convict us so we will know from God's Holy Word what He expects of us. God was not hesitant to tell the Israelites of His promises and of His wrath if they ignored His commands (Deuteronomy 28). Read this entire chapter to make yourself certain that God demands righteousness. In Deuteronomy 28:15 God admonishes the Israelites, "However, if you do not obey the Lord your God and do not carefully follow all His commands and decrees I am giving you today, all these curses will come upon you and overtake you:". The rest of this chapter describes in detail how God would punish Israel if they did not take His commands seriously. Please take the time to read these verses. Do you think it is any different today, for Christians? Just because Christ died for us on the cross do not allow Satan to deceive you into thinking this gives us a license to do whatever we want. God does not change. He is still the same today as He was yesterday. God demands an obedient heart and faith, regardless which side of BC/AD you were born.

How God presents what He wants of us and what will happen if we do not abide with His will should be our model for teaching others. Our church leaders are to direct and guide us. We all need a course correction periodically. Pastors who tell the crowd only what they want to hear and in a manner that is always pleasing to their ears are little more than motivational speakers. This is nothing new though – Jeremiah wailed against this in the Old Testament (Jeremiah 14:14-16). In Jeremiah 23:16 we are told, "This is what the Lord Almighty says: "Do not listen to what the prophets are prophesying to you; they fill you with false hopes. They speak visions from their own minds, not from the mouth of the Lord. They keep saying to those who despise me, 'The Lord says: You will have peace.' And to all who follow the stubbornness of their hearts they say, 'No harm will come to you.' But which of them has stood in the council of the Lord to see or to hear His word? Who has listened and heard His word? See, the storm of the Lord will burst out in wrath, a whirlwind swirling down on the heads of the wicked. The anger of the Lord will not turn back until He fully accomplishes the purposes of His heart. In days to come you will understand it clearly." The days to come are now. It is true that God is love but it is also true that He is not to be taken lightly or mocked (Galatians 6:7). If these verses do not get your attention, then your heart has been sadly led astray. Do not follow the stubbornness of your heart or the follies of our culture to where you no longer believe God will hold you answerable for your thoughts and deeds.

El Elyon's other attributes are extremely important. There is no better place to learn of these attributes than the Old Testament. By combing OT and NT study, we get a much more complete picture of our Triune God. Yes, God is a God of love and prefers to interact with us on that basis. More than that though, our God is a holy God. He is the Most High God. He cannot allow those who are sinful to manipulate righteousness for their own gain. While Jesus seeks to redeem us all, we have to have a willing spirit and an obedient heart. Those who deceive themselves and others are addressed in the above quoted verses from the book of Matthew. Jesus delivers a stern warning to those who are casual or uncommitted in their faith and obedience. We (and the Father) will know the constitution of a person's heart by the fruit which they produce. Is your character reflecting good fruit which leads to the glory of God and the benefit of mankind or are you exhibiting fruit which only benefits you? Additionally, with God, it does not matter how good your intentions are. What matters is what you <u>do</u> to advance His holy kingdom. Do not deceive yourself or allow others to deceive you. Not by words but by faith and deeds will God judge your participation in kingdom work. As C. S. Lewis says, our works and our faith are like the two blades of a pair of scissors. They are both necessary and both work together to accomplish the goal (<u>Mere Christianity</u>, page 148). Our works come from the character of Christ which is within us. While faith is what saves our souls, deeds are the produce of our hearts.

### The Parable of the Sower Explained

For the explanation of the parable about the different soils in Matthew 13:3-23 the NIVDSB commentary gives the following insights: "The Word of God, the good "seed", is powerful but it must be planted in good soil to germinate and to produce a crop. Hearing the parable we must ask: what sort of "soil" am I? That determines how we will receive the Word of God. God's Word will always have a mixed reaction. The four reactions which the seed encountered on different grounds are the way in which people respond to the revelation of God: unreceptive, unfaithful, unfruitful, and unexpectedly productive. The hearers, represented by the varied types of soil, are different.

1. The hard-hearted – these hearers, like the soil, have heard and rejected the message so often they have become gospel-hardened. They cannot understand its beauty or its life-giving hope.
2. The emotional responders – so many people make spur-of-the-moment emotional decisions which quickly fade because they have made no personal commitment. The first bit of spiritual trouble sends them running looking for the next emotional pick-up.
3. Those unwilling to pay the price – many people are attracted to Jesus but are unwilling to pay the cost of following Him.
4. The faithful disciples – God has always prepared a fourth type of hearer, those with willing hearts who respond to the good news. They have three characteristics: (a) they hear the word willingly; (b) they understand it and respond to it in true commitment and faith; and (c) with the power of God within, they are changed and produce fruit, that is, they enlist other followers of Jesus."

The Believer's Bible Commentary by William MacDonald gives this additional understanding on pages 1255-1256: "The hard-packed pathway speaks of people who refuse to receive the message. They hear the gospel but do not understand it – not because they can't but because they won't. The Pharisees were hard-soil hearers." In discussing the rocky soil folks, MacDonald makes this interesting statement about what ministers face. "At first the sower might be elated that his preaching is so successful. But soon he learns the deeper lesson, that it is not good when the message is received with smiles and cheers. First there must be conviction of sin, contrition, and repentance. It is far more promising to see an inquirer weeping his way to Calvary than to see him walking down the aisle light-heartedly and exuberantly. The shallow earth yields a shallow profession; there is no depth to the root." Of the soil infested with thorns, MacDonald says, "They appear outwardly to be genuine subjects of the kingdom but in time their interest is choked out by the cares of this world and by their delight in riches. There is no fruit for God in their lives." Of the fourth soil MacDonald explains what the fruit is which they produce. He says, "Fruit here is probably the manifestation of Christian character rather than souls won to Christ. When the word "fruit" is used in the New Testament, it generally refers to the fruit of the Spirit (Gal. 5:22-23)."

Obviously this parable is meant to encourage us to take seriously our pledge of faith in God Almighty. We are to be "doers" of the Word and not just "hearers" of the Gospels. The Good News is to transform us into being inwardly and outwardly true believers, not just acknowledgers. It also prepares us for the reality that only a few will accept the teachings of our Bible. MacDonald tells us on page 1256, "As for the disciples, the parable prepared them and future followers of Jesus for the otherwise discouraging fact that relatively few of those who hear the message are genuinely saved."

This parable further reveals the truth about eternal security following the continuum of faith: (1) no faith, (2) little faith, (3) casual, moderate, unproductive faith, and (4) genuine, sincere, productive faith. Eternal security is ours when we step out in steadfast, unwavering faith that Jesus is the Son of God and His promises are true. His promises give us hope and purpose. **Until we make a resolute, unwavering commitment to Christ Jesus that He and only He is our personal Lord and Savior, whatever faith we might have is only preparatory faith**. **It is the initial phase of faith (a precursor to genuine faith), but it is not yet redemptive faith**. Jesus has been very clear with us. The Father only wants those who will reverently surrender their will to His and be earnestly sold out for the kingdom. We are either with Him or we are against Him (Matthew 12:30, Mark 9:38-40). There is no middle of the road, moderate position acceptable to our Lord. There is a very good reason for God's position on this. Our world is full of temptations and trials. If the body of Christ is not made up of genuinely committed believers, then we will fall.

Satan is too crafty for the uncommitted "quasi-believers". Those who intellectually think they can reserve certain doubts about the validity of God's Holy Word in order to show their special insights or worldly wisdom are only deceiving themselves. All or none is God's requirement for admission into His kingdom. With God, it is all about your heart. If El Elyon cannot have all of your heart, then you might as well give Him none of it. What do we know that substantiates such a statement? Turn to Exodus 20:3-5, Deuteronomy 6:13-17 and Joshua 24:16-20. All three of these passages refer to our God as being a jealous God. By jealous, it means He is possessive; He demands your complete allegiance. God Almighty is not willing to share someone's faith with any other god. You cannot pick what you like about Christianity and then combine it with Buddhism or Islam in order to create your own new brand of religion. If you allow anything else other than the Triune God of heaven to be worshipped by you, the Holy Trinity will turn against you and you will suffer righteous judgment. God the Father, God the Son, and God the Holy Spirit created us and as such they can set the rules.

Frankly, I agree with this position. I do not want to be surrounded with people who I think are solidly supporting my beliefs, only to find that they are the ones who are stirring up dissension. Let the tests and trials come! This will separate out those of little and moderate faith. This ultimately makes room for those who are sincere in their faith to operate in a more productive environment. The sooner these folks realize they are not participating in Christ's salvation, the better. They are usually the ones who are the complainers in our churches anyways. Perhaps we should shun these folks in order to make them uncomfortable, so they will leave. This may solve two problems. It would free us of some dissenters and would make finding a parking spot as easy on Sunday mornings as it is on Sunday nights.

That would be fine but in doing so, we would be the ones committing the sin (I trust you caught my humor). This is absolutely not what we should do. In doing this, we would be playing the role of judge. We would be judging them as not being worthy of God's grace and salvation. That is a role reserved solely for Christ Jesus. What we should do is the exact opposite. God purposely puts some difficult people in our paths to help us to grow in the fruits of the Spirit. If we are not tested, how else will we know if we have become patient, loving, kind, and good to others? They are both a test and an opportunity. These are the very folks we should work the hardest to get. At least they have some knowledge of Jesus. We do not have to spend thousands of dollars and get on an airplane to witness to them. They live in our communities and some are even attending church with us. If we save them, not only do we add to God's kingdom but we also help by developing another good citizen for our country. For America to remain strong, we have to work at developing God fearing citizens who will call on the name of Jehovah God to bless our country. Therefore, we need to witness to these deceived souls and help them see how alive Jesus is in our lives.

Give these quasi-believers a chance to express their doubts and fears. When this happens, we are to lead them along in biblical passages which address their concerns. We are to pray with them, for them. All of us were on the proverbial spiritual fence prior to our conversion. <u>Every one of us has benefited from some kindhearted Christian who has worked with us through our season of doubt and confusion</u>. We should have empathy for them, not disdain or distaste for them. Every effort should be made to include these confused souls in our family of believers. Remember, we all started out as nonbelievers. Then we progressed along the continuum of faith until we reached the point where we knew deep in our hearts that God is who He says He is and He does what He says He will do. Once we came to this decision, it then became incumbent on us to lead others along the same path. God is so wise in His plan for our salvation. It is so wonderful that He allows us to participate with the Holy Trinity in planting seeds and growing a crop of new Christians.

One of the major differences between genuine believers and CINO's is repentance. This is where they desperately need our help. These quasi-believers must come to the realization that God does not play favorites; He will not grant them any exemptions. Even though He loves them, God cannot allow them to casually disregard His commandments and rules. In order to be obedient to God, you must turn away from your sins. Faith without true repentance is only nominal faith. Repentance involves the positive action of turning away from sin and toward a life centered on obedience to Jehovah God. Confession leads to repentance, which merits forgiveness if done with a pure heart. No repentance, then no forgiveness. Redemptive faith and God-oriented repentance are intrinsically linked. CINO's just do not seem to accept the necessity of actually leading a 7 day a week life centered on Jesus. Our Redeemer teaches us we can recognize these pretenders by their lack of fruitful living. Some will be wolves in sheep's clothing. Some intentionally deceive while others are ignorantly deceived. Regardless, the same fate awaits all three.

## *Why do not All People believe in the Holy Trinity*

Let's extend the discussion of the parable of the soils a little further. Since Elohim put an inherent nature in each of us to seek Him, why do not all people follow the Triune God of the Christian Bible? The following are some of the reasons but this list is by no means exhaustive. As you read these points of discussion try to think of the four different soil types in the Parable of the Sower (Matthew 13:3-9, 18-23). Many of these points interrelate, so conversion is an even greater challenge in some cases. These interwoven, dynamic human conditions are suggestive of why Christianity is the road less traveled. Human beings are extremely complicated social creatures when it comes to our interests, attitudes, beliefs, emotions, and motivations. As evident here, the free will which God gives us can be either a blessing or a curse.

(1) Most live for the moment. Most people are seekers of pleasure rather than righteousness. What makes them happy is what they want at that moment. The aspect of denying themselves any perceived pleasures is not to be considered. Such thinking is attributable to the misguided desire not to be held accountable to a higher authority. This is why evolutionary theories are so intriguing to the spiritually bereft. If there is no God, then they are free to decide their own set of morals. Without a God as our creator, then they are only accountable to themselves and their cultural group. This conveniently allows them to have less spiritual conflicts and greater carnal pleasures.

(2) People do not like to submit to authority. Most people do not like submitting to an ultimate authority where there are absolute right and wrong behaviors and these behaviors carry consequences. Most people like living in the "gray areas" of life where they are able to justify

any of their emotions and subsequent behaviors. Many prefer to have someone to blame other than themselves and to be answerable to no one. Additionally, the word "submission" carries a connotation of weakness. To submit their free will to a righteous God who demands obedience is not what most people desire. While not wanting to admit it most people lack the focus and determination to live a life surrendered to God. Following God requires self-discipline. Our obedience to Him should become the major priority in our life. Christians are not believed when we tell others of how empowering and rewarding a surrendered life to the Lord actually is. This sounds foreign to their present cultural views and they want nothing of it.

(3) Pride and intellectualism combine to war against one's spiritual faith. As we marvel at our own reasoning powers, we become self-absorbed in the pursuit to explain our existence in rational terms. Paul expresses this well in Romans 1:20-22, "For since the creation of the world God's invisible qualities—his eternal power and divine nature—have been clearly seen, being understood from what has been made, so that men are without excuse. For although they knew God, they neither glorified Him as God nor gave thanks to Him, but their thinking became futile and their foolish hearts were darkened. Although they claimed to be wise, they became fools..." It has always been amazing to me how many who have advanced intellects allow their self-absorption to render them inept in understanding the true wisdom of the ages. Many who are of this persuasion are too prideful to surrender their wills to God. The worldly values of power, pleasure, wealth, and status all lead to pride. Jehovah God teaches against pride. He wants us to be humble in our interactions. Intellectualism seems to be coupled with pride. The

two appear to go hand in hand (in fact, the first three reasons all relate to each other). You do not have to actually be smart – all that is required is that you think you are smart. From this pride takes hold. Most of us want to be the "captain of our own ship" but we are too arrogant to realize we have a fool as the captain. While it may appear contradictory, it actually takes a very secure person to completely surrender their life to Christ. The insecure try this but when trouble comes, they quickly take back the control seat.

(4) <u>Many are content in their own ignorance</u>. These are those poor souls who are simply too lazy to read the Bible and learn God's revealed plan for their lives. They may believe in eternity and even reference some ethereal notion of some type of deity. Nonetheless, they seem to always find some rationalization to excuse themselves from gaining any real knowledge of our holy God. Their excuses are many but their reasoning is always flawed. To be certain, the process of sanctification is hard, disciplined work. These people lack the determination and dedication to earnestly pursue a life where suffering and self-discipline are parts of the total composite.

(5) <u>Family heritage is very strong and extremely hard to overcome</u>. The sins of the father as they relate to their lack of belief or misdirected beliefs are often visited on their offspring. Most family leaders do not want to admit that they have been in error with regards to spiritual guidance. They exert their considerable familial power in maintaining their group. This preserves their power, status, and prestige in the larger social network. Our missionaries and church planters have great difficulties in breaking through generations of cultural norms. Most people find it much easier and safer to simply go along with the crowd. This is why most people accept

the commonly held religious beliefs of their cultural group. When conversions do happen, these people are often ostracized and shunned from participating in family and cultural events. The power of the pack is strong, even in humans.

(6) <u>Satan is masterful in his deceptions</u>. At times, life can be very harsh. Due to this, many people do not see a loving, holy God at work in our world. They see how pervasive evil is. This makes them doubt that a loving, righteous God could exist and allow all of this to happen. <u>Most do not recognize that the evil which happens to them is not God's choice</u>. This evil which distresses them so is the result of mankind rejecting God's desires and following their own selfish nature. These confused souls blame Jehovah, not Satan or themselves, for the wickedness of this world. They ask "How can a loving God allow such and such to happen?" These deceived people absolutely wear me out. If they would only stop to critically examine their own question, they should be able to see the fallacy in it. This question leads to a blasphemous assertion. They attribute something bad (the evil in this world) to something good (God). They incorrectly reason since God is sovereign, He must be to blame for all the bad which happens. This implies if He were truly a loving God, then Elohim would not allow such suffering. The truth is, Satan prompts evil and these people are so drenched in ignorance of God's character and His Holy Word that they end up questioning God. This has got to be one of Satan's greatest triumphs. They do not stop to think that God gives each of us a free will and the bad things which happen are the results of people's free wills in action. Moreover, we are not puppets. By this I mean God allows us to make choices. What we face in life is *often* due to the choices which we have made. These duped souls seem

to be quick to blame God for any misfortunes – whether natural or man made. They seldom stop to think these misfortunes are the direct result of the actions of people around them, including themselves. The correct question should be: How could mankind, which has been so richly blessed by God Almighty, have become so corrupt in its nature that we bring such suffering to this world? Even with natural disasters, it is often traceable back to man's poor decision making as to why such resulting suffering occurs. But then, let's not blame ourselves. Where would the politicians get their power if we each started holding ourselves and others responsible for the suffering we endure?

(7) <u>Discouragement rules paramount</u> in stealing away a person's ability to believe in a divine Being. With many cultures being so mired in darkness, Satan has stolen their trust in the goodness of anything meaningful. These are the people who I have the greatest sympathy for in their spiritual bleakness. Life has beaten them down. Their God given spirits have become weakened by years of disillusionment and distrust in any form of religion. As they lose trust in what can be seen, it becomes even harder to trust in what is not seen. Their lives do not testify to the goodness of the Lord. If we can give them the gift of hope, then at least they may be able to endure their present conditions for the promise of a future of peace, joy, love, and happiness. <u>What we most often fail to realize is if God punished evil immediately when it happens, then none of us would be here</u>. The man who wrote "Amazing Grace" was a former slave ship captain. John Newton repented and spent the remainder of his life working for the abolition of slavery in England. His life illustrates Divine grace. Our patient and loving Father does not immediately dispense justice because He wants to give all of us a

chance to repent and turn to Him. In the meantime, we wreak havoc on ourselves and others.

(8) Peer pressure can be enormous. People reject God's calling to them because the allure of worldly values is very strong. Social pressure is very hard to resist (John 12:42-43). Many of these people may already belong to another world religion. The Jews rejected Jesus because their social mores craved a conquering king like David rather than a suffering servant like Jesus. Most of us want to fit in with the world around us. This is a natural inclination. In contrast, if you are a Christian God gives you a different set of marching orders. You are to set yourself apart from this world. That is an impossible task for some who are so controlled by their desires to be liked and accepted.

(9) Being short-sighted is a common characteristic of people. Many think they can wait until they are older to make these types of decisions. They prefer the pleasures of today and are perfectly willing to postpone consideration of eternity until a later date. Why is this? You have to realize what these folks are really saying is they believe being faithful to God will be limiting to them in some way. How can obeying a God who demands righteousness be fun? Add to that His decree for us to tithe and serve others. These misguided souls do not know that God will transform you. The Holy Spirit will help you develop interests and habits which are both rewarding and of service to God. Surprisingly to many, being a Christian is not a boring lifestyle.

(10) Many have been turned off to Christianity because of some perceived hypocrisy by a Christian acquaintance or church. It is my opinion that pseudo-Christians (CINO's) have done more to discredit the Christian religion than any other group (including the evolutionists). These hypocrites give credence to the attacks

of the world against Christianity. Who do you think instigated the famous "Holy Wars" and the persecutions of the Middle Ages? It was not sincere, genuine Christians. These wars and persecutions went against everything which is taught in the Bible. The perpetrators of these evil events were false believers masquerading as church leaders. They were the Pharisees of that era. These men whitewashed themselves in the banner of the church but they were actually seeking power and wealth. This led to an enduring, discrediting blemish on our Christian faith in the eyes of the world. This is what is so sad (but exactly what Satan wanted) – God gets the black eye and Satan gets the victory. In our modern day, these hypocrites are the CINO's who may attend church but they hardly ever pick up their Bibles and read. For them to tithe would be akin to expecting them to give up some of their precious indulgences. They have no real, intimate relationship with God Almighty, nor do they seek one. That would require too much effort. These people like being seen as first-rate Christians because it makes them feel good inside. Church attendance occurs because of how it makes them feel rather than because it is their chance to refine their personal relationship with the Holy Trinity. These are the ones who are quick to judge and criticize others. Those who make prayer and the study of God's Word a priority are guided by the Spirit to be encouraging. Those who show up at church and use it as a social event are more like the Pharisees of old. They are quick to lay heavy burdens on others but are not willing to exercise the self-discipline required to walk righteously with God.

(11) People in general seem to prefer a religion of convenience. Most want to worship at their convenience and under conditions which they feel easily accom-

modates their lifestyle. Many have deluded themselves into thinking they are believers (of some form of god or ethereal being) and that all beliefs lead to the same destination. This is true; there are many paths which lead to the same destination. However, as one of the ladies in my Sunday School class pointed out, the problem is the destination is not the one they have in mind (Matthew 7:13). I think this is where Satan gets most people. The Great Deceiver looks at the values, attitudes, and beliefs of a cultural group and then molds false gods to draw them away from a life-altering experience with El Elyon. This makes it very convenient for that cultural group since their gods reflect their established beliefs. Satan offers up false gods who seem to demand very little in the way of requirements for righteous living. Some of these false gods are in the form of other world religions. They hold a kernel of truth but deception is sprinkled all through them. We can make a false god out of anything which we put our faith in as opposed to worshipping the Triune God of Christianity. Think about where many people spend their time and money, or in what they put their faith. We have: wealth, success, status, government, nature, entertainment, sports, science, self-sufficiency, self- indulgence, and many other pursuits. These things, when they replace our faith and service to God, can all become modern day idols. They are convenient and many offer expressions of worldly pleasures and ambitions while worshipping them. To say the least, a Christian commitment is not convenient for most people's way of life. God demands a portion of both your time and your money. Attending church, reading your Bible, praying, witnessing – these all take time and effort. For people who tend to be self-centered, these are commitments which they do not care to make.

(12)  <u>Money is a big reason</u>. More people are willing to give of their time rather than their money. Even to secular causes, people will often donate their time but they do not want to be relied on for regular contributions. Celebrities offer their services as spokesman for a certain cause. This makes them feel good about themselves. How much of their money did they give? We seldom hear of this. God demands an offering and greedy people resist this. People who cling to their money often try to justify this behavior by accusing churches of misspending. Sure, this happens but those who do it will pay a heavy price one day. It is our responsibility to give unto God and it is our leaders' responsibilities to wisely account for the money. The two are separate. If someone feels their church is mishandling the funds, they should approach the stewardship committee. If they do not get satisfaction, then perhaps they should find another church. At no point are we to refuse to tithe. Jesus gives us a glimpse at this problem in the story of the rich young man (Matt 19:16-24). Money means power, status, privilege, security, and provision. These are values which most societies treasure. Christ teaches us to store for ourselves treasures in heaven, not on earth (Matt 6:19-21). Jesus continues with this wisdom in verse 24, "No one can serve two masters. Either he will hate the one and love the other, or he will be devoted to the one and despise the other. You cannot serve both God and Money." Many will allow their love of money to rob them of a wondrous eternity.

(13)  <u>Some simply do not believe the accounts of the Bible</u>. Such a person may have a cursory knowledge of the events and teachings of the Bible and reject them because these events do not make logical sense in their world view. As Jesus explains this, the person's heart has become hardened because, "the evil one comes

and snatches away what was sown in his heart" Matt 13:19. Examples of this type of rejection are: the story of creation requiring only six days; Noah getting all of those animals in the ark; Jesus being an incarnate Deity where He is simultaneously fully man and fully God; the resurrection and subsequent appearances of Jesus after dying on the cross. These and many more biblical stories cause them to doubt the validity of the Bible as a whole. *Just because something is hard to understand or explain does not make it less real.* After all, our senses tell us the earth is flat.

I own a business based on a particular type of computer software. If someone sat me in front of a PC and demanded I write a program from scratch, including the operating system, I would be completely lost. I cannot explain precisely how a computer works, yet I make my living in that industry. For me to require that I have to understand everything in the Bible and to be able to explain it completely in logical terms in order for me to place faith in its content is laughable. If I do not demand that of myself in my professional life, why should I require that of myself in my spiritual life? Yet some seem to try this argument as though it has substance. Sadly, they miss the point. Religion speaks to your heart. This is how God designed it. Your intellect flows with your growing knowledge of biblical stories, but where there are things which exceed your understanding or areas of ambiguities, it is your heart which gives substance to the "mystery". <u>Faith fills the void where man's intellect fails him</u>.

Skeptics deprive themselves of the hope and assurance of God. That is a very high price to pay for cynicism. Some of these individuals who reject the truths of the Bible may be members of some of the other world religions. They probably feel their religion has a better presentation of theological truths and concepts than the Christian religion does.

Others have accepted the various idols of modern man as their objects of faith and worship.

### *How do We Know the Bible is Truthful*

The concept that the Bible is inerrant is another hard teaching for many to accept. Knowledge is constantly under attack, whether it is man's knowledge or God's enlightened revelation. This helps establish an atmosphere of doubt and uncertainty. It is true that biblical translations have had challenges with the original language of some passages. Some of the terms which Moses used had become vague and unfamiliar as expressions of speech even by the time Jesus preached the Good News. How much more so are they now for our scholars to translate? For instance, the early Hebrew use for the word "son" could also apply to "grandson". When Noah placed a curse on Canaan (Genesis 9:24-25), it is not exactly clear whether the curse originally applied to Ham or for something which Canaan did (<u>Believer's Bible Commentary</u>, William MacDonald, page 44-45). For Noah's curse to be on Canaan because Ham pointed out his nakedness seems overly harsh and misdirected. Had Canaan done something as well? The interchange between son and grandson can be part of this confusion. As you can see, translating and taking the various connotations into account can be very challenging. This does not mean God's message is in error though. All it means is <u>man does not yet have complete knowledge</u>.

<u>We should not be surprised if when we get to heaven we find out God worked His wonders in many amazing and magnificent ways which were not recorded in the Bible</u>. If everything which God has done for us were recorded, how many libraries would be required to house these volumes (John 21:25)? This should not be a problem for us though. For instance, if God created more people after Adam and

Eve, that does not change the truth of Him being God, the Creator of all the heavens and the earth. To continue with the Great Flood, if there were survivors in addition to Noah in other parts of the world this would not change the truth that God does what He says He will do. The account which Moses recorded about the flood concentrated on Noah and his ancestral relationship with the Jewish people. There is certainly ample evidence this was a universal flood, not merely a localized event. The biblical account is emphatic in its presentation that all of life was wiped out except for those on the ark. If so, then how do we account for other cultures having various versions of this flood? Do some research on Google for the Great Flood. There are numerous stories from cultures all over the globe which tell of this event. It seems logical that someone would have had to have survived this in each culture in order for it to be passed from one generation to the next. These cultures were separated by great distances (even continents), so the exchange of these stories from the Genesis rendering is rather doubtful. We also know anything is possible with God (Luke 18:27). Our heavenly Father could have done whatever He saw fit in order to continue His divine plan for this world. Adonai is not limited by power, locality, or cultural groups in how He interacts with His creation. If our Lord judged it righteous to have other survivors, this would clarify some of the confusion surrounding these global accounts.

This may possibly be one of those instances where our understanding of the survivors differs from what God actually did at that time. Interestingly, we may not know what we think we know. The Babylonian description of the flood is amusingly similar in the natural history of the event yet very different in the basic theological teachings. The Babylonian portrayal however was recorded long before Moses wrote the book of Genesis (The New Unger's Bible Dictionary, Merrill Unger, pages 433-435). All this means is it is somewhat doubtful the Babylonians borrowed their version of the event from the Hebrews. Regardless, this does not change the theological teachings of the flood though. God poured out His holy wrath against sinful man. In the commentary in the NIVDSB on page 14 it states, "God loved His creation; but when it defied His moral standards, He knew He must vindicate His holiness by sending punishment. Because creation was good, however, He wished to preserve it. He established propagation as His method of perpetuating His creation. Even as He punished sinners, He made provision for propagation of the species to continue. We can be certain God's world will go on today until He wills to consummate history with Christ's return. The world is so constituted that it adjusts to any shock or tragedy. God controls creation's destiny." This is an excellent synopsis of the Christian understanding of the Great Flood. The question is: Could God have provided for the continuance of mankind in other areas of the world in addition to Mt. Ararat (where the ark came to rest – Genesis 8:4)? If it served His purpose, why not?

Unger gives a very interesting treatment to this discussion. In explaining the similarities between the Hebrew and Babylonian versions, Unger asserts on pages 434-435, "the most widely accepted explanation is that the Hebrew borrowed from the Babylonian account. The likely explanation is that both the Hebrew and Babylonian accounts go back to a common source of fact, which originated in an actual occurrence. The Flood occurred sometime long before 4000 B.C. The memory of this great event persisted in tradition. The Babylonians received it in a completely corrupted and distorted form. Genesis portrays it as it actually occurred, and as the Spirit of God gave it to meet special needs in the history of redemption." I thank Unger for this insight but I wish he had taken it a little further to explain to us how all of these stories persisted in areas which were supposedly wiped out from the flood. Unger does not seem to be inclined to think the various cultures borrowed them from each other because so many of the details are so disparate. I tend to agree but I really do not know where to go from there. This is where the fun of speculation based on what we know about the character of God and His basic truths can guide us as we explore the possible avenues for a better understanding of this puzzle.

First, we should ask ourselves: Did the Babylonian culture have people who survived the flood in their region? Logic seems to dictate this since they have the basic facts correct in their account (as do other cultures who had no likely communication with the area where Noah lived). I do not know how to reconcile this conclusion though in light of Genesis 6:17-18 where God declares to Noah, "I am going to bring floodwaters on the earth to destroy all life under the heavens, every creature that has the breath of life in it. Everything on earth will perish. But I will establish my covenant with you, and you will enter the ark—you and your sons and your wife and your sons' wives with you." This account seems very specific to me as it continues in Genesis 7:23, "Every living thing on the face of the earth was wiped out; men and animals and the creatures that move along the ground and the birds of the air were wiped from the earth. Only Noah was left, and those with him in the ark." To me, this sounds like no one else on earth survived the flood. This has always been my understanding. The enigma is then how is it that all of these other cultures have their version of the flood? Rational thought would aver that some of the ancient people in these cultures must have survived in order for the knowledge of the flood to have passed on to subsequent generations. This is especially troubling since these cultures were all separated by great physical distances.

While most Christians feel comfortable that other cultures simply reinvented their own version of the biblical account as man moved into these areas, this presents a definite quandary for those who are not of our persuasion. Their questions are due our respect if we are to strive to help them see that belief in God does not require you to abandon your intellectual reasoning. After all, God gave us inquisitive minds, so we should use them.

Perhaps this is another instance where biblical translation has presented us with a challenge. What if in the Genesis narrative, the ancient Hebrew word for "earth" could be interpreted as meaning "that region of the world"? When you place this phrase in the above verses, it seems to work. Now, if this same Divine message was given to all the cultures which have stories of the Great Flood, then we possibly have some reconciliation. God may have offered His warning to all people groups of this earth but only a few heeded it. If the ancient Hebrew word for "earth" could have the connotation of a geographic region, then the assertion that all life being destroyed in a particular locality (except for the assumed survivors of each cultural group) would account for this confusion. The biblical account highlights Noah because all the others completely missed God's message. As such, God may have seen no need to include any reference to them as He was guiding Moses to record this event.

This is purely speculative with very little Scriptural support, so take it with a grain of salt. For biblical suppositions to have any value though, they must be in keeping with the attributes of our Lord. Where guesswork goes awry is when it abandons or goes against what we know as the character of God. However, this present conjecture is consistent with certain of Elohim's character traits. This speculation is based on: (1) we know God is the God of second chances; (2) we also know He does not render His wrath without warnings; and (3) He is always wanting all of His creation to fellowship with Him. El Elyon is not the Most High God of the Jews alone. While the Bible is God's revelation through the Jewish people, our God is sovereign over all of creation.

Since we know these things about God, it is possible (and highly likely) that He reached out to more than Noah. It is in keeping with His character that El Shaddai gave warning to all people groups throughout the world of the impending deluge. It is also probable, knowing human nature, that all others ignored His divine warnings.

As I have gotten older, I realize I am not a particularly intelligent man (so I could be wrong in this conjecture). Yet this line of thought does help explain how the various cultures have their version of the flood story. In addition, it even helps with understanding how the various races of people came to populate the earth. That is another dilemma for mankind. If we all came from Noah, then how did the various races develop? I do not accept that the various global environments alone produced such marked differences. The races exist alongside each other all over this world and none of them change from one race to another after having been in a certain locality for whatever length of time. I feel God has had a more distinct hand in creating the various racial groups, so this environmental explanation does not seem to fully explain the issue. Racial differences seem to be God's way of enjoying His creations as they adapt to their various geographical regions. They display their own unique mixture of cultural attributes, which seem to add pizzazz to His grand mosaic. God's design for mankind seems to be much greater than our merely living in a certain local.

To the Judeo-Christian mind, the Genesis version of the flood is the only one which combines Godly truth with a plausible story. As is evident with Noah and his sons, even the most righteous of men continued to fight against sin (Genesis 9:20-27). The flood certainly did not eradicate sin from the world. As man survived the flood, so did Satan's influence on our spiritual life. These other stories of the Great Flood show that man did not ultimately heed the warning of their gods. They continued on much as they had in the past. One of the main differences which these other cultural accounts have with the biblical presentation is highlighted in the Babylonian story. The account of the Babylonians failed to present the accurate moral lesson of the event. God's truth is His holiness necessitated judgment being administered to an unholy and unrighteous world. Man had gone too far. We know God is patient and He wants all to turn to Him. Nevertheless, at this point in world history, God decided His justice must prevail. The people had become too distant from Elohim's original plans for mankind. Their free wills betrayed them. Rather than following Jehovah, they pursued their own sinful desires. By this, they grieved God. It is also certainly conceivable in the face of all this, He still warned *all* people to repent and turn back to Him.

As it appears, even if there were survivors in Babylon, they were too steeped in sin to understand the deliverance God provided them. Other cultures have their own corrupted versions of the flood as well. The historicity and the theological implications have been distorted by all of them. They show little or no understanding of why the earth was deluged. Some have a rudimentary understanding of the great battle between good and evil, but that is about as far as it goes. Their explanations of how some people survived the flood are often comical though. At best, perhaps God was giving these cultures another chance. I do not know if I really accept this as my explanation for all these versions of the flood story, but it does have a certain rationality to its reasoning. Christians can be sure of this – the flood happened just as described in Genesis chapters 6 through 9. If others in various regions survived, it just shows that the Babylonians (and others) missed the point of it all. Whether they had survivors or they borrowed their stories from the biblical account, one thing is for certain – Satan once again has been able to confuse mankind in its relationship with God Almighty and how He operates in our lives.

Have we by chance then discovered an inaccuracy in this biblical account? Possibly, but more probably, we have discovered yet another area where man simply does not have sufficient knowledge to rationally explain this conundrum. This is where faith steps in and fills the gap. However, this still does not necessarily challenge the inerrancy of the biblical account of the Great Flood. All this means is: (1) man has had some difficulties at times in accurately translating and/or understanding the Word of God, and (2) the Bible does not include the complete, exhaustive record of all God's interactions with mankind since the beginning of creation. Keep in mind, it does not matter how skillfully modern man processes (or fails to process) God's wisdom and revelations. God's truth is ultimate truth, regardless of man's attempts at understanding. The Bible is inerrant but it is not exhaustive in recording all which the Holy Trinity has done for this world.

With all this said, please do not put trust in human speculation. It is fun to ponder these mysteries; to allow your mind to attempt to make sense of the various bits of knowledge and events which are not clear to our present day understanding. The mysteries of this period are truly perplexing. Yet their enigma is the intrigue of this biblical account. Of course, there is the very real possibility these verses read exactly as God intends them to read. This is why we should never get emotionally involved in defending our personal speculations – we could be wrong. There is no way of proving these thoughts. Never argue with fellow believers when the Scriptures are a little unclear. Have fun allowing your thoughts to form a plausible construct. Listen to others as they explain what they believe. To argue would not promote the harmony which Jesus desires of the church family. One day we will have the exhilarating joy of listening to the actual participants in these events explaining all the details. Imagine the thrill of taking a class in "Ark Building 101" from Noah, or "Basket Weaving" from Moses' mom, or one which the guys will really enjoy, "Pulling a Building Down" by Samson. What a wonderful eternity God has in store for us.

This challenge to our understanding of God's word is a good example of why Jehovah God does not present any of His truths only one time in the Bible. Go to any of your favorite verses and see how many other verses are listed in the cross reference section. The holy truths which Jehovah Jireh provides us are interwoven throughout the 66 books of the Bible. While ancient stories and legends seem to go through a progressive metamorphosis as they are being passed down, this has not happened with the Bible. Why? Because the Holy Spirit has been the inspirational force behind each stroke of the pen. The Holy Spirit has inspired and guided each of the 40 authors so that the accuracy of God's word has been inerrantly preserved. The only problem in the inerrancy of the Bible has been in man's understanding, not in the veracity of the Scriptural content. This interconnecting of Scriptures allows for anything which some might consider being minor flaws in translational choices or manual copying errors from the original text to be self correcting. This applies to whatever biblical translation you prefer. I use the NIV and the King James versions for most of my studying. There is nothing about these translations which makes me think there are any errors whatsoever in them. They vary by the choice of words in some verses but the overall message is preserved in both. I am confident that *if* a translational error happens to occur in one passage, the truth which God is wanting to present will be made known through subsequent, related Scriptures. This is why it is best that you interpret passages as a collection of interrelated bits of wisdom.

In light of all this, please do not allow what you do not and cannot know to derail what you do know. God's truths are abundantly clear. Some facts and some holes in the story line may be ambiguous to us now but El Shaddai's message is clear. The ultimate truths which are certain about God and the Great Flood are:

(1) God is in control – now and then (Genesis 7:11-12, 8:1-4; Exodus 7:17-19; Matthew 27:45, 50-54)
(2) Man is to bring honor and glory to God (Genesis 6:9, 22, 8:20; Isaiah 43:7; Revelation 4:11)
(3) Jehovah Tsidkenu's holiness necessitates Him being righteous in His interactions with us (Genesis 6:9,13-14; Psalm 33:4-5; Jeremiah 23:5-6; Romans 3:21-26)
(4) His righteousness means He cannot allow man's rebellion to go unchecked or unpunished forever (Genesis 6:11-13, 7:22-23; 2 Kings 23:36- 24:4; John 3:36)
(5) Jehovah God wants us to repent and return to Him (Genesis 6:5-8; Psalm 103:12-18; Ezekiel 18:18- 23)
(6) Yahweh always prefers to interact with us in love rather than judgment (Genesis 9:1, 8-11, Psalm 145:17-20; Revelation 15:4)
(7) Jehovah Jireh is the God of second chances (Genesis 6:18-21, 7:13-16; Matthew 18:21-27; 2 Peter 3:8-9)
(8) God loves His creation and it will remain under His control (Genesis 8:15-17, 9:12-17; John 3:16; Revelation 11:15)
(9) At times our Lord does not provide us with all the details (Genesis 6:7-8, 11-13, 9:22-27; Isaiah 55:8-11; Romans 11:33-34).

Our faith in Adonai's trustworthiness fills in the gaps when rational thought fails us. This story, like many of the others, is a test to prove whether we are willing to live by faith or do we require scientific-like proof before we will believe. Steadfast faith in God's promises allows for the ambiguities in our understanding without these questions derailing our belief, trust, and commitment to Him as our sovereign God.

When this elusiveness to precise understanding occurs, we are to place the blame on ourselves rather than His message. The Holy Bible is exactly as Paul describes it in 2 Timothy 3:16-17. "All Scripture is God-breathed and is useful for teaching, rebuking, correcting and training in righteousness, so that the man of God may be thoroughly equipped for every good work." Righteousness is living in harmony with God and others. It is not a complete intellectual understanding of the "mysteries" of God; it is the obedient actions of living in accord with God's will.

The inerrancy of the Bible is that God's truths as revealed in the original Holy Scriptures make up ultimate truth. The verses are all absolutely and perfectly pure in their correctness. God does not give us stories which are only partially true. El Elyon's revelations through commandments and stories are flawless. As such, there are absolutely no errors in their truthful content. Yes, there is such a thing as absolute, ultimate truth. It is not relative to what someone believes truth to be. One group does not define it for another group. One person does not have their brand of truth and another person have something different as their truth. God's Word is ultimate truth and it does not matter how much modern man tries to confound and confuse the issues. El Shaddai's truths reign supreme. While linguists may have had problems with translations at times, each story in the Bible is factually true. All of these things happened as described. The Christian Bible is not a book of myths or folklore.

Each Scriptural account reveals a greater understanding which God wants man to possess. However, the Bible certainly does not include all of God's history with mankind. Even with the short 3 year ministry of Jesus, John tells us in John 21:25, "Jesus did many other things as well. If every one of them were written down, I suppose that even the whole world would not have room for the books that would be written." God has provided the seeker of His truths with sufficient stories so that we will know His will for our lives. We can know that He is who He says He is and that He does what He says He will do. This is further validated by El Elyon Himself in Revelation 21:5, "for these words are trustworthy and true." The Bible is not the exhaustive text of God's interaction with man. However, what measure it does reveal, it is inerrant in its message.

It is perfectly fine for the various Christian denominations to have interpretational differences over various Scriptures. We do not have to all believe exactly what each other believes in order to be part of God's kingdom. What we should unite behind though is the absolute authority of God's Holy Word. Christians talk about the inerrancy of the Bible, and then some disregard the parts which conflict with their preferences and attitudes. Worse yet, we now have groups which do not even agree with the basic tenet that the Scriptures are inerrant. We are not to pick and choose which parts of the Bible make us feel good about ourselves or justify our actions, and then disregard those passages which condemn us.

Additionally, we have churches which are so concerned with membership rolls that they forfeit their boldness for Christ. Why is this? Possibly they are concerned more with the offering plate than their witness. If a preacher starts really trying to focus on the application of various Scriptures to our lives, they run the risk of alienating certain individuals and groups. When this happens, then the money stops flowing. Some are bowing to this pressure and compromising the urgency of the message of truth for the sake of the bank balance. For this, these ministers will ultimately answer. The church which will not take a stand for the plain and apparent message of the Word is a church which has compromised its soul (Revelation Chapters 2-4). Please take the time to read these chapters in Revelation. Jesus' words are timeless. Be certain of this, God will judge us individually and collectively. I believe the greatest challenge in the Christian faith is not from outside but from within. Too many want the approval of this world. Too many are willing to compromise convictions for bank balances. <u>We are so fortunate that the Holy Spirit is a more loyal fighter for our souls than we are for the inerrant truth of the Scriptures</u>. <u>We are to try with every effort to positively affect the lives of others, but we are not to weaken our commitment to Christ in order to make the unbelievers among us feel comfortable and righteous</u>.

In summation, Jesus provides us the answer to our question posed earlier about why not all people accept our Lord as their God. All that is required to find this answer is to read His Word. These reasons for rejecting Christ as a person's Lord and Savior are much like the mixing of the primary colors – various combinations yield different shades of this issue. This makes our appreciation for what ministers and missionaries do even the more praiseworthy. The first three types of soils in our focus parable (Matt 13:3-8, 18-23) explain why most people do not believe. With reference to the 13 reasons why people do not accept the Triune God of Christianity, here is how they interrelate. The first type of soil relates to: #1, 2, 3, 6, 7, 8, 9, 11, 12, and 13. The second type of soil relates to: #1, 4, 5, 7, 8, 9, 10, 11, and 12. The third type of soil relates to: #5, 7, 8, 10, and 12. This little exercise has hopefully been thought provoking, along with conveying the essence of Jesus' message. The world has many complicated situations which war against accepting Christ as one's Savior. Couple this parable with the Parable of the Weeds (Matt 13:24-30, 36-43) and Jesus provides us with much insight into the spiritual condition of mankind.

Our Lord Jesus sums up these teachings with His admonition in Matthew 7:13-14. "Enter through the narrow gate. For wide is the gate and broad is the road that leads to destruction, and many enter through it. But small is the gate and narrow the road that leads to life, and only a few find it." These three lessons reveal that God realizes only a few will accept His plan for their eternal existence. Yahweh does not make salvation impossible for us by setting stringent rules and rituals which have to be performed flawlessly. A believer does not have to live a perfect life in order to reap the benefit of eternal salvation. If this was required, then we would have an excuse since living such a life is unattainable. God does require though that we seek Him and only Him as the object of our spiritual faith. When we are sincere in our faith, then we will correspondingly pursue the righteous life style to which He calls us. The problem is that many people in this world are, to varying degrees, spiritually confused, weak, oppressed, apathetic, self-centered, undisciplined, deceived, or decadent. Sadly for these deceived souls, Satan adeptly exploits these tendencies. Of course, these same people think Christians are likewise described. Many of them hold as strongly to their belief systems as we do. This is why missions work has to be given such respect and support. Satan loves nothing better than separating God's creation from Him.

# Chapter Eight How You can Know That You Know You are going to Heaven

———ফ্রর———

There are many, many references to the human heart in the Bible. What is God referencing when He speaks of our hearts? Certainly the physical heart is one of the most important organs in our bodies. Mankind has understood since antiquity that all of life is bound in the heart. Why in 1 Samuel 16:7 did God tell Samuel, "...Man looks at the outward appearance, but the Lord looks at the heart"? The heart in Old Testament religious terms is the seat of one's intrinsic nature. It is the center of life. It is my impression that God used the heart to refer to the center of our intrinsic spiritual nature in the Old Testament because men at that time only had a very rudimentary understanding of the nature of the heart and the mind. Ancient men assigned the heart much more duties than merely pumping blood through the body. They did not have the scientific understanding of the vast complexities of the human mind. Blood is life and without the heart, there is no life. That they understood. Correspondingly, we have gained greater insights into the functioning of the human spirit as we move from the Old Testament to the New Testament. Mankind has progressed in our knowledge over the centuries of the higher order mental functions so now our terminology can become more precise. Without man's higher level intrinsic nature as revealed in his spirit, he is nothing more than any of the other beasts which God created.

## *Body, Soul, and Spirit*

As man's walk with God became more enlightened, the concept of man having a soul became more understood. Originally, God directly interacted with Adam. After the "fall", God only spoke with select individuals. As the centuries progressed, Jehovah God sent His prophets to reveal Himself to us. Through these prophets, we became more knowledgeable about God. The prophets had various messages from Jehovah Jireh. This provided us with an increasingly greater awareness of God's desire for us to grow into a more righteous relationship with Him. These messages also helped us to better understand God's nature and His plans for us. The apex of this understanding is presented in Matthew 3:16-17, "As soon as Jesus was baptized, He went up out of the water. At that moment heaven was opened, and He saw the Spirit of God descending like a dove and lighting on Him. And a voice from heaven said, "This is my Son, whom I love; with Him I am well pleased." This is where God further introduces in a very precise manner the understanding that we serve a Triune God – God the Father, God the Son, and God the Holy Spirit. God has progressively revealed Himself to us through the ages. When you read that God is concerned with your heart, does that not mean He is concerned with your inner spirit? Yes it does. When God wants you to love Him with all your heart, does that not mean He wants your spirit centered on Him as the Lord God Almighty? As a person advances in their sanctification process, they will increasingly come to a much higher understanding of the Holy Trinity.

As we learn more about God, we should be learning more about what God wants from us. In Haggai 1:12-15, v.13 God declares, "I am with you." How certain are we of God's commitment to us? If you need reassurance, then read Genesis 26:24, 28:15; Joshua 3:7; Isaiah 41:10, 43:5; Jeremiah 1:8-9, 42:11; Matthew 28:20; Acts 18:10. God models the commitment He wants from us by being committed to us with this same steadfast promise. I prefer the definition of faith as "having the heartfelt inner confidence that God is who He says He is and that He does what He says He will do." This comes in part from Exodus 3:14, "I AM WHO I AM". God is who He says He is. From that, we can also believe in His promises. More than that, we can be absolutely certain of God's promises. These verses are our evidence. The Holy Trinity is committed to us and we should respond likewise.

Which is God most concerned with – your body, your soul, or your spirit? Your body is what is physically observable. It is the part which is often the subject of our prayers. We want safety, nourishment, and physical healing for ourselves and our loved ones. One's soul is the collection of immaterial (nonphysical) aspects of the inner you – your intellect, will, emotions, motivations, interests, attitudes, and beliefs. In other words your personality (that which distinguishes you from all others and makes you a unique creation of God). Your spirit is that part of your inner being which reaches out to God for communion and worship (Psalm 105:1-4, Matthew 5:6, John 3:6). In John 4:23-24 Jesus clarifies the matter by saying, "Yet a time is coming and has now come when the true worshipers will worship the Father in spirit and truth, for they are the kind of worshipers the Father seeks. God is spirit, and His worshipers must worship in spirit and in truth." Paul teaches in Romans 8:16, "The Spirit Himself testifies with our spirit that we are God's children." One's inner spirit, that which defines our core being, is the highest level of functioning within a person. It is that part of man which reaches out and yearns for Yahweh. In the inner spirit of man we find that which is noble and pure. I know skeptics think there is nothing noble and pure about man, but they probably have not held a 3 month old baby lately. Look into a child's eyes. Watch a 3 year old play with a puppy. Their spirits have not yet been corrupted. In small children we find the reason God created us. He wants our spirits to see Him as does a 4 year old who looks up and suddenly spots their mother. A bright smile appears on their face and they run to get a hug. Man is at his best when he can rekindle the spirit of his youth. Is God then more concerned with your spirit than with your body or your soul?

I think of our inner spirit as like a white t-shirt covering our body to give us a little protection from the elements and to keep us warm. Imagine wearing that t-shirt each and everyday of your life. In the winter it is underneath all your other clothing, so it does not get soiled but it can get rather malodorous. In the summer it may be your outer layer of clothing. It gets all of the dirt, grass stains, and food stains. The smell may become down right rank. If you cut yourself, it may even get a little blood on it. Year after year this t-shirt gradually loses its resemblance to that clean, white, shirt which you put on many years prior. This is where the cynics are partially correct. As we get older, it sometimes becomes increasing more difficult to recognize a person's original nature. Our lives can gradually become like the dirty, tattered t-shirt. They can become offensive at worst. Otherwise they are mostly unproductive and soiled.

Then an amazing thing happens. Christ comes into your life. The Holy Spirit indwells your being. The dirty, ragged old t-shirt becomes washed as white as snow. It returns to the form which God originally designed. A protective layer much like Scotch guard but a bazillion times stronger is sprayed on this shirt. It may get a small stain from time to time, but with prayer, confession and repentance, these spots disappear, never to be seen again. I know this is simplistic, but I'm a simple guy. It's the best I can do. I believe in my heart that God created us a good. I believe there is something noble and pure in each of us. As we get older, we just need the right washing detergent and a good spot remover (Revelation 22:12-14). Our God declares in Isaiah 1:18-19, "Come now, let us reason together," says the Lord. "Though your sins are like scarlet, they shall be as white as snow; though they are red as crimson, they shall be like wool. If you are willing and obedient, you will eat the best from the land;"

In the spirit we find a section which is commonly referred to as our conscience. This part of our spirit functions at the most basic level. The conscience is the part which relates to our cultural norms and mores as well as to our parental guidance. God gives each of us a conscience in order to guide our interactions with one another. Each culture puts its on twist to these basic rules to reflect the nuances of its people. In addition to a conscience, God gives each of us within our spirit an even higher functional dimension. It is this higher level of functioning in our spirit which drives us to seek Jehovah God as the object of our worship and praise (Acts 17:26-27, Romans 2:14-15, Hebrews 11:6). It is important we understand the dynamic functioning of our spirit as it communes with the Holy Spirit because this linkage is where we get our greatest evidence that we are part of God's kingdom family. In light of this, it is this part of our inner spirit where we find man displaying his highest level of functioning. Nothing we ever do will exceed our reaching out to God Almighty. **We are at the apex of our existence when we correctly identify the source of all life; we place our faith in God Almighty that He is who He says He is; and we surrender our will to God the Father, God the Son and God the Holy Spirit**. This series of decisions will extend us into all eternity.

What is so perplexing is this apex of functioning *may* come at a time when our human strength, as the world sees it, is at its lowest. It may be when we have the innocence of our youth driving us to a full acceptance of God (Matthew 19:13-14). A young child is seldom seen as being strong, but when they are full of faith, they are often mightier than some battle scarred adults who have forgotten their first love (Revelation 2:2-5). It may also be when we are suffering with emotional, financial, or physical problems that, though we are weak in fleshly strength, we are mighty in faith. *A noteworthy reality is that at times we Christians are at our best when we are at our lowest* (2 Corinthians 12:7-11). God loves the contrite at heart and the meek of spirit. These are the times when it seems our spirit has the clearest communication with the Holy Spirit. We refocus the very fabric of our being to receive whatever message our holy God has for us. It is a very remarkable person who can be at their highest functioning level both as a person of earthly achievements and as a servant of God. Thankfully, God refines us. For most spiritual warriors who, on the whole, function at this higher level there is a common experience. They can trace back to a time when they were on their knees as being the beginning of their explosion into spiritual faith. This humble, contrite action then propelled them to a higher level of worship and communion with El Shaddai, Lord God Almighty. To God belongs the glory.

Many of us who have extensive experiences with animals recognize that animals also have souls – that intangible quality which makes each one of them unique. As best I know, animals do not have spirits. This is where man is unique. Only man seeks to know God the Creator. So, since animals share with us having both bodies and souls, does that mean that God values our spirits the most? Read the book of Revelation. It seems to me God has made eternal provision for all aspects of our being. We will receive resurrected bodies and these new bodies will be united with our souls and our spirits in a glorious celebration as He unveils His new earth and the new Jerusalem (1 Corinthians 15:40-54, Revelation 21:1-5). <u>God made each of us unique and it appears to me He is concerned with all aspects of our lives</u>. Did Jesus seem to emphasis the spirit over the body in His ministry? No, Jesus lets us know that God cares about even the most minute of details of our lives (Matthew 10:30).

In many places in the Bible the writer will use soul and spirit synonymously. Paul separates the soul from the spirit in his teachings (Romans 11:8, 1 Cor. 4:21, 2 Cor. 7:1, Galatians 6:18). In 1 Thessalonians 5:23 Paul encourages, "May your whole spirit, soul and body be kept blameless at the coming of our Lord Jesus Christ." This separation is reasonable. Since we speak of the Holy Spirit why should we not refer to that part of us which reaches out to the Holy Spirit as being our human spirit? Do not let this bother you though. If you prefer to use soul and spirit interchangeably, do so. What is important is the understanding that part of you is physical and part is intangible. God cares for both. The part which is intangible is what is united with Christ at the time of your death (2 Cor. 5:4-8, Philippians 1:21-23). The part which is tangible is refashioned and united with your intangible part at the resurrection (1 Cor. 15:42-44).

## *Spurious Transformations*

Is it possible to turn your life around without the help of Jesus and the Holy Spirit? Yes, you can turn certain aspects of your life around without God. Psychologists, psychiatrists, and other mental health facilitators help people every day learn to deal with their emotional challenges. Financial planners help people struggling with debt to turn their economic crises around. The medical profession restores the health of a sick patient, regardless of their spiritual orientation. Much of what happens in this world can be done without a close, personal relationship with God. Keep in mind Matthew 5:45, "He causes His sun to rise on the evil and the good, and sends rain on the righteous and the unrighteous." God does not play favorites with us based on our righteousness. What we have to remember is that God loves <u>all</u> people. He waits patiently for each of His creation to repent and turn to Him. None are valued more highly than any of the others. The thing which all of the above situations with psychologists, physicians, and financial planners have in common is that they are all temporal. This is what separates all of us – some have temporal solutions, others have eternal solutions.

There are many people who seem to lead well adjusted lives, but do not have Jesus as their spiritual guide. We all know people who are kind, considerate, enjoyable people, but their souls are without God. Christians do not have the market cornered on psychological, biological, and financial health. In fact, Christians have much the same challenges with mental, physical, and financial health as the rest of the population. <u>Believers are not special by the absence of misfortunes – we are special by the presence of a reassuring Lord</u>. The same challenges are faced by all of God's creation. What Jehovah does for believers is He comforts us in ways no healthcare or financial professional can ever match (2 Corinthians 1:3-4).

Most nonbelievers consider themselves to be spiritual in some way or another but just not believers in the Triune God of the Christian Bible. They have deluded themselves into thinking they are believers in some form or fashion in an acceptable god (whatever that might be). Many further confuse themselves into thinking all beliefs lead to the same destination. They claim God is too big to be contained in any one religion. Put bluntly, what they are doing places them in danger of intellectualizing themselves straight into hell. El Shaddai is not a God to be contemplated, mixed and matched, then made into what you prefer Him to be (Isaiah 29:13-16).

These deceived souls may even have head knowledge of our Lord Jesus. Sadly, they have not made Him their Savior. Any transformation they think they have experienced has been spurious. Only through a genuine, steadfast faith in Christ Jesus can a person's life be authentically transformed into being righteous with God Almighty (John 3:14-18). Paul further teaches us in Philippians 3:18-21, "For, as I have often told you before and now say again even with tears, many live as enemies of the cross of Christ. Their destiny is destruction, their god is their stomach, and their glory is in their shame. Their mind is on earthly things. But our citizenship is in heaven. And we eagerly await a Savior from there, the Lord Jesus Christ, who, by the power that enables Him to bring everything under His control, will transform our lowly bodies so that they will be like His glorious body." Only then will your faith and works reflect the true nature of your inner spirit.

Most people consider Christ Jesus to have been basically a great prophet. They feel perfectly fine sprinkling in beliefs from other religions and various diverse politically correct ways of thinking to come up with their own unique theology. They may through some convoluted logic even consider themselves to be a Christian. Unfortunately, the god they then worship is very different from the Holy Trinity (Matthew 3:16-17, Romans 1:18-22, 2 Peter 2:1-9). These people are deceivers, not believers. They not only deceive others about their true spiritual status, they also often deceive themselves. This is what is so sad about their existence. They do not know enough about God to know how perilous their eternal fate actually is. More importantly, they have no way of assessing the accuracy of their present spiritual status. Christians do.

## *Being Absolutely Certain of Your Salvation*

I recall one Sunday in 1991 when I was speaking with my pastor at that time, Rev. Marty Brown, when a retired minister for whom I had great respect joined us in the conversation. I do not recall exactly what we were discussing but I do recall the emotional and spiritual confusion which resulted. What the retired minister admitted to us rocked my spiritual foundation. He shared that he did not truly get saved until after he had started his ministry. I thought, "How could he be confused about his salvation, especially after having attended seminary? How could he have been mistaken about his salvation after having preached so many sermons as a young man?" To say the least, this made me doubt the validity of my own salvation experience. Had I been mistaken all these years about my ultimate destiny? As the result of this conversation, I wanted to learn how I could be absolutely certain of my salvation. More than that – I wanted to not only know how I could be certain of my salvation but I wanted to "know that I know" that I am saved. I sought absolute biblical certainty of my eternal status. With this goal in mind, I turned to the Scriptures.

It has mystified me ever since why more Christians do not know how they can tell if they are saved. Many rely on a "feeling of being saved". Rightfully, emotions do play a prominent role in our relationship with our Lord Jesus. Christian salvation is more than a feeling though. Remember the words of Jesus in Matthew 22:37, "Love the Lord your God with all your heart and with all your soul and with all your mind." Certainly, we worship God with our hearts (our emotions). We are to praise and worship Him with our minds (our intellectual knowledge of who He is and what He promises) and our spirits (which commune with the Holy Spirit - even in ways we do not always understand). <u>Since in spirit and intellect we are to relate to God, it only stands to reason</u>

that God would not have us to rely solely on emotional feelings to help us maintain a steadfast belief system in Him as our one true God. Our Lord can be mysterious in many of His ways. However, Elohim does not leave the question of our salvation as a mystery for us to find out only when the Great White Throne of Judgment occurs. I wanted to be certain I was not basing eternity on my remembrance of an event which happened at age 8. We know memories are facilitated by having emotions attached to them. Were my emotions accurate and I was actually saved or were my memories and related emotions faulty. I wanted to "know that I know" that I am saved.

How *do* we know we are saved? This is the $64,000 question (remember the old TV show by that name – however in today's economy it would be the $1,000,000 question). There is no greater authority than Christ Jesus and He tells us "by our fruit" we will be known. Jesus urges us in Matt 7:15-23, "Watch out for false prophets. They come to you in sheep's clothing, but inwardly they are ferocious wolves. By their fruit (their characteristics) you will recognize them. Do people pick grapes from thornbushes, or figs from thistles? Likewise every good tree bears good fruit, but a bad tree bears bad fruit. A good tree cannot bear bad fruit, and a bad tree cannot bear good fruit. Every tree that does not bear good fruit is cut down and thrown into the fire. Thus, by their fruit you will recognize them. Not everyone who says to me, 'Lord, Lord,' will enter the kingdom of heaven, but only he who does the will of my Father who is in heaven. Many will say to me on that day, 'Lord, Lord, did we not prophesy (teach) in your name, and in your name drive out demons and perform many miracles?' Then I will tell them plainly, 'I never knew you. Away from me, you evildoers!" He continues in Matt. 12:33, "Make a tree good and its fruit will be good, or make a tree bad and its fruit will be bad, for a tree is recognized by its fruit."

If we are to be known by our fruit, what does that tell us about this fruit? It must be pretty important. Fruit here is not referring to our works (that would be the fruits of our labor). Fruit is a reference to our Christ-like attributes. A tree is known by the fruit which it bears. This is its distinguishing characteristic. We are to be known by our distinguishing characteristics. What are these attributes? Think about it. Where else does the Bible speak of fruit? In Galatians 5:22-23 Paul instructs us, "the fruit of the Spirit is love, joy, peace, patience, kindness, goodness, faithfulness, gentleness and self-control." These qualities are given to you by the Holy Spirit to help you in your transformation process so you can become like Jesus (Philippians 1:6). Do these attributes accurately describe our Lord? They certainly do. If your family and friends would not describe you in these terms, then either you do not have the Holy Spirit or you are not allowing Him to have a powerful influence in your life.

In Romans 8:9 Paul tells us "You, however, are controlled not by the sinful nature but by the Spirit, if the Spirit of God lives in you." Has it ever occurred to you the striking similarity between what is required of us as taught in the Beatitudes (Matthew 5:3-12) and what is provided us through the fruit of the Spirit? God is so awesome. Did not Jesus promise us the Holy Spirit in John 14:15-26, 15:26, 16:5-16, and 20:22 once we place our faith and obedience in Him? **By the presence of the Holy Spirit in your life is how you can absolutely know that you are saved** (Romans 5:5; 8:1-17; and 8:22-27). Jesus promised the Holy Spirit to us and we know He is within us if we have the fruit of the Spirit guiding us in our lives. If this fruit and His presence are not apparent in your life, then you have cause to worry that your very salvation is in question.

In 2 Corinthians 13:5-6 Paul urged them, "Examine yourselves to see whether you are in the faith; test yourselves. Do you not realize that Christ Jesus is in you – unless, of course, you fail the test? And I trust that you will discover that we have not failed the test." How do we test ourselves? By examining whether we are allowing Christ, through the Holy Spirit, to grow in strength and influence in our lives. Be very honest with yourself during this examination. This is the most important thing about yourself which you, as a person who longs for eternity with Christ, have to know. You have to know that you know.

The various characteristics of God which He chooses to reveal to us are done so for multiple reasons. First, so we can know Elohim better. If we do not know Him, then how are we to obey Him? Solomon teaches us in Proverbs 9:10, "The fear of the Lord is the beginning of wisdom, and knowledge of the Holy One is understanding." Secondly, so we will know the traits which the Father wants to see in us. We are to take these characteristics and make them our own. Jesus is a light to us so we can be a light to others. John tried to help the early Christians to know that they know God by select verses in 1 John. In 1 John 2:3-6 we learn, "we have come to know Him if we obey His commands... This is how we know we are in Him: Whoever claims to live in Him must walk as Jesus did." Now go to 1 John 3:24, "And this is how we know that He lives in us: We know it by the Spirit He gave us." Chapter 4:7-21 teaches us about God's love and how He has put love in all of us. This supports what Paul said in Romans 1:20-2:16 about God placing an awareness in all of us to know Him and to seek His Righteousness. John ends in verse 4:21 with, "And He has given us this command: Whoever loves God must also love his brother." Above all else, we are to love God and one another. This is the most important attribute by which we are to be known.

Have you ever heard the expression, "the main thing is the main thing"? The main thing in the Christian walk is love (Matthew 22:36-40). In the front cover of my Bible I have the inscription: "It is not who I am, nor what I am, but

Whose I am that I rejoice." God continues to refine me and to shape me into being a better person. It is the love which God has brought into my life which makes me want to be a better man. I do know this: it is by the power of the Holy Spirit that we love the lost, the hurting, those who disappoint us, those who attack us, and those who are just plain hard to love. As Jesus chides us, anyone can love those who love them back (Matthew 5:46-48). Christian love is to involve action. Love is shown through tangible acts of service and charity toward others, especially the poor and the oppressed. Listen to the Holy Spirit when He is prompting you in some act of Christian love. Both the doer and the receiver will be blessed.

Love for others is a major piece of evidence of your salvation. We must be willing to answer the needs of others if we are sincere about kingdom service. Good intentions alone do not count. C. S. Lewis in Mere Christianity tells us, "Love in the Christian sense does not mean an emotion. It is a state not of the feelings but of the will" (page 129). We choose to love others, as an act of obedience to our Lord. These are not the result of some mysterious urgings which we inexplicably follow. Christian love is something which we purposefully cultivate. Lewis goes on to explain, "The worldly man treats certain people kindly because he 'likes' them: the Christian, trying to treat every one kindly, finds himself liking more and more people as he goes on" (page 130). As we exercise our "will to love", we discover a very joyous result – we come to love more people, with an even deeper love than when we first started this transformation. This love is not without an emotional element. On the contrary, the will to love seems to produce some of the closest of friendships which you will ever develop. Your Sunday School class is an excellent place to start exercising this love. Find a way to serve them; fill it with purpose; then watch how your emotional feelings get in line with your acts of service.

Turn now to Romans 12:9-21 to read Paul's encouragement to us to on how we should live according to the Spirit. Test yourself with respect to the fruit of the Spirit. Do you feel love only towards those who love you back? What did Jesus say about this type of love? Do you feel joy when worshipping God during church services, or do you mainly feel good about yourself for having taken the time to attend church? Do joy and hope fill your life, or do worry and pessimism characterize your emotional outlook? Do you do acts of kindness for people without expecting anything in return? Are you patient when someone is causing an interruption in your day? Do you have a gentle spirit for the foolish, the poor, and the oppressed? Or do you feel they have what they have because of poor life choices, so they should learn to make the most of it? Is your faithfulness characterized by accepting what life brings you, with a heart looking to God for strength, guidance, and support, or do you find yourself blaming God for your misfortunes (I mean, after all, if He really did love us, none of this bad stuff would be happening to us, right)? What about self-control – are you upset if someone in a car ahead of you slams on their brakes, causing you to brake hard, without any regard for what may have caused the person in front of you to stop so suddenly? Jesus teaches us in Luke 6:43-45 about the fruitful man. "For out of the overflow of his heart, his mouth speaks." Do your words indict you? Without the Holy Spirit exerting His influence in my life, I could be just as mean, uncaring, quick tempered, ego-centric, and ill-mannered a person as the next guy. The Holy Spirit will change you, if you'll let Him!

God never asks anything of us for which He does not equip us beforehand. "May the God of peace, who through the blood of the eternal covenant brought back from the dead our Lord Jesus, that great Shepherd of the sheep, equip you with everything good for doing His will, and may He work in us what is pleasing to Him, through Jesus Christ, to whom be glory for ever and ever" (Hebrews 13:20-21). Each of the attributes which of the Spirit brings us will prepare the believer for the tasks which God desires them to undertake. When you combine them with the traits of the Beatitudes, you can gain a glimpse into what life will be like when God restores the eternal earth and dwells with us for ever and ever (Revelation 21:1-5).

Each of these character traits will require a sacrifice of your time or the way you spend your money. Serving the kingdom of God is a series of opportunities by which we either involve ourselves in a specific manner or we neglect that act of service. We learn in 1 John 5:2-3, "This is how we know that we love the children of God: by loving God and carrying out His commands. This is love for God: to obey His commands. And His commands are not burdensome." God has equipped us for His service. The question is whether we only want the blessings of God or do we want to play a role in His blessing someone else? As Jesus says, even the pagans are loving to those who love them back. Much more is expected of believers. We are to use these fruits of the Spirit to bring glory to our Savior. When we look at what Jesus saved us from, this is the least we can do.

The law teaches us what sin is and that we cannot achieve righteousness by our own power. The Beatitudes teach us kingdom behavioral traits so we can properly approach God and man. <u>This is an additional way you know if you have been saved – are you passionate about serving the kingdom of God</u>. The Beatitudes are not mere words which we are to contemplate. These are character traits which we are to develop. They help us to feel God's presence. Then we are to take these traits and help others to feel God's presence through us. We get in order to give. We receive so we can share. The fruits of the Spirit are character traits which enable us to live lives oriented toward God and mankind in love and righteousness. God is mysterious in some of His ways but

He does not leave it a mystery as to how we are to relate to Him and to each other.

Jehovah Jireh does not leave it to each person's own devices to live a righteous life. He provides us through His revealed Word with the knowledge required to walk in accordance to His ways. John summarizes this line of thought rather well in 1 John 2:4-6. "The man who says, "I know Him," but does not do what He commands is a liar, and the truth is not in him. But if anyone obeys His word, God's love is truly made complete in him. This is how we know we are in Him: Whoever claims to live in Him must walk as Jesus did."

## *Evidence of the Holy Spirit in Your Life*

### *Self-Control*

Now is an excellent time to critically examine each of these nine character traits which the Holy Spirit brings to the Christian believer and how we should apply them to our daily lives. Self-control is covered extensively in Proverbs. Solomon teaches us in Proverbs 17:27, "A man of knowledge uses words with restraint, and a man of understanding is even-tempered." He continues this line of thought in 20:22. In 23:4 Solomon gives some sound financial advice. Solomon instructs us on the restraint of our anger in 29:11. "A fool gives full vent to his anger, but a wise man keeps himself under control." Other verses which relate to self-control are Proverbs 25:28 and 29:18.

Paul lends his wisdom in 1 Thessalonians 4:3-4 by declaring, "It is God's will that you should be sanctified: that you should avoid sexual immorality; that each of you should learn to control his own body in a way that is holy and honorable…" Paul continues in 2 Timothy 3:1-3 to warn us, "But mark this: There will be terrible times in the last days. People will be lovers of themselves, lovers of money, boastful, proud, abusive, disobedient to their parents, ungrateful, unholy, without love, unforgiving, slanderous, without self-control, brutal, not lovers of the good..." Peter encourages us in 2 Peter 1:5-6, "For this very reason, make every effort to add to your faith goodness; and to goodness, knowledge; and to knowledge, self-control; and to self-control, perseverance; and to perseverance, godliness..." What does all of this mean for us today? <u>God expects us to restrain ourselves so that we represent Him as a glowing light to the rest of the world</u>. We are not to do as many nonbelievers do who act out of their own self-interests and emotions. Self-control is the trait which saves us from saying things on the spur of the moment, then living to regret them later. Self-control will have us keep our emotional outbursts to ourselves until we have had time to reflect on WWJD (what would Jesus do). I am so thankful when I do not give vent to my first reaction to many of the situations which are around me.

To what measure can we achieve self-control in our lives? At one time I thought it was unreasonable to think that we could exercise any real measure of control over our thoughts, especially during dreams. These thought patterns are controlled by our unconsciousness, thereby not submissive to our willful censorship. An amazing thing has happened though in my life. As I am progressing in my sanctification process, the Holy Spirit is helping me to gain at least a small measure of control over these unconscious thoughts. As I read the Bible daily, these stories and characters have eventually invaded my dreams. I am finding that when I have the occasional violent or immoral dream, certain biblical lessons will suddenly appear in the dream and interrupt the dream sequence. It is as though the Holy Spirit says, "Enough of that. Glenn needs help." Then He sends thoughts into my mind which counteract the dream pattern. I would not believe this if it had not happened to me. This also happens when we day dream or just have random thoughts running through our minds during the day.

I have previously thought that it is unfair of God to hold us answerable for our thought processes. He should only hold us accountable for our observable behavior. How much I have had to learn! What about temptations which flood our consciousness? Are we responsible for these enticements? True, we are not held liable for temptations. What we are held accountable for is how we respond to those temptations. Our thoughts are a form of response though (Matthew 5:27-28). When someone is rude or provokes us, the next thoughts we have will be influenced by what we have been bringing into our minds throughout the day. What we feed our minds during the day becomes grist for the mill of all our conscious and unconscious thoughts. I have heard people say Christians need to watch and read what nonbelievers watch and read in order to counter their arguments. I find this thinking pure folly. These thoughts will work their way into our thinking more quickly than most realize. I have come to learn that if you feed your mind biblical stories during the day, it will interweave them into your thought patterns. This is a long and deliberate process. It takes consistent nourishment to counteract the years of pure garbage which comes to us from all angles. If you feed your mind the common trash which our society seems to think is entertainment, then that will be what you think about at various times. These thoughts will become your behavior. The Holy Spirit will help you gain control over your thoughts, emotions, and outward behavior if you will center your thinking on the lessons of the Holy Bible. The more good nourishment we feed our minds, the more the Holy Spirit has to work with for our betterment.

## *Gentleness*

Gentleness is always prized in a grandparent, parent, spouse, teacher, and best friend. Why? This is mostly because the world can be so harsh and unrelenting. It is nice to have someone who shows us love through their gentle manner. The Lord God appeared to Elijah as a gentle whisper. In 1 Kings 19:11-12, "The Lord said, "Go out and stand on the mountain in the presence of the Lord, for the Lord is about to pass by." Then a great and powerful wind tore the mountains apart and shattered the rocks before the Lord, but the Lord was not in the wind. After the wind there was an earthquake, but the Lord was not in the earthquake. After the earthquake came a fire, but the Lord was not in the fire. And after the fire came a gentle whisper. When Elijah heard it, he pulled his cloak over his face and went out and stood at the mouth of the cave. Then a voice said to him, 'What are you doing here, Elijah?'" With all of El Shaddai's mighty powers, why did He appear as a gentle whisper to Elijah? Think about the Beatitudes. <u>Gentleness is being willing to graciously consider the others person's needs and to act in humble sensitivity towards them.</u> You are exerting self-control over your interests in the interest of someone else. Then you do whatever it is you are doing in a spirit of compassion and tenderness. <u>The Golden Rule is God's guide for us in our pursuit of gentleness.</u> Meekness in the Beatitudes is another characteristic of gentleness. Meekness refers to: obediently accepting God's guidance and His vindication; it is gentle strength with restraint; power under control; yielding your will to the will of the Holy Spirit. We are not meek because we are weak. We are said to be meek when we choose to use our power under submission to God to do good rather than using our power to achieve selfish desires. God displayed for Elijah exactly how He desires His Christian children to display themselves. Anybody can be loud and boisterous. To be omnipotent, yet to come as a gentle whisper is a profound revelation. Couple this with what Solomon says in Proverbs 15:1. "A gentle answer turns away wrath, but a harsh word stirs up anger." Being mighty of spirit does not require us to be loud of mouth.

To train animals, we learn to be calm and assertive. This also works well with children, employees, coworkers, and friends (in fact, with most anyone who values being treated in a respectful manner). For the Christian, we are to go a step further and add gentleness to this. Since people have the advantage of language, it should be our pleasure to be gentle in words and deeds when dealing with God and all His creation. Kind words make a difference, even to our pets. Go to the prophecy in Zechariah 9:9 to see how the King of Kings was to present Himself. Self-pride has no grounds in a life sold-out for Christ. The Master teaches us in Matthew 11:28-30, "Come to me, all you who are weary and burdened, and I will give you rest. Take my yoke upon you and learn from me, for I am gentle and humble in heart, and you will find rest for your souls. For my yoke is easy and my burden is light." How much more apparent does it have to be?

Paul extends this by imploring us in Ephesians 4:2, "Be completely humble and gentle; be patient, bearing with one another in love." Paul covers gentleness in Philippians 4:5, Colossians 3:12, and rounds it out with his urging Christians in 1 Timothy 6:11 to pursue gentleness. We are not just to exhibit gentleness; we are to pursue it. Then our blessed Peter in 1 Peter 3:15 instructs us, "But in your hearts set apart Christ as Lord. Always be prepared to give an answer to everyone who asks you to give the reason for the hope that you have. But do this with gentleness and respect..." Peter had come full circle in his sanctification process. He embraced the Beatitudes and exhibited the fullness of the Holy Spirit. The brash fisherman grew into a kind and gentle pastor, calling on his brothers to uphold the integrity of his friend Jesus with gentleness and respect. You can't help but love Peter.

## *Faithfulness*

What does the fruit of faithfulness bring to the life of a Christian? Solomon once again graces us with his wisdom in Proverbs 16:6, "Through love and faithfulness sin is atoned for; through the fear of the Lord a man avoids evil." Faithfulness is being steadfast in your belief, trust, and commitment to our Lord. We are not to waver between God and some current, false religions or cultural idols. We are not to seek first, as some do, the various agencies of government as the answer to our problems, but when it fails us, only then do we turn to God. After 911 the churches were filled with people seeking God's wisdom and solace. Where are these people now? God is not like a water faucet – willing to be turned on and off at our whim. We, as genuine believers, are not to separate God from our work, our play, our socializing, or even our politics. We are to seek El Elyon during the good times and the bad times, in all that we do. Our spiritual beliefs are to permeate all aspects of our lives. The political sphere is where I am amazed the most with regards to a person's breakdown of faith and lifestyle. It is as though people think it is perfectly fine to separate their religious beliefs from their political persuasion. <u>Faithfulness demands that our spiritual belief system flows into everything we think, say, and do</u>. If you vote for pocket book issues or lax moral positions, you are not being faithful to God. Those who represent us should reflect the values which God wants each of us to share. There is <u>no</u> separation of God and state for the faithful believer. To set the record straight, our country was not founded on the principle of freedom from religion but rather on the principle of freedom for religion. Our faithfulness to God is shown by all avenues of our lives being in concert with God's will. To God, all means all.

Jehovah God is forever faithful with us. Hebrews 10:23 states, "Let us hold unswervingly to the hope we profess, for He who promised is faithful." Adonai never leaves us nor forsakes us (Joshua 1:5). Correspondingly, our Lord asks the same of us. Joshua delivers one of my favorite quotes in Joshua 24:15. "But if serving the Lord seems undesirable to you, then choose for yourselves this day whom you will serve, whether the gods your forefathers served beyond the River, or the gods of the Amorites, in whose land you are living. But as for me and my household, we will serve the Lord." This quote hangs in the hallway of my home. It is not there to impress visitors. It is there to serve as an ever present reminder to our household of what we pledge to God. Joshua lived his faithfulness. Not only that, he led his family in faithfulness. He lived his life as God desires each of us to live.

Isaiah prophesied in Isaiah 11:5 that the Messiah would be characterized as, "Righteousness will be His belt and faithfulness the sash around His waist." Is this how you picture Jesus? Is this not how we are to be pictured? Our Lord chastises the Pharisees as hypocrites for not showing justice, mercy, and faithfulness in Matthew 23:23. John regales his friend Gaius in 3 John 1:3 for his faithfulness to the truth. In Revelation 13:10, John talks about the patient endurance and faithfulness which will be required during that terrible period. Faithfulness is what this entire book is about. <u>Without faithfulness to the truth of God as revealed in His Holy Scriptures, your life is devoid of any real meaning, purpose, hope, and joy</u>. All other pursuits in this life are for show. Only in a sold-out life for Christ Jesus can we maintain the steadfast hold on our beliefs. Partial faith leads to partial faithfulness. All of us experience episodes where our faith is challenged. This is why it is imperative that we be as Joshua and proclaim before all men, "as for me and my household, we will serve the Lord." With this public proclamation, we are more inclined to follow in faithfulness than if we merely hold this as a personal goal. Commitment brings conviction.

## *Goodness*

Goodness to each other seems to be sorely lacking in our society today. We had a repairman do some work on our house. When he totaled his invoice to us, he made a mistake. He under billed us by $175.00. I called to point out the error and to request a new invoice. Ronnie brought it to my work the next day and said he wanted to shake my hand. He said in ten years of repair work, I am the first customer to have called him ever about a mistake like this. Please note, I am not trying to pat myself on the back with this example. God expects this of us. He gives us these fruits so we can be a blessing to others, in His name. It is for His glory that we are good to each other. Seldom does God give us anything which is meant to be held within ourselves. I know in my business we occasionally make innocent mistakes. We expect our clients to allow us to make corrections when we find these errors. It saddens me to think people are so quick to take advantage of innocent mistakes. This man delivered a service to my family. He deserved fair payment.

In Psalm 31:19 David sings the praise of God by proclaiming, "How great is your goodness, which you have stored up for those who fear you, which you bestow in the sight of men on those who take refuge in you." How would we feel if God short-changed us? As Christians we are to be the standard bearers of God's inherent goodness. In Psalm 116:12 the question is asked, "How can I repay the Lord for all His goodness to me?" The answer is simply this – be good to your neighbors. What does this mean? Goodness refers to being virtuous. It is living in righteousness. Doing the right thing is the hallmark of goodness. We are not good because we are weak or that we have no other option. We are good because God is good and He tells us to be like Him. A good person is someone who others can count on to be virtuous and righteous because it is his characteristic manner. Paul explains this in Ephesians 5:8-10. "For you were once darkness, but now you are light in the Lord. Live as children of light (for the fruit of the light consists in all goodness, righteousness and truth) and find out what pleases the Lord." What pleases the Lord? Peter answers this in 2 Peter 1:5-7, "For this very reason, make every effort to add to your faith goodness; and to goodness, knowledge; and to knowledge, self-control; and to self-control, perseverance; and to perseverance, godliness; and to godliness, brotherly kindness; and to brotherly kindness, love." When these qualities become characteristics by which others describe us, then we can be certain we are pleasing the Lord.

## *Kindness*

How nice is it when a stranger sees your arms full and they open the door for you? How pleasant is a kind word spoken to you during a hectic day? God intends for Christians to regularly display random acts of kindness to others. We do these acts expecting nothing in return. That is what makes them so special. They are special to the person who receives them and special to us for having the presence of mind to know what God would have us to do in that situation. Kindness displays one's consideration for others. It is benign goodness. When you think of Jesus, can you not picture His kindness toward the masses as they huddled around Him? They wanted His healing and His compassion. Kindness requires our time. In our fast paced lives, we trample over many opportunities for these random acts of kindness. All that is required is that we slow down a little. Then we need to think of how we would like to be treated in a particular situation. In Psalm 103:13-14 we are reminded of God's kindness. "As a father has compassion on his children, so the Lord has compassion on those who fear Him; for He knows how we are formed, He remembers that we are dust." How completely we depend on the kindness of El Elyon! Pass it on.

What do you think Solomon had in mind in Proverbs 14:31? "He who oppresses the poor shows contempt for their Maker, but whoever is kind to the needy honors God." All of us are needy in one respect or another. All of us are in need of kindness. The anthem for kindness can be found in 2 Corinthians 1:3-4. "Praise be to the God and Father of our Lord Jesus Christ, the Father of compassion and the God of all comfort, who comforts us in all our troubles, so that we can comfort those in any trouble with the comfort we ourselves have received from God." It makes sense that if God is the Father of compassion, then He must want His children to exhibit that same kindness to others, doesn't it? This kindness is not restricted to those of our kind. It means everyone. Paul states it simply in Ephesians 4:32. "Be kind and compassionate to one another, forgiving each other, just as in Christ God forgave you." If Jesus does it for us, then it is only reasonable that He expects us to do this for others. He came to earth to model kingdom behavior. So when we recognize a character trait of Jesus', then pick it up and make it part of your makeup. Do as Paul instructs us in Colossians 3:12 and 1 Thessalonians 5:15. Become the person God put you here to become.

## Patience

With hectic schedules come hectic attitudes. We seem to have lost the desire to "stop and smell the roses". Patience is partly self-control, followed by a large measure of peace and contentment. <u>Being patient reflects an indulgent willingness on your part to allow someone to impact your time without any consequence to them</u>. For this to happen, a person must be contented with who they are and what their purpose is in life. On the other hand, frustrated people seem to be at war with themselves and everyone else. On a spiritual level, the patient person is one who looks at their lot in life as being God's representative. The impatient person only represents themselves.

What must we do to cultivate this character trait? Tolerance is much like meekness in that it is the power of our will under restraint. Where I have one of my greatest challenges is revealed in Psalm 27:14. "Wait for the Lord; be strong and take heart and wait for the Lord." I have the bad habit of doing what I think I should do, then praying about it. Just as bad is when I do stop and pray before making a decision. If I do not get what I think is an answer in a timely manner, I go ahead and do what I think God wants me to do. I have to learn that sometimes no answer is the answer. Other times, an answer is forthcoming, just not yet though. Putting our lives on God's schedule is a very hard task.

Another side of patience is reflected in Proverbs 19:11. "A man's wisdom gives him patience; it is to his glory to overlook an offense." Time can be our ally if we learn to use it properly. <u>Most of us find as we mature that patiently waiting to collect our thoughts before responding to a volatile situation will usually produce our best response</u>. Solomon shares his wisdom with us on this subject in Ecclesiastes 7:8-9. "The end of a matter is better than its beginning, and patience is better than pride. Do not be quickly provoked in your spirit, for anger resides in the lap of fools." The end of the matter is only better than the beginning if we have exercised patience in our judgment and words. Solomon gives us the following insight in exercising patience in Proverbs 16:24. "Pleasant words are a honeycomb, sweet to the soul and healing to the bones." We usually associate pleasant words coming from a patient person. Brash words come from haughty, self-absorbed people.

Paul provides us with the best of all reasons why we should exercise patience in Colossians 1:10-12. "And we pray this in order that you may live a life worthy of the Lord and may please Him in every way: bearing fruit in every good work, growing in the knowledge of God, being strengthened with all power according to His glorious might so that you may have great endurance and patience, and joyfully giving thanks to the Father, who has qualified you to share in the inheritance of the saints in the kingdom of light."

How patient was Jesus in working with the disciples to help them to become the leaders of the early Christian church? His labor paid off. Today you and I are saved souls because of Him and the patient work which His disciples, in turn, did with the early Church. Paul sums it up rather well in 1 Timothy 1:16. "But for that very reason I was shown mercy so that in me, the worst of sinners, Christ Jesus might display His unlimited patience as an example for those who would believe on Him and receive eternal life." We should learn to exercise patience not so that we will be thought of well but to represent our Lord in a fashion where He is thought of well. In doing so, this will add to the enjoyment, contentment, and peace in our lives.

*Peace*

Peace is something which most of us yearn to have. Our souls cry out for it. Our psychological framework seeks harmony in order to function at its best. Unfortunately, many have lived so long with disharmony that they seem to no longer seek what is tranquil. It is as though they would not know how to function. Peace can mean different things to different people. To the Christian peace means inner tranquility, contentment, and harmony through the spiritual restoration which is brought to us by our Savior, Christ Jesus. Ultimate peace is achievable in only one way – through the Way (John 14:6, Isaiah 9:6-7).

Being content in what God has blessed me with brings peace to my life. As I try to live as God intends, harmony in my relationships both with God and man becomes more prevalent. It produces a balance which makes all aspects of my life flow into a more meaningful, cohesive plan for living. Warring within yourself with spiritual discord takes a heavy toll. Psalm 29:11 teaches us, "The Lord gives strength to His people; the Lord blesses His people with peace." If you are without peace, then perhaps you have not been receptive to the Holy Spirit's urgings in your soul. Perhaps you are struggling with pride, envy, or jealousy. These three emotions will rob you of your peace.

Just as Paul urges us to pursue gentleness, Psalm 34:14 prompts us to, "Turn from evil and do good; seek peace and pursue it." How do we pursue peace? We do this by following Psalm 37:11. "But the meek will inherit the land and enjoy great peace." This applies to one's mental condition as well as to geography. In this context, as well as in the Beatitudes, meekness is not weakness. Meekness is power under restraint. This power is self-controlled and is to be used for God's glory. When we are working within God's framework, peace comes to us because of what is conveyed in Psalm 29:11. God will give us the strength to pursue peace, if we will seek it.

Even in challenges, God can make our efforts peaceful if we seek His will in what we are doing. Psalm 119:165 amplifies this. "Great peace have they who love your law, and nothing can make them stumble." When we follow the plan which our Triune God has set for us, inner peace is one of the rewards. This does not mean that we walk around with perpetual smiles plastered on our faces. You can be fighting cancer, yet have peace. How is this? It can be so because you are <u>earnestly trusting in God's provision for your life</u>. You may not know what is going to happen and you may not like what is happening, yet internally there exists an inexplicable peace. This is because you are His and He is yours. God will never harm us out of neglect or whim. Regardless of whatever is happening, we can be assured, He is in control. He is our loving heavenly Father. As such, we can have a peace which surpasses all understanding. We are reminded in Philippians 4:6-7, "Do not be anxious about anything, but in everything, by prayer and petition, with thanksgiving, present your requests to God. And the peace of God, which transcends all understanding, will guard your hearts and your minds in Christ Jesus." It is very hard to explain this peace if someone has never felt it.

Our peace is <u>not</u> some type of fleeting, mystical, nirvana experience either. God's peace penetrates throughout your life – in each area where you turn in meekness to His will. Solomon tells us in Proverbs 14:30, "A heart at peace gives life to the body..." As far as fruits go, Isaiah teaches us in Isaiah 32:17, "The fruit of righteousness will be peace; the effect of righteousness will be quietness and confidence forever." Jesus promises His peace to His believers in John 14:27 and Paul substantiates this in Romans 5:1. Paul then lays a heavy challenge on us in Romans 12:18. "If it is possible, as far as it depends on you, live at peace with everyone." Does this sound like what Jesus tells us about loving even our enemies? If we do these things, then Paul's wish for our lives in Romans 15:13 is certainly achievable.

James rounds out our discussion on peace by relating it back to the Beatitudes. James 3:18 teaches, "Peacemakers who sow in peace raise a harvest of righteousness." Jesus means it when He says "Blessed are the peacemakers, for they will be called sons of God" (Matthew 5:9). These are people who actively intervene to make peace. The role of the peacemaker is to restore relationships and bring them back to harmony. By making peace, believers manifest themselves as sons of God, and God will one day acknowledge them as people who bear the family likeness. Jesus is known as the Prince of Peace, so that should tell us something of the value which God puts on peacemakers.

## *Joy*

Is your life characterized by strife, conflicts, and internal struggles? Give it a rest. Joy is assured us when we invite Jesus to be the Lord of our lives. If, as a Christian, you do not have joy, then please reassess your interests and priorities. The Holy Spirit is trying to tell you something. <u>Spiritual joy is the delight we have in being the sons and daughters of El Elyon, the Most High God</u>. In Psalm 51:11-12 David cries out to God, "Do not cast me from your presence or take your Holy Spirit from me. Restore to me the joy of your salvation and grant me a willing spirit, to sustain me." Notice the value David put on the joy of his salvation. He was not asking for earthly pleasures. God's salvation is what gave David so much joy. David further instructs us in Psalm 19:7-9, "The law of the Lord is perfect, reviving the soul. The statutes of the Lord are trustworthy, making wise the simple. The precepts of the Lord are right, giving joy to the heart." <u>David gained immeasurable joy from his relationship with God because he found everything about God to be utterly amazing</u>. He feasted on God's Holy Word. He prayed for God's guidance, deliverance, protection, and blessings. God was completely entwined in all aspects of David's life. Sure, David had sorrows in his daily life, but his inner spirit soared with an everlasting joy which only the Father can provide.

The writer of Hebrews promises us in 1:9, "You have loved righteousness and hated wickedness; therefore God, your God, has set you above your companions by anointing you with the oil of joy." What is this oil of joy? The oil of our joy is the Holy Spirit (the object of our joy is Christ Jesus). The Holy Spirit has been poured on us and in us. We are lubricated with His eternal Being. Believers are anointed with the Holy Spirit as a sign of membership in the family of God. It is the oil of the Holy Spirit which fuels our flame for our Lord Jesus. The Holy Spirit helps us to keep Christ Jesus at the center of our being.

1 Peter 1:8-9 reveals, "Though you have not seen Him (Jesus), you love Him; and even though you do not see Him now, you believe in Him and are filled with an inexpressible and glorious joy, for you are receiving the goal of your faith, the salvation of your souls." <u>What can give us more joy than to know our spirits will be joined with our resurrected bodies to dwell with our Lord forever and ever in a world totally free from sin?</u> If joy does not permeate your life, then either you have not genuinely accepted Christ as your Savior or you have not laid claim to the fruit which the Holy Spirit desires you to have.

Seize hold of Romans 14:17-18 and claim it for your own. "For the kingdom of God is not a matter of eating and drinking, but of righteousness, peace and joy in the Holy Spirit, because anyone who serves Christ in this way is pleasing to God and approved by men." Then move to Romans 15:13. "May the God of hope fill you with all joy and peace as you trust in Him, so that you may overflow with hope by the power of the Holy Spirit." Joy has no room for pessimism. Where God is, hope abounds. Where hope abounds, joy reigns.

Living in the Spirit is like having a warm coat on during the winter (Luke 24:49). You are still in the cold weather but you have something which makes the cold weather more bearable. The Spirit transforms us and makes this world more bearable. This life (and world) is a test (Rev. 3:10) to determine where for all eternity you will spend your existence (we will all be somewhere – it's a matter of faith where that somewhere will be). It should make you joyful to "know that you know" the purpose and direction of your life. <u>A believer should find it impossible to be a pessimist in the presence of our Triune God.</u> <u>It is not that only good things happen to us but, most importantly, that we have a God who turns our failures into victories.</u> "And we know that in all things God works for the good of those who love Him, who have been called according to His purpose" (Romans 8:28). When this verse becomes alive in your life, then joy never leaves you, ever again.

### *Love*

With respect to love, Peter says it best in 1 Peter 4:8. <u>"Above all, love each other deeply, because love covers over a multitude of sins."</u> Love not only covers a multitude of sins, it also covers a multitude of failures as a parent, a child, a sibling, a spouse, a fellow believer, or whatever the relationship. If the person we slight knows we love them, the offense is often rendered inconsequential. Our heavenly Father is much the same way. The sheer enormity of Scriptural references to love is a telling study. In the NIV Bible, you will get 551 references when doing a word search on love. Faith has 270 hits and hope has 166 hits. Since all Scripture is God-breathed, then it should be obvious to us how important God feels love is in a Christian's life.

The Apostle Paul gives us an excellent narrative on what love is in 1 Corinthians 13:1-13. "If I speak in the tongues of men and of angels, but have not love, I am only a resounding gong or a clanging cymbal. If I have the gift of prophecy and can fathom all mysteries and all knowledge, and if I have a faith that can move mountains, but have not love, I am nothing. If I give all I possess to the poor and surrender my body to the flames, but have not love, I gain nothing. Love is patient, love is kind. It does not envy, it does not boast, it is not proud. It is not rude, it is not self-seeking, it is not easily angered, it keeps no record of wrongs. Love does not delight in evil but rejoices with the truth. It always protects, always trusts, always hopes, always perseveres. Love never fails. But where there are prophecies, they will cease; where there are tongues, they will be stilled; where there is knowledge, it will pass away. For we know in part and we prophesy in part, but when perfection comes, the imperfect disappears. When I was a child, I talked like a child, I thought like a child, I reasoned like a child. When I became a man, I put childish ways behind me. Now we see but a poor reflection as in a mirror; then we shall see face to face. Now I know in part; then I shall know fully, even as I am fully known. And now these three remain: faith, hope and love. But the greatest of these is love."

John continues this in 1 John 4:7-12. "Dear friends, let us love one another, for love comes from God. Everyone who loves has been born of God and knows God. Whoever does not love does not know God, because God is love. This is how God showed His love among us: He sent His one and only Son into the world that we might live through Him. This is love: not that we loved God, but that He loved us and sent His Son as an atoning sacrifice for our sins. Dear friends, since God so loved us, we also ought to love one another. No one has ever seen God; but if we love one another, God lives in us and His love is made complete in us." <u>Love is God's fingerprints on our lives</u>. He, who seeks to love his fellowman, seeks God also, whether he is Jew or Gentile or someone who has never heard the Gospels. John's discussion about God's love and how He put love in all of us supports what Paul says in Romans 1:20 – 2:16 about God placing an awareness in all of us to know Him and to seek His righteousness. The unfortunate reality is that some get derailed by false gods as they pursue these inherent urgings.

Solomon teaches us in Proverbs 3:3-4 that love should be that for which we are known. Love and faith atone for our sins (Proverbs 16:6). In Proverbs 21:21 Solomon gives us the promise of future glory by stating, "He who pursues righteousness and love finds life, prosperity and honor." Though our life, prosperity and honor may be different than what this world seeks, it is of eternal consequences on which we set our sights (Hebrews 11:40). One of the most memorable announcements by Jesus concerned love. When asked which is the most important commandment, Mark 12:30-31 notes His reply. "Love the Lord your God with all your heart and with all your soul and with all your mind and with all your strength.' The second is this: 'Love your neighbor as yourself.' There is no commandment greater than these." Jesus continues with His disciples in John 13:34-35 teaching them how they are to be known. "A new command I give you: Love one another. As I have loved you, so you must love one another. By this all men will know that you are my disciples, if you love one another." If a person considers themselves to be a Christian but when they are in the midst of a Christian gathering, if they do not feel close, familial love for all who are present, then they need to consult their minister or a close spiritual friend. Either they have been deceived about their conversion or their hearts have become hardened in a very improper way. Jesus commands it, so it should be so. Love is to characterize the life of the Christian believer.

In John 14:15 Jesus urges us, "If you love me, you will obey what I command." Unfortunately for many a broken heart, people's words of love can merely be the platitudes of their social graces. It is one's actions which portray their true emotions. Jesus knows this all too well and this is why He gives us this directive. Is this lack of true commitment typical of our many of our earthly relationships? Sadly it is. If I genuinely love my wife, will I not give careful consideration to following her wishes? If I love my friends, will I not want to live in harmony with them? Our love for each other is reflected in our willingness to seek mutual cooperation and harmony. Christian love therefore involves holding the other person in high esteem. When we hold someone in high regard, we value them and cherish their being part of our lives. We do not want to disappoint them with anything which we might do and thereby risk harming the relationship. The difference in our loving relationships is often seen in the degrees of our willing cooperation. When Jesus, Peter and Paul talk about Christian submission they are referring to *a spirit of willing cooperation* (not lowly servitude or cowardly surrender). Submission reveals inner strength, commitment, and trust. Jesus is our Lord and Master, therefore we are to give Him our total submission. With Him, we are to follow – plain and simple. Jesus is to be first in our lives, with our spouses, families, and friends following in relational order.

Someone who is not willing to follow the teachings of Christ but thinks they are a Christian is only fooling themselves. You cannot pick and choose which commands to follow. Christ does not give us multiple choice answers. We are to follow all His commands. Our Lord furthers this line of teaching in John 15:12-14, "My command is this: Love each other as I have loved you. Greater love has no one than this, that he lay down his life for his friends. You are my friends if you do what I command." Our Lord lived out His example. He loved us enough to die for us; the least we can do is to live for Him. The childhood song is right – "what a friend we have in Jesus."

In John 15:19 our Lord explains the cost of loving Him. "If you belonged to the world, it would love you as its own. As it is, you do not belong to the world, but I have chosen you out of the world. That is why the world hates you." The cost is high for now but it will be worth incalculable value when the great trumpet sounds and Christ calls us home

(Revelation 4:1). Many believe this verse ushers the rapture of the church. This sounds fine with me because I plan on being one of those who is ushered home!

As an aside: Christian love does not mean people are free to do to each other as they wish, without any consequences. Sin has consequences and behavior has boundaries. Christian love does not give others the license to heap abuse on us. We can love someone without allowing them to be manipulative of our good heartedness. We see this often when churches are approached by people wanting money but who are not willing to help in providing for themselves. When the answer is "no", they try to make the pastor feel guilty for turning them away. Pastors have to be sufficiently insightful to know when to help someone and when someone is merely trying to manipulate their sense of Christian charity. Christians do not have to be the doormat for the rest of the world. We do have to be willing to love the sinner though. The person who attacks us today may repent and become our brother tomorrow. Only God knows the heart of others, so we have to be willing to take risks and allow God to sort out the results.

Where we do not have to worry about what kind of stand we should be taking is when our faith is under attack. Jesus was bold in His defense of the gospel when challenged by the Pharisees and so should we be when the politically correct crowd attempts to make us mitigate our faith in order not to offend others who have no faith. If your belief in Jehovah God is not worth fighting for and resisting the politically correct crowd's persistent attacks, then you have not made a steadfast, heartfelt commitment to your faith. This is a sure sign your faith in Jesus as Lord has not become a core belief system for you. Our love for God should be filled with such passion and tenacity that nothing said by man can ever dissuade us from holding God Almighty in our utmost esteem. <u>If your theology is so fluid that you are susceptible</u>

to altering your religious beliefs to suit the "world view", you will wind up believing in nothing but thinking it's something.

When you explore the book of Romans you will find it contains many wonderful verses which illuminate the concept of Christian love. In Romans 5:8 Paul teaches, "But God demonstrates His own love for us in this: While we were still sinners, Christ died for us." Go to Romans 12:9-21 and read Paul's instructions for us concerning love. Paul encourages us to live at peace, if possible, with everyone. We can do this only if love directs our actions. Love, faith, and joy are the hallmarks of Christian living.

It is often strange to our world how Christians can find such fulfillment and love in something which is not apparent to the senses. The concept of the Triune God leaves many questions which are challenging to answer. Our spiritual reality truly appears subjective in many ways, especially to nonbelievers. That does not stop it from being real though. As I have said previously, just because something does not appear logical or rational in our minds does not make it any less real (the earth was thought to be flat for how many centuries?). On the other hand, most of this world's spiritual existence is often bleak and self-directed. A Christian can be experiencing trials and tribulations, yet have peace within their spirit. It is not phony. It is not naïve thinking. It is the recognition that God has a plan for us and if we will submit our spirits to the Holy Spirit, He will fill us with all the qualities necessary to achieve a purposeful life. The Holy Spirit brings these qualities to us to prepare us for the road to sanctification. As we are told many times in the Scriptures, the greatest of these qualities is love. A caritas love where we hold God in highest esteem facilitates the spreading of love in our lives to all aspects of our existence. We are blessed when we surrender our lives to the One who came in love so that those who place their faith in Him can be made righteous in the eyes of the Father.

The fruit of the Spirit helps you to refocus your life from being "all about you" to being "all about Jesus Christ, our Lord and Savior". <u>An additional benefit of a life focused on righteousness is that your growing commitment to our Lord Jesus will lead you to an increasing contentment with your life</u>. Our heavenly Father does an amazing thing with our wants and desires when we sincerely commit to His kingdom. He changes us (for the better). While earthly possessions are still valued and treasured, they are not our "eternal treasure". When this change happens, contentment has a real possibility for your life. <u>We can "know that we know" by the fruits which are apparent in our reborn lives</u>.

For a greater understanding of what God wants to be paramount in our lives, read Psalm 51:1-17 and Isaiah 57:15. These are excellent verses which point to what God is looking for – He wants us to have a contrite heart, to go along with the fruit of the Spirit and the traits of the Beatitudes. In Isaiah 57:15 the Lord declares: "I live in a high and holy place, but also with him who is contrite and lowly in spirit, to revive the spirit of the lowly and to revive the heart of the contrite." If these verses do not describe your heartfelt attitude toward your sins and how they grieve both your spirit and the Holy Spirit, then you need to question what sort of transformation you think you have achieved. Ask yourself if you have truly given the Holy Spirit dominion over your life.

Another way you can test your transformation is to see where you spend your time and money. Is regular attendance at Sunday worship an opportunity or a burden? Do acts of Christian service regularly appear on your calendar of scheduled events or just on special holidays? We are to serve the kingdom daily. As you grow in kingdom service, it will become a blur as to who is actually benefiting from these acts of kindness. As to money, do you give first to

God, or just whatever is left over? Do you give a full tithe or just what allows you to feel good about yourself? <u>Time and money are excellent barometers of our spiritual commitment</u>. If after asking yourself these questions, if you realize you have not started the process of spiritual transformation, then you need to seek a trusted pastor or Christian friend who can lead you along the path for salvation. If a person is not sure about their salvation, then they should read the book of Romans. After reading that book, if they are not sure, then they need to seek a minister or a Christian friend.

Let me encourage you as you engage in your biblical scholarship to go out to <u>www.blueletterbible.org</u> when you need to search by a word or phrase as you are trying to remember a verse but you cannot recall the location in the Bible where it can be found. You can select which one of many biblical translations you prefer; then hit "search". It is that easy. Select "study tools" to pull up the online encyclopedia and dictionary. With these you can research a topic more fully and get the correct pronunciation of a word. In the Blue Letter Bible there are extensive commentaries associated with Scriptures and topics. This is an excellent way to augment you biblical studies. At lunch time or during breaks, you can grow in your faith as you recuperate from your hectic day. Bible study has never been easier. It still helps if you know basic words in a verse for which you are searching but this online help is much more extensive than most Bible concordances. Maps and charts are available on this site as well. Sometimes I will go out to <u>www.Google.com</u> to research a topic, phrase or name. In Google, Wikipedia is an online encyclopedia which provides quick access to almost any topic you can desire to research. Google links you to thousands of sites where you can get a broad overview on down to the latest in scholastic discourse on a topic. Of course you have to exercise discretion in choosing which articles back up our doctrinal beliefs and which might lead to confusion or blatant deception. I know there are many areas where the worldwide web has been exploited for carnal purposes but it has also greatly opened the knowledge base of Christian topics as well. With so many tools available to us today, we no longer have the excuse that biblical study is too difficult.

In conclusion to this discussion, the answer to "how do you know that you know you are going to heaven" has been around for 2000 years. Why is it that so many Christians do not feel they have actual evidence they have been saved? Possibly the reason lies in the word "feel". Many people when asked how they know they are saved answer they feel it in their heart that they are saved. To many, religion is a feeling. It is mysterious and hard to define or express. What a shame. Sometimes I think we absolutely must wear God out. He reveals through His prophets; He sends His Son to teach us; yet most still miss the message. How to know that you know you are saved has been revealed to us in many, many Scriptural verses. Rather than reading these verses and feasting on their meaning, many people seem perfectly content to rely on their emotions to provide them some measure of assurance of their eternal fate. There is nothing wrong with allowing your feelings to enhance your spiritual faith. Jesus tells us to love God with all our hearts; in other words, our emotions have a proper place in our worship of God. He also tells us to love Him with all our minds. God has given us an incredible amount of evidence to assure us intellectually that God is who He says He is and that He does what He says He will do. Furthermore, God has also given us the Holy Spirit so we can love God through our inner spirit as it communes with the Holy Spirit. However, nothing takes the place of self-directed biblical exploration. Worship of God Almighty should involve our total being. As such, we can gain a greater understanding of our relationship with God as we grow in our knowledge of His presence and subsequent involvement in our daily lives.

If you were going on a cruise to Alaska, would you not read some articles about Alaska before departing? Wouldn't you go online to get a visual overview of the ship on which you would be sailing? Why do so many not go to the Word for the final word? Our biblical translators have done magnificent jobs of making Scriptural study interesting and easy. Take up the challenge of no longer relying on feelings and pastoral sermons to get your only understanding of God's plan for your life. Get active; take charge. The answers are there; pursue them.

# Chapter Nine The Final Outcome – Heaven for Some, Hell for the Others

—∞∞∞—

"**B**ut as I have told you, what is written in the Bible must be preached, whether it be gloomy or cheerful." These are the words of the famous British minister, Charles Spurgeon, in 1855, in his sermon entitled, "Heaven and Hell" (Blue Letter Bible Commentary). I fear most congregations have not heard many sermons about the reality of hell these days. There exist among the Christian populace tremendous discrepancies in congregational knowledge of the two places which our Lord declared will be the eternal abode of believers and nonbelievers. Jesus refers to hell in numerous passages (Matthew 5:22, 5:29-30, 7:13, 10:28, 16:18, 18:9, 23:15, 23:33, Mark 9:43-47, Luke 12:5, 16:23-31, and John 17:12). If it was important enough that Jesus spoke about hell this often, we should become knowledgeable of why it exists and likewise with the reality of it. <u>Jesus never avoided a topic because it was too controversial. He never failed to reveal the truth because He worried it might upset someone. If we are to take this sanctification process seriously, we must cover ground from which others shy away.</u>

Is this confusion or lack of knowledge about hell because pastors do not have the insight or understanding to preach about such difficult topics, or is it that most congregations do not want to hear the unpleasant reality of God's righteous judgment and subsequent wrath? I feel reasonably sure most pastors know more about hell than they present in their Sunday sermons. The fault for not preaching fervent sermons concerning the wages of sin and the consequences of rejecting our Savior probably can most often be spread to both the pastors and the congregations. Is this not what God decried in Isaiah 6:8-10? The Lord speaks out against the Israelite people in Isaiah 30:8-11. He chides them, "Go now, write it on a tablet for them, inscribe it on a scroll, that for the days to come it may be an everlasting witness. These are rebellious people, deceitful children, children unwilling to listen to the Lord's instruction. They say to the seers, "See no more visions!" and to the prophets, "Give us no more visions of what is right! Tell us pleasant things, prophesy illusions. Leave this way, get off this path, and stop confronting us with the Holy One of Israel!" In 2 Peter 2:1-4 Peter admonishes his people, "But there were also false prophets among the people, just as there will be false teachers among you. They will secretly introduce destructive heresies, even denying the sovereign Lord who bought them—bringing swift destruction on themselves. Many will follow their shameful ways and will bring the way of truth into disrepute. In their greed these teachers will exploit you with stories they have made up. Their condemnation has long been hanging over them, and their destruction has not been sleeping. For if God did not spare angels when they sinned, but sent them to hell, putting them into gloomy dungeons to be held for judgment..." Believers need to hear these prophetic words of Isaiah and Peter and thirst for the whole Gospel message, not just the parts which bring pleasing reassurances to their ears.

I know moms do not want their darling little children upset. Imagine how frightened they would be hearing about how the devil will torment you for all eternity if you reject God's plan of salvation. Think of how those poor souls who were demon-possessed in the Gospels were ravaged by Satan's minions. It will be worse and it will be for all eternity! What questions these kids would ask if their pastor actually described what happened to Jesus for those three days between His death and His resurrection. I can tell you what happened. He spent them in hell, on our behalf (Matthew 12:40, 1 Peter 3:18-19). Our Christ Jesus experienced the worst of God's wrath against mankind's sins so we can experience the best of His blessings. Henry Blackaby in Experiencing the Cross tells us, "When Paul said 'Christ died for the ungodly,' (Romans 5:6), he didn't just mean that Jesus stopped breathing. No, that word *died* meant that Jesus walked straight into the terrible night of rejection and eternal separation resulting from sin...He endured all of it – praise His name! – so you and I wouldn't have to go through it... Jesus took the long journey for us. He took upon Himself the full-depth, deepest-death, that should have been ours" (pages 49-50). Our precious Redeemer experienced from Friday afternoon until sometime Sunday morning the full magnitude which hell had to offer – in our place!

A good sermon on hell will generate a lot of questions for a minister. Some he would probably just as soon not have to address. Others will just wear him out because the people will resist hearing what the Word actually says about the wages of sin. Even in the ministry, there are tremendous pressures to be "politically correct." Additionally, there is much confusion about hell – not because the Bible is so mysterious about it – rather because most people do not want to take the time to learn about the realities of eternal damnation. As in ancient times, we hear what we want to hear. Unpleasant realities are not something which most of this world care to confront. Give us the easy path; the one lined with love, feel good feelings, and eternal acceptance.

Peter reveals to us that Christ Jesus preached to the spirits in hell prior to His resurrection (1 Peter 3:18-19). Yes, He did preach there as Peter tells but you can only imagine under what unbearable circumstances He must have had to endure in delivering the message of His triumph over sin and death. The content of His message is not revealed but there is nothing in the Scriptures which would make us think Jesus was offering these souls a second chance at salvation. You have only the time while you are alive on this earth to seek the Lord as your object of redemptive faith. There will be no second-chances after death. What we do know is that sin has to be atoned for and our blessed Jesus took on sin for all who will believe in Him as their Lord and Savior. Sin is a very serious matter with God. Be certain of this – our Messiah most certainly did not enter into a peaceful "soul sleep" during that three day period. He paid in full our sin debt. That for sure was no easy payment for Him to make.

Now extend this line of thought and consider what will be on these kids' little minds when the pastor explains the three levels of hell. It may give them some bad dreams (it certainly did for me), but hopefully these dreams will motivate them (and the adults as well) to start taking sin more seriously. Do not worry about the permanent damage to their little psyches. Most likely, after listening to a good ole "hell fire and brimstone sermon", these same kids will go home and play video games which are more blood-curdling than anything which I have ever heard from the pulpit. We protect our children too much these days from certain things and then we turn around and allow them to pollute their minds with the most disturbing forms of anti-social behavior which can be produced by this world's entertainment industry. Thankfully God did not overly protect His Son, or else we would all have a most unpleasant eternity. Of course, you may think that was different – and you're right – it was much worse!

There are countless fine ministers in our nation. I am sure many would like to preach about the consequences of misguided faith, but something probably is holding back those who shy away from preaching, as Charles Spurgeon calls, "the gloomy" side of the Bible. It could be they do not want to hear all the criticism they would endure if they actually preached the entire Bible. If you have a pastor who teaches the whole Bible – from Genesis through Revelation, then you have an excellent minister. An excellent pastor will emphasize God's holiness, righteousness, providence, sovereignty, justice, and judgment as well as His loving nature. If your minister preaches that we have individual accountability for our sins to where each will face the consequences for their sins (yes, even saved people will endure consequences for their sins), then you have an exceptional pastor. Exceptional ministers focus on making their congregations aware that "they must take up their crosses daily" if they are to be steadfast servants to our Lord. The Christian life is not all about praying a "shopping list" to God, then going about your day expecting God to bless you as you wish to be blessed. If your preacher delivers an occasional sermon teaching that God considers *all* sins as serious breaches of our relationship with Him, then goes on to explain the three levels of hell and that contrary to what modern political correctness espouses, unbelievers do not simply cease to exist when they die, then you have yourself a truly remarkable pastor. These pastors do not want their flocks to live delusional lives, resisting hearing what may be unpleasant or downright convicting.

Pastors should not shy away from the book of Revelation because it is filled with symbolic language and that it deals extensively with the damnation of unbelieving souls in a place called hell. To preach about hell takes a lot of knowledge as well as intestinal fortitude. To preach the entire Word of God requires a pastor to rise above the populace and to reach for the approval of only one – the One. In lay terms, it kind of depends on who the pastor considers his boss to be. Our congregation is thankful we sit under the tutelage of a full gospel minister who is bold in his convictions (he knows who his boss is). Perhaps because he is older, he may see things more clearly. Dr. Doug Sager certainly does not wear the glasses of political correctness. For that, we love him dearly. Toes get stepped on. Yet we keep coming back. Why? Because seekers seek the truth – the whole truth.

### *Death and Eternity*

What happens to someone when they die? We know from John 3:16 and many other favorite passages what is promised to those who have a redemptive faith in Christ Jesus. What about those who have mistakenly put their faith in some other god (whatever form it might be)? Do they merely cease to exist after a reasonable period of punishment for rejecting Christ as their Savior? Does eternal damnation sound overly harsh to you? What does the Bible teach us about the duration of God's judgment and wrath?

Americans are alarmingly confused on the topic of death and eternity. If you give any credence to the surveys covering what most people think happens to us at the point of our death, you recognize that most do not have a biblically correct comprehension of this topic (as opposed to being politically correct). According to the Pew Forum on Religion and Public Life, "70 percent of Americans with a religious affiliation said they believe many religions can lead to eternal life. This evidence shows Americans dismiss or don't know fundamental teachings of their own faiths" (Fox News.com, June 2008). In this report it quotes D. Michael Lindsay, a Rice University sociologist of religions as saying, "The survey shows religion in America is, indeed, 3,000 miles wide and only a few inches deep." This certainly reflects Jesus' statement about "broad is the road which leads to destruction but narrow is the one which leads to eternal life" (Matthew 7:13-14).

Other similar studies have shown that most people simply think all good people go to heaven and bad people just cease to exist (or they are punished for only a short while). In the Pew report, most Americans believe many religions can lead to eternal life: Protestants – 83%, Roman Catholics – 79%, Jews – 82%, and Muslims – 56%. It is as though all religions are on equal footing. They naively accept the politically correct view that all paths lead to the same destination. Jesus is thereby rendered to be "a Way", not "the Way". Sin is minimized and rejection of Christ is neutralized. Obviously most Americans prefer to contemplate God and to shape what they believe by what their opinions are of Him, without getting concrete biblical facts. Few seem to actually pick up their Bibles and read. It truly is as Catholic Archbishop Charles Chaput summarizes the Pew report by saying, "the church ought to work harder at evangelizing its own members."

There are three main points which seem to need to be made here. First, our Triune God is eternal, so any rejection of the Holy Trinity (or any member thereof) will thereby be eternal. This is first and foremost. El Olam, the Everlasting God, does not force Himself on us, but neither does He take our rejection lightly. Secondly, Jesus used the same word to describe life with Him in the kingdom and life apart from Him in hell. If you accept "eternal life" as meaning everlasting life, then you must accept His use of the same word to describe the everlasting nature for the condemnation of those who reject His offer of salvation. Thirdly, the effects of our sins often live longer than we do. Henry Blackaby warns, "All sin is deadly, and the deadening effect of our own sin goes beyond ourselves. What do you suppose is the consequence of *your* sins? You can never sin in private. You may be able to sin in secret, but you can't sin in private, because your sin will immediately affect everything around you (Experiencing the Cross, p.105)." I would like to now examine each of these three points in further details. It is an absolute shame that so many people pick and choose what they like in the Bible and then they dismiss the parts which convict them and make them feel uncomfortable.

The Holy Bible teaches that sin has to be paid for in full. This is a requirement by God Almighty. Since this is the case, we can, in our own human reasoning abilities, logically assess that its payment should last at least as long as its effects do. Of course, in our society where we are such enablers, one might say, "at least until they have sufficiently repented of their sins." The problem is – God does not offer this option. There is absolutely nothing in the Bible which offers any hope for another chance once someone has taken their last breaths. More importantly, to help put this in God's eternal perspective, we need to consider how long the effects of your rejection of His offer for salvation continue to influence not only yourself but others as well. Let us say your name is Charles. You first study medicine and then later theology at Cambridge. Your family's introduction of God to you was very liberal in nature. Your grandfather's ideas about how man came into being were much different than what the church taught you. You grew up celebrating the wisdom of men while yet vaguely flirting with the ministry as a profession.

You learn how to skillfully write your thoughts on how the world came into being. New ideas are presented to you by many apparently highly respected and educated men. Your thoughts come to differ greatly from what the Bible presents. Not to be held back by what you have come to consider religious restrictions, you push your new ideas onto the world under the guise of "scientific discovery." Hundreds, thousands, millions, and even billions of people are impressed with your thoughts on the creation of man. These ideas prompt them to mistakenly think they are now released from any moral codes passed to them from previous generations. This is something new. Yes, it is quite intriguing. According to your theory people can live their lives without being encumbered by spiritual laws since man is merely a biological animal. Mankind's creation and existence is no different than any other living, breathing life form on this earth.

You win worldwide fame. Many misguided individuals come to accept your theory as replacing the Gospel message. As with all things which oppose God, problems start to arise. As things take a turn for the worse, unsavory people use your ideas to justify their total disregard for the urgings which God Almighty put in the hearts of each of us. Evil, cruel men with oppressive military forces absorb your theory denouncing God. You have succeeded into making man a mini-god. Though these unsavory political powers may oppose each other, they hold your theory as a common ground. Having a social structure which has no spiritual guide proves useful for them. Men like Vladimir Lenin, Joseph Stalin, Adolph Hitler, and Mao Zedong brought death to millions. The communists replaced any spiritual essence in man with your total rejection of God as the Creator. This allowed them to look on the masses as mere instruments to be used for their social revolutions. The Nazis took another dimension of your theory. While Hitler claimed to be a Christian, he used the natural selection and survival of the fittest ideas of evolutionary theory to justify ridding society of groups of people who he deemed repulsive (and this applied not just to the Jews – it applied to the gypsies, the physically and mentally handicapped, as well as other groups he viewed as blights on Aryan society). The Nazis aggrandized one group while attempting to annihilate others. This was a total aberration of biblical teachings.

All these corrupt governments took aspects of your theory and molded them to support their malevolent regimes. For certain, these evil men would have been evil even if they had never read of your work. The question is how useful have your ideas been to them in justifying to others that man can only be properly understood when viewed as an evolved being. When you took God out of the equation for creation you provided excuses for all these godless people to justify their actions. So, what part did you play in the deaths of all those people these men had murdered? The godlessness of your theory fits well with those who exploit others (in the name of racial, social, or national superiority). They valued human life less since it has no spiritual dimension. Your groups of high minded thinkers have changed the world, but not for the better. Wherever your theory triumphs, people suffer. Governments become the god for dispensing "blessings". Faith is destroyed; hope is lost. People become mere animals; not any better than any other creature fighting to survive on this earth. In fact it is this struggle for survival which feeds the pride of those who enjoy exploiting the weak and the oppressed. It gives affirmation to their power to exploit. Their superior strength comes to be admired, regardless how it is used.

Unfortunately, what you have proposed starts falling apart under the scrutiny of objective scientists – men and women who are not out to prove something which better fits their carnal appetites. These men and women, who are truly using their scientific skills to better understand this world which God has given us, become the objects of scorn. When holes and falsehoods are found in your so-called scientific data, deceit is employed to bolster acceptance. People publish articles with known flaws – but then, the end justifies the means. Careers of opponents are besmirched by fellow advocates of yours. Your theory takes on the mantle of a new religion – one not impeded with spiritual laws but rather bolstered by the so-called laws of nature. People start worshipping the environment and the physical world as their source of existence. Scientists who hold to their sacred beliefs in Jehovah God are ridiculed. In your new world view only the highly enlightened are to be given positions of power. Old ideas have to be removed. As these grand thoughts of yours become theories, they are accepted as truth. As this "new truth" of yours stands in direct opposition to God's truth, then what should be your punishment? How many lives have you turned from worshipping the One true Creator? Your sin extends from generation to generation. When does it end?

You may not be Charles Darwin but your thoughts and attitudes will be shared by your family and friends. They will, in turn, share these thoughts and attitudes with their families and friends. If these are righteous thoughts, then good. You will have done as God desires of you. If they are corrupt thoughts, then how long have these thoughts lived in the lives of those you have influenced? The job of being God, the righteous Judge of mankind, is not an easy one. We weave such tangled webs of deceit. If you are Charles Darwin, the duration of your punishment would seem to dictate a rather lengthy punishment in light of all the lives you misled into serving a false set of counter-religious beliefs. No, we are not all Darwin, but we do extend our influence much further and longer than most of us ever consider. Who started the idea of abortions? Who taught others to steal? What man first influenced his friends into pursuing their carnal nature? Now you have these tendencies. Who are you influencing? When will the chain be broken? No, the job of being the supreme Judge of mankind is far more difficult than any of us can grasp. If you have put your faith in the Triune God of Christianity, rest assured that all judgment will be righteous.

Of course, their have been religious groups who have brought terrible carnage to mankind, all supposedly in the name of God. This accusation can be made against the men who perpetrated the Holy Wars. These wars were somewhat the reverse from what evolutionary theories try to do. Evolution denies the very existence of God. During the Middle Ages, the Catholic hierarchy tried to use the passion of godly people to spread the Gospel message for their own corrupt gains. These were actions taken by allegedly religious men. However, these men were more like the Jewish Sanhedrin with their ulterior movements for self-promotion rather than doing the business of the Lord. The truth was these endeavors were undertaken to satisfy their greed and lust for power. Being the "good men of God", they covered it in the mantle of religion (much like the current day Islamic extremists cloak their violent behaviors in the guise of religious pursuits). What these men were pursuing was power – both political and economic. In the Middle Ages these church men, who were actually godless (as indicated by their behaviors), used God for their own purposes. Is God to blame for this? Absolutely not. Then what is the difference? The purpose of evolutionary theory is to deny the existence with God, thereby destroying any relationship with Him. The purpose of the Holy Wars was more to build up the coffers of the Catholic Church than to evangelize the Arab world. We know this because sincere Christian evangelists do not use the point of a spear to convert people (and neither did Jesus and His disciples). Whenever we remove God from the source of our activities, godlessness triumphs (Proverbs 14:22; 21:30). It does not matter whether you are standing on a Bible or on a biology textbook. Both groups were pursuing their own self-serving interests rather than the good for a godly society. This is why Jesus warned us to "beware of wolves in sheep's clothing (Matthew 7:15-17)."

The sincerity of your motives will be shown by what fruit your labor produces. Whether your sin is of denying God or of subverting His holy name to aggrandize yourself, the sin carries long term consequences. Do not think for one minute Satan does not relish in sullying God's reputation with mankind. It makes no difference with him whether we disguise our motives based on natural laws or God's laws. If he perverts the outcome, he wins. The problem is mankind, with all its high-minded ideas, is too often the willing accomplish of Satan and his minions. We think ourselves wise, yet we are fools. As Paul teaches in Romans 1:18-22, "The wrath of God is being revealed from heaven against all the godlessness and wickedness of men who suppress the truth by their wickedness... For although they knew God, they neither glorified Him as God nor gave thanks to Him, but their thinking became futile and their foolish hearts were darkened. Although they claimed to be wise, they became fools..."

An excellent biblical reference for this discussion of the duration of hell can be found in Matthew 25:41-46. Jesus is teaching the gathering about the Day of Judgment. He warns the crowd in verse 41, "Then He will say to those on His left, 'Depart from me, you who are cursed, into the eternal fire prepared for the devil and his angels.'" Jesus ends this lesson with verse 46, "Then they will go away to eternal punishment, but the righteous to eternal life." <u>If eternal life means the righteous will live forever with their resurrected bodies, spirits and souls, then I think it is safe to conclude that the unrighteous will spend all of eternity in the payment for their sins.</u> As William MacDonald states in <u>Believer's Bible Commentary</u> concerning Matthew 25:41-46, "The Lord Jesus spoke of eternal fire (v.41), eternal punishment (v.46), and eternal life (v.46). The same One who taught eternal life taught eternal punishment. Since the same word for *eternal* is used to describe each, it is inconsistent to accept one without the other (p. 1300)." The Hebrew word for eternal is "olam"; the Greek word is "aion". These words are used to describe the eternal nature of God, our eternal salvation, and the eternal damnation for those who reject Jesus Christ as their Lord and Savior. Both mean forever. Neither has any connotation as to being of a temporal duration.

Now turn to Mark 9:47-48 where Jesus is teaching about the price for sin, "And if your eye causes you to sin, pluck it out. It is better for you to enter the kingdom of God with one eye than to have two eyes and be thrown into hell, where "'their worm does not die, and the fire is not quenched.'" This refers to Isaiah 66:24. The symbolism of "their worm" references the worms and maggots which were ever present in the trash dump outside of Jerusalem, called Gehenna. The burned and rotting flesh is to conjure up the worst of visual images for what is to happen to rebellious sinners. "Their worm" is meant to represent the continuous pain and torment which these unredeemed individuals will experience. Jesus wants to draw an image in our minds of our bodies being slowly and eternally eaten away.

Some might say that since Christ uses the metaphor of a worm eating a decomposing body, that eventually it will finish the task. From this they draw an incorrect conclusion that punishment must have an element of duration. At some point, the sinner is totally consumed, thereby no longer experiencing the torments of hell. Their condition is forever removed from any chance of salvation (hence eternal condemnation) but at least their suffering ends. Let us examine this reasoning. True, as far as worms and dead bodies go, the decaying process is just that – it is a process which has a finality. Careful now; stop for a moment and think about Who we are discussing. With God, things can be different. Think of the burning bush which Moses encountered in the desert (Exodus 3:2-3). Remember what caught Moses' eye. Here was a burning bush, yet it was not being consumed by the fire. Now that got his attention. If God can do that with a bush, why can He not do it with the eternally condemned? With God, all things are possible (Matthew 19:26). The spiritual truth which Jesus wants us to comprehend is that

in Gehenna, your spirit and soul will face unending pain
and torment. Unbelievers will receive a physical body on
the Day of Judgment as death and Hades give up their dead
(Revelation 20:11-15). However, the dead to Christ will
not have the gloriously resurrected bodies which will function for them in the same fashion as what the believers will
receive. The unbeliever's body will be destroyed in the lake
of fire (the second death – for those who reject God's plan
of salvation), yet their spirit will survive for all eternity. It
is their spirit which will continue to experience this eternal
suffering.

With the above passage from Mark 9, the duration of
their punishment sounds pretty eternal to me. No, Jesus did
not leave us with the impression that unbelievers simply
cease to exist. Their spirit will experience the total separation and desolation which Christ experienced when He died
on the cross. He died on the cross so they would not have to
spend eternity in hell. Since nonbelievers will have rejected
His gracious offer of salvation, guess what?

Where do you suppose we get this idea that the payment
for sin should have some duration limit? Is it because our
penal codes generally have a time limit attached to most
of them? Do our sentimental hearts tell us at some point a
person's payment for their rejection of God's plan for salvation must have a reasonable end? Are we mistakenly thinking
man's laws should be the guide for Divine laws? Here is the
problem with that thinking. Turn to 2 Thessalonians 1:8-9
where Paul assures us of God's justice through His judgment. "He will punish those who do not know God and do
not obey the gospel of our Lord Jesus. They will be punished
with everlasting destruction and shut out from the presence
of the Lord and from the majesty of his power." Since our
God is eternal, their rejection of Him must be eternal. He
will therefore honor their desire to not be in His presence,
for all eternity. As already stated, the Jews had a specific

name for God to reflect this aspect of His character. They called Him El Olam, the Everlasting God. This was to help them keep their attitude toward Him in proper perspective. Unfortunately, many of our world have lost this perspective on God. It seems right to me that if someone rejects God, this rejection will last as long as God lasts.

We can see the end of this discussion point by turning to Revelation 20:11-15, "Then I saw a great white throne and Him who was seated on it. Earth and sky fled from His presence, and there was no place for them. And I saw the dead, great and small, standing before the throne, and books were opened. Another book was opened, which is the book of life. The dead were judged according to what they had done as recorded in the books. The sea gave up the dead that were in it, and death and Hades gave up the dead that were in them, and each person was judged according to what he had done. Then death and Hades were thrown into the lake of fire. The lake of fire is the second death. If anyone's name was not found written in the book of life, he was thrown into the lake of fire."

As Dr. Doug Sager teaches in his lecture series on the book of Revelation, "Christians are born twice but die once. Nonbelievers are born once but die twice." The resurrected bodies of the apostates (those who have rebelled against God) last only long enough for them to receive His judgment. Then they are thrown into the lake of fire (which is the second death). Suffice it to say, it is the understanding of most biblical scholars that the lake of fire is an eternal damnation. The body dies in the lake of fire but their spirit and soul never die. Once again, it does not matter what modern man thinks; it does not matter if many "feel" this is overly harsh. God's word on this subject is rather clear. Sin is rebellion against God Almighty. He takes this rebellion very, very seriously. Additionally, our sins have an eternal dimension. They endure beyond the immediate act of committing that particular sin. They influence others to sin. As such, someone has to pay for them. <u>Either Christ paid your sin debt in full or else you will</u>. Either you spend all of eternity in His presence or all of eternity in an absolute absence of anything holy and good.

Merrill Unger in <u>The New Unger's Bible Dictionary</u> gives an excellent summary of this topic. As for "death" he says, "The general teaching of the Scriptures is that man is not only a physical but also a spiritual being; accordingly, death is not the end of human existence, but a change of place or conditions in which conscious existence continues (p. 293)." On the subject of "immortality" Unger explains, "By immortality theologians frequently mean the survival of the spiritual part of man after physical death. However, it must be clearly kept in mind that immortality is not mere existence after death. Death does not end human life, whether in the case of the saved or unsaved. In fact, the tenet of the immortality of the soul alone in unknown in Scripture (p. 610)." Unger goes on to explain that, "Unsaved people who do not possess eternal life possess a mortal body that will never be immortal. <u>Their soul and spirit will go on existing forever but their body, raised for judgment, will suffer "the second death" at the sinner's judgment of the white throne</u>. <u>This is not annihilation. This is eternal conscious existence in separation from God, and thus torment and what is called 'fire which burns with brimstone'</u> (p. 611)."

I must be honest, what the visual imagery of hell conjures up is a much larger epic punishment than I can possibly comprehend. Admittedly, the same is true of heaven as well (of course, on the other end of the spectrum). In most references, Jesus describes hell as a fiery, tormenting, painful existence which is eternal in its duration (Matthew 13:42, 13:50, Mark 9:43-48, Luke 16:24). In a few passages, He describes it as being dark and gloomy (Matthew 8:12, 25:30). The reconciliation of these two impressions may possibly be achieved if we consider that hell just might have a timeline. I believe the lake of fire is (as Jesus describes Gehenna) the fiery pain and tormenting part of the second death (Revelation 20:14-15). I think *after* the physical body of the unbeliever has been consumed in the lake of fire that their spirit and soul survives only to then be moved into the darkness and isolation phase of eternity.

Perhaps there is a duration to the burning lake of fire phase of punishment. This might be dependent on the evil a person has committed in their lifetime (Matthew 10:15). Jesus gives this ominous warning in Luke 12:46-48, "The master of that servant will come on a day when he does not expect him and at an hour he is not aware of. He will cut him to pieces and assign him a place with the unbelievers. That servant who knows his master's will and does not get ready or does not do what his master wants will be beaten with many blows. But the one who does not know and does things deserving punishment will be beaten with few blows." It seems to me Jesus is trying to leave the impression that not all unbelievers will be treated as equally evil. To be certain, they are all unbelievers, with no chance of salvation. However our Lord seems to imply there will be some measure of accountability levied against the occupants of hell. I am not saying that having multiple phases of hell is something which the Bible clearly teaches. This is only my surmise in order to try to make sense of the various descriptions which Christ gives us of eternal punishment.

If you have ever visited an old fashion trash dump you will know what an unsettling visual image Gehenna presented for the Jews and early Christians. I lived in the country as a boy and it seems every young boy had to make a foray to explore the burning trash heaps at the city dump. It was mound after mound of smoldering trash where the flames never quite extinguished. On the edges of the dump where the dying embers of the smoldering fire were hidden underneath the mounds, the smoke would give off an eerie darkness. In the center, the mounds were ablaze, like towering, fiery infernos. Old tires were particularly fun to watch as they would blaze up and give off great bellows of smoke. As the blazes would die down to where these heaps were merely smoldering, the bull dozers would push trash out from the center to allow the refuse which had been packed in tight to be exposed to the air. This would aid in the continuation of the "slow burn". On the fringes, the smell was bad (obviously we boys never got in the center of the dump). The stuff on the edges of the burn piles was still on fire but this was more of a low grade burn. At night, the dump gave off some pretty awesome images. I know for most people today they will find my description of the city dump to be mildly humorous. They might wonder why in the world someone would go there other than to merely drop off their trash. To an eight year old boy, it was a great place of discovery. Also, you got to dare your buddies to do things which our moms would have killed us if they knew what we were doing.

Since I accept Jesus' teachings that an unbeliever's punishment is eternal, this makes me think the spirit and soul may be moved from the center of fiery hell after a period of time. They are moved to the dark and gloomy edges of hell, for an eternal separation from God. If this is what happens, then this would reconcile these two images of eternal condemnation. Take my personal explanation of the phases of hell with a grain of salt. It is only a construct, allowing me to attempt to understand something which I do not clearly understand. I do know this – being separated from all things holy and good would certainly be tormenting. Being in darkness and isolation would certainly be punishing. I do not think Jesus gives us these seemingly contradictory images of hell as a mistake on His part. It may simply be the sequential view of a hellish eternity.

## *Immediate Relocation or Soul Sleep*

In our Sunday School class, some of the most interesting discussions we have had have centered on what happens to people immediately at the point of biological death. There are passages in the Bible which support our spirits and souls being immediately relocated to heaven. There are also excellent passages which support the notion of a "soul sleep". Is it always one or the other? Can it sometimes be soul sleep for some and immediate relocation for others? I love it when we discuss what we think God is trying to reveal to us through His Scriptures. I relish hearing how these Scriptures come alive in our personal lives. Full understanding cannot be achieved until we have turned to the Scriptures to gain as much biblical evidence as we can. This is one area where there can be fervent discussion points in favor of either position. Do not base your personal understanding of this topic merely on what you have heard in sermons. Pastors do not always agree on this topic. These are good men who happen to interpret the same Scriptures a little differently. That is what makes biblical scholarship so interesting.

Not all people have to experience the same things from God. Perhaps Lazarus (John 11:1-44) did experience soul sleep in order for Jesus to teach us a particular lesson. Jesus raised him from the dead to teach the gathering that as the Son of God He had command over life and death. Lazarus certainly did not come out of the tomb protesting that Jesus had returned him from the comforts of heaven. Not a word is recorded of Lazarus speaking of any bright lights or heavenly experiences. It appears his spirit and soul remained with his body waiting for Jesus to call him forth. As with the little girl whom Jesus raised from the dead (Mark 5:35-43) not a word is recorded of any celestial experience she might have had while her body lay dead to the world. Part of the explanation for this is that in this passage Jesus gives the specific command for the family not to talk of this.

Jesus gives an intriguing parable concerning what the unbelievers will experience in hell. This is recorded in Luke 16:20-31. Lazarus, the beggar, experienced physical death yet he had an awareness of an eternal state apart from his earthly existence. The rich man cited in this lesson realized he was in hell. Both were conscious of being relocated from their earthly domains. This is viewed as an allegorical lesson because nowhere else in the Bible are we taught that those in Hades have any communication with the saints in heaven. The commentary in the NIVDSB gives the following amplification. "Jesus contrasted the destinies of two persons. One died and entered a condition of blessedness. The other died and entered one of misery. Both were presented by Jesus as entering their future condition immediately following death. The suggestion in Jesus' story is that the spirits of the righteous enter a conscious state of blessedness. Similarly, the spirits of the unrighteous go into a state of conscious torment." The commentary continues with the following ominous statement. "Death ends the opportunity to confess, repent, and seek salvation. The prayer of the former rich man was unanswerable. It was too late; the gulf was fixed." I have also read commentaries calling this account an actual event, not a parable. Regardless how you categorize this teaching, the basic truths remain. Despite what the Sadducees thought, there is life after physical death. Additionally, hell ain't no fun – which is Southern for: if you find yourself eternally condemned in the abode of the most reprehensible characters who have ever walked this earth, your experiences will be of the most unpleasant sort.

To say the least, biblical study can be very challenging at times. Some passages are much harder to decipher God's intended lessons. Even with the topic of death, there are variations in content. Not all biblical stories have the heroes dying in the end. Take the events of the ascensions of Enoch (Genesis 5:24, Hebrews 11:5) and Elijah (2 Kings 2:1-18). They did not die. That was different from the norm. The events of the crucifixion provide us two different examples supporting spiritual relocation. The thief on the cross was told by Jesus "today you will be with me in paradise." This denotes relocation. Jesus Himself went into Hades during the period of His physical death (Matthew 12:40). These four stories support the belief that relocation is what happens immediately after the body biologically dies. However Jesus said Lazarus and the little girl were merely sleeping. Perhaps some have soul sleep; others have immediate relocation. Our sovereign God can do whatever His infinite wisdom leads Him to do. His purpose is always to instruct us. These lessons reference facts exactly as they were. The misunderstanding may be in our improper interpretation of the message our heavenly Father is giving us.

I believe spiritual relocation is the more likely of the two possibilities. The examples of soul sleep were used by God to teach us of the power which Christ Jesus has over life and death. The Transfiguration (Luke 9:28-36) certainly points to Moses and Elijah having an awareness of the situation here on earth at the time of Jesus' approaching crucifixion. Their spirits were still engaged in the events of earth or why else did they come to minister to Jesus? Had they been experiencing soul sleep all those years, they would not have had such knowledge of the events facing Jesus. Why would God have brought two sleeping prophets to minister to His Son? No, I believe their souls and spirits had been in heaven and God sent them to Jesus with a specific mission in mind.

Paul adds further grist for the mill in the following two passages. In 2 Corinthians 5:6-9 Paul writes, "Therefore we are always confident and know that as long as we are at home in the body we are away from the Lord. We live by faith, not by sight. We are confident, I say, and would prefer to be away from the body and at home with the Lord. So we make it our goal to please Him, whether we are at home in the body or away from it." Seems pretty clear to me Paul is proposing a relocation of the spirit immediately when death occurs. He goes on to say, "For to me, to live is Christ and to die is gain. If I am to go on living in the body, this will mean fruitful labor for me. Yet what shall I choose? I do not know! I am torn between the two: I desire to depart and be with Christ, which is better by far; but it is more necessary for you that I remain in the body" (Philippians 1:21-24). To be apart from the body and to be with Christ is Paul's ultimate desire. These verses appear to point to Paul having the understanding that when a believer dies, they shed their physical body and their spirit and soul go immediately to be with Christ Jesus in heaven.

However, this is where it gets real interesting. I have read commentaries by pastors who believe in soul sleep. The amazing thing is they cite these very verses as substantiation for death being a resting place and no relocation taking place until the Second Coming (see 1 Corinthians 15:51-55, 1 Thessalonians 4:16-18). These are good men with tremendous hearts for the truth. Equally good men with hearts for the truth draw different conclusions. How can this be? Our families, our friends, our cultural groups, our mentors, our pastors – all have powerful influences on how we individually interpret the Bible. I do not believe anyone is willfully trying to influence others in an evil manner so to deceive them by robbing them of the truth of God. No, we are all products of many factors. Therefore, we will reason a little differently; we will interpret and misinterpret based on who we are and where we are at a particular point in life. <u>Be cautious in assigning negative labels to others who interpret Scriptures differently than you.</u> <u>The reason this is not alarming or unsettling to me is that these men are not debating issues over how you get to heaven; they are debating *when* you get to heaven.</u>

This is very different from those who try to mislead us about the truth of salvation. Look at their hearts. If their hearts are pure, then marvel at how God works differently in each of us, according to His plan.

In John 14:1-3, Jesus says He will come back for us. Does that mean we will not be with Him in any form or fashion until the Second Coming? Could this not mean that our spirits and souls relocate to heaven at the time of our death but our physical bodies wait on earth for the promised resurrected bodies at the Second Coming? By "preparing a place for you" Jesus could mean He would be preparing a place for us in heaven. Jesus could also mean that He would be busy preparing the new Jerusalem which will descend out of heaven and be our city of great joy on the new earth (Revelation 21). With either interpretation, the basic end result is the same – we will be gathered with Jesus, for all eternity.

Since Revelation 6:9-11 talks about the martyrs asking God "how long must they wait for their blood to be avenged", it makes me think there is an awareness after the body stops biologically functioning. This awareness may not be limited to celestial things. It looks like there is an awareness of what is happening on this earth as well. This observation is additionally supported by the Transfiguration (Luke 9:28-31) involving Moses and Elijah ministering to Jesus prior to His crucifixion. If they were not aware of the events unfolding on earth, then how were they ministering to Jesus? The passage alludes to them discussing the coming trial and all that Jesus would be facing. How would they know all of this if they were not in heaven, looking down on Jesus during His time on earth?

Of course, you can stop and ask yourself, if you immediately go to heaven, then why did Paul revive the young man who fell out the window (Acts 20:9-10)? Why did he not let him go on to heaven? If the young man was headed to Hades, then Paul gave him a second chance at salvation. We know that is not possible. When all is said and done, it really makes no difference to me whether there is soul sleep or immediate relocation. I will be happy either way. This is a good lesson where we need to learn to be tolerant of the interpretations which others have of Scriptures. The truth is in the Scriptures. It is nonetheless beyond my understanding currently to reconcile these points of view. I look forward to God continuing His work in me so that I will come to a clearer understanding of exactly what happens immediately when your heart stops and your brain flat-lines. Until then, I lean toward your body being biologically dead, yet your spirit and soul relocating to heaven or Hades immediately when you take your last breath.

Many people get great solace when a loved one dies thinking that person's spirit and soul have departed to be with the Lord. As I see it, there is more evidence supporting this view than soul sleep. However, if you prefer believing that the next moment of someone's consciousness is when "that great trumpet sounds" (Revelation 11:15) then by all means, continue to believe that. Bottom-line, with either interpretation, the righteous in the Lord will receive a resurrected body, uniting with their eternal spirit and soul when our Lord and Savior comes to reign on the eternal earth. I do not know why there is this discrepancy in the Scriptures but we should not allow this to divide us. It appears that if anyone wants to take a hard line and say that the Scriptures emphatically prove one side or the other, they must bend certain of the above cited verses to fit their purposes. Be careful not to do this. Rather, glory that others are studying the Bible so intently that they see things in light of their understanding, regardless whether it perfectly matches your understanding. The Holy Spirit is doing a separate work in each of us; bringing each along the path of sanctification in a manner which is best for them. Glory be to God in the highest.

This is much like what we have discussed concerning eternal security. Recognize there are legitimate differences in interpretation of various Scriptural passages. Regardless what you believe, live as if there is no eternal security. Keep away from sin. Refocus your life daily. Pray to our Father that He supplies you with the strength and guidance that is necessary for you to live in a manner which is glorifying to Him. For those of us who believe in eternal security, thank God for this blessed assurance but do not take advantage of it by having a casual attitude toward sin. For those who do not believe in eternal security, do not worry that our God is so wrathful that He will sentence you to eternal damnation because you happen to have committed a sin prior to death. Remember, God looks at our believing hearts as being reflective of our redemptive faith. With either interpretation, keep your heart right with God and you will have nothing about which to worry. With regards to soul sleep vs. immediate relocation, keep your heart right with God and you will have nothing about which to worry.

### *The Book of Hope*

When one accepts the challenge to study the book of Revelation, they will find there exists ample commentary to guide them. However, much of this commentary is based on the author's particular understanding of what the Holy Spirit is trying to convey to us. The same is true here. I am presenting my thoughts and the thoughts of others who seem to make the most sense to me. If you disagree with these thoughts or you feel you have a better understanding, that is fine. By all means, uncover whatever meaning you can possibly find in the wonderfully powerful book of Revelation. No one group of thinkers will have all the answers to this final book in the New Testament.

My personal understanding is undergirded by a strong sense of hope which this book provides us. As Christians, we know how the final battle ends – our God wins! The rewards which were mentioned at the start of my book referencing Hebrews chapter 11 are presented to us in Revelations. All of our faith is affirmed. Christ comes back to rule the earth – a restored earth – where people will live in a fashion as to how our heavenly Father originally intended us to live. Our free wills will mesh in perfect harmony with our Lord's will. Divisions between nations and people will disappear. Pride will vanish. Healing will be complete. Purpose and fulfillment will rule the day. The fruit of the Spirit will guide our every action. <u>We will finally be free to be the persons God originally intended each of us to be</u>. No more oppression by the evil powers of Satan, holding us back from achieving our true potentials. Every talent, every ability, will be finely tuned. Peace will be the order of the day. Think about it – an eternal earth, devoid of the influence of sin. This is a place our spirits yearn for and it has been promised to us by El Elyon Himself. I can't wait.

My pastor, Dr. Doug Sager, encourages us as we study the book of Revelation that we should keep it in proper perspective. Dr. Sager teaches us above all the mystery of the symbolism of the book of Revelation, it is a book of hope and encouragement. This is precisely why it should and must be taught. I have read this final book of the Bible numerous times. Each reading has been supplemented by various biblical commentaries. At first I would become lost in all the obscurity of the symbolism. Later I learned to glean would I could and be assured that with each future reading, I would come away with whatever the Spirit wants to impart to me at that time. This is why Bible study never becomes monotonous. Each time you read a chapter or a verse, something new will be revealed. The Holy Spirit is an awesome teacher (John 14:26).

The book of Revelation is the ultimate book of redemptive faith. It reveals what God promised us way back in Jeremiah 29:11-13. "For I know the plans I have for you," declares the Lord, "plans to prosper you and not to harm you, plans to give you hope and a future. Then you will call upon Me and come and pray to Me, and I will listen to you. You will seek Me and find Me when you seek Me with all your heart." And what a future He has planned for us! If we will walk in righteousness, what we consider our best days on this earth will pale in comparison to what the Triune God has in store for us.

On the other hand, for those who have given our Lord nothing but rejection and derision – what they consider their worst days on this earth will seem glorious compared to what Elohim has in store for them. Yes, there is a place called hell. Jesus spoke of it often (Matthew 5:29, 10:28, 18:9, 23:15, 23:32, Mark 9:43, 9:45, 9:47, Luke 12:4-5, 16:22-23). Those who will reject Him will discover someday just how right He is and how wrong they have been. All of their arrogance and pride will vanish into tears and wailing. They will discern a vast difference between the gods they held so dear while ranting about our narrow-minded ways and our Jehovah Tsidkenu (The Lord Our Righteousness). Yes Adonai (Our Lord and Master) is a loving God but above all else He is holy. This holiness is made evident in His righteousness. Revelation means unveiling. This earth *will* see His ultimate righteousness. The humble will be vindicated and the wicked will bear His wrath. All of the previous books of the Bible come to fulfillment in Revelation. As MacDonald says in his book, Believer's Bible Commentary, "…this book ties up the loose ends of the first sixty-five books of the Bible. In fact, that is how the book can best be understood, by knowing the whole Bible!" (p.2349). For those of us who have read this book, we know the ending – our Lord Jesus, the King of Kings, the Lord of Lords wins! Forevermore evil is relegated to that great "lake of fire". We will live on the resurrected, eternal earth with our Lord Jesus as our King. Life, from that point on, will be all that God originally intended it to be.

Dr. Sager in his lesson series on the book of Revelation puts a proper perspective on how Christians and Jews are dealt with at the end of time. Although I have said I identify in certain ways with the Israel of the Old Testament that is not to say the Christian church is the "new" Israel. Israel failed miserably in being a light to the rest of the world for God, our Father. The Christian church picked up that banner though and has done a remarkable job of trying to fulfill the Great Commission (Matthew 28:19-20). Dr. Sager makes the point that, to be precise, we are still the church and Israel is still Israel. The Christian church is dealt with in the early chapters of Revelation (1-3). As you go through chapters 4-19 you will see that God will still be doing a work with His chosen people. We Christians will be long gone in that great rapture in the sky. We do not come back into play until chapter 19 – The Marriage Supper of the Lamb. I am so thankful for that!

### The Message to the Churches

William MacDonald said it well in his introduction to Revelation. "For all children of God, the book teaches the folly of living for things that will shortly pass away. It spurs us to witness to the perishing, and encourages us to wait with patience for the Lord's return. For the unbeliever, the book is a solemn warning of the terrible doom that awaits all who reject the Savior." (Believer's Bible Commentary, p.2351) My inclusion of an overview of the book of Revelation is intended to help Christians to solidify in their thinking what God holds for all mankind. The review of the following churches which Christ addresses is meant to call us to intro-spection. If you are walking in faith as shown through your obedience, then you have a glorious anticipation forth-coming. If you are an individual whose faith has weakened or your church's faith and obedience have slipped, then please repent and refocus. This is what Jesus is asking of each of these following churches to do.

In Revelation 2:4 the church of Ephesus is accused by Jesus of having forsaken its first love. What was this first love? Paul established this church and it was centered on the Word of God and the loving fellowship of its believers. The Nicolaitans were a sect of worshippers who had an "anything goes" lifestyle. Whatever made them happy was what they intended to do. This went for worship as well. As such, they incorporated various sexual aspects of pagan practices into their worship behavior. This was much like the worship-pers of Baal and Molech against which the Old Testament prophets so often fought. The Nicolaitans compromised their faith in order to feel free to seek worldly pleasures. Christ commended the Ephesians for resisting this tempta-tion. Jesus lovingly calls these worshippers to refocus and to continue in their bonds of faith and obedience.

Jesus encourages the church in Smyrna in 2:9-10. The issue of false believers raises its ugly head with this New Testament church. In the KJVLASB commentary on verse 10 it states, "The message to the Smyrna church is to remain faithful during their suffering because God is in control and His promises are reliable. Jesus never says that by being faithful to Him we will avoid troubles, suffering, and perse-cution. Rather, we must be faithful to Him *in* our sufferings. Only then will our faith prove itself genuine." Churches are made up of people. Some churches experience more turmoil than others by the nature of the people within and outside of their congregations. When persecution comes, the sincere believers must dig deep in their souls to withstand these hardships. As an encouragement, Jesus promises those who with-stand that they will not be destroyed by the "second death."

Pergamum is the church which is like many of the compromised denominations of today. They practice an insipid theology rather than living a vibrant, Bible-centered relationship with God. Jesus admonishes this church in 2:14-16 against being lenient. The social pressure to be open-minded was as corrupting then as it is now. This angers our Lord and He calls them to keep steadfast in their faith and worship. Does this not sound like some present day Christian churches who try to accommodate the practices of various groups into their worship services? This church is embracing what the Ephesians are resisting. Pergamum is much like the churches of today who celebrate diversity. They are blending in with the world and our Lord Jesus is speaking out against this. God is a jealous God. Jehovah God wants diversity in church membership in that the church is open to all people. Be crystal clear on this – the Christian church *is not to be open* to all worship objects and practices which others may want to impose on us all under the pretense of being "inclusive." The Holy Trinity is to be the one and only object of our worship. When we compromise to include other religions and their practices, we are violating God's commandment against idol worship. When we dilute the true message of Jesus in order to be politically correct and to not hurt the feelings of seditious parties, we alienate ourselves from the One power which grants us forgiveness and redemption. If this describes you or your church, act now by following what has been written in your heart. Christians are to play to an audience of One. Do not allow our upside down world to confuse you and dilute your boldness for the Word. When they are through with you, they will cast you off as filthy rags. If you fail to stand up for Jesus, He will cast you off as well.

For the church in Thyatira Jesus has harsh words against those who rebel against God's teachings. Disobedience and the drawing of others away from God will carry a heavy price when the final judgment comes. False teachers will pay the heaviest of prices when God searches their hearts and repays them for their deeds. God's condemnation of false teachers is recorded in Jeremiah 23:25-32. "I have heard what the prophets say who prophesy lies in my name. They say, 'I had a dream! I had a dream!' How long will this continue in the hearts of these lying prophets, who prophesy the delusions of their own minds? They think the dreams they tell one another will make my people forget my name, just as their fathers forgot my name through Baal worship. Let the prophet who has a dream tell his dream, but let the one who has my word speak it faithfully. For what has straw to do with grain?" declares the Lord. "Is not my word like fire," declares the Lord, "and like a hammer that breaks a rock in pieces?" "Therefore," declares the Lord, "I am against the prophets who steal from one another words supposedly from me. Yes," declares the Lord, "I am against the prophets who wag their own tongues and yet declare, 'The Lord declares.' Indeed, I am against those who prophesy false dreams," declares the Lord. "They tell them and lead my people astray with their reckless lies, yet I did not send or appoint them. They do not benefit these people in the least," declares the Lord."

We all know well what Jesus teaches in Matthew 7:22-23. "Many will say to me on that day, 'Lord, Lord, did we not prophesy in your name, and in your name drive out demons and perform many miracles?' Then I will tell them plainly, 'I never knew you. Away from me, you evildoers!'" It should be evident to those who are seekers of His truth that God has fought throughout human history to keep our worship of Him righteous, reverent, pure, and respectful. Every generation has those who try to combine worldly pleasures with

Godly worship. This unfortunately attracts a lot of uncommitted worshippers. In Revelation 2:26 Christ continues though with a promise for those who remain steadfast. He will use the faithful believers to reign over the nations when the resurrected earth is established.

To the church in Sardis (3:1-6) Jesus is speaking to a church which has become lifeless. We know these churches. They are the ones who need no water in their baptistery. If a church is not in the business of winning new souls, then it has lost the Great Commission. When a church loses its heart for the conversion of new souls, it loses its life. Jesus does not want us to become complacent or too tired to fight the good fight. He encourages them to continue in much the same spirit which Paul cheered on Timothy in Titus 1:18. "Timothy, my son, I give you this instruction in keeping with the prophecies once made about you, so that by following them you may fight the good fight, holding on to faith and a good conscience. Some have rejected these and so have shipwrecked their faith." Some at Sardis had shipwrecked their faith and Jesus is calling out to them.

The church at Philadelphia is the church where we all want to be members. In Revelation 3:10 Jesus makes the Philadelphia church the greatest of promises. "Since you have kept my command to endure patiently, I will also keep you from the hour of trial that is going to come upon the whole world to test those who live on the earth." As I understand this verse, Jesus is promising these Christians they will be raptured prior to the period of tribulation. It is also the verse where Jesus confirms to us that this world is a test.

Revelation 3:15-18 presents us with the harshest of accusations by Jesus for any church. Laodicea is a church in deep trouble with God. Jesus says, "I know your deeds, that you are neither cold nor hot. I wish you were either one or the other! So, because you are lukewarm—neither hot nor cold—I am about to spit you out of my mouth. You say, 'I am rich; I have acquired wealth and do not need a thing.' But you do not realize that you are wretched, pitiful, poor, blind and naked. I counsel you to buy from me gold refined in the fire, so you can become rich; and white clothes to wear, so you can cover your shameful nakedness; and salve to put on your eyes, so you can see." Laodicea is like many churches and denominations today. They see their wealth, their buildings, their social status, and it deceives them. They have become secure in these things rather than trusting God for His promises. Political correctness is rampant in these gatherings. They hardly deserve to be called churches! They are CINO's who Christ will reject, as by His promise in these verses. Take heed of these verses. They are the strongest of incrimination for the lukewarm, deceived believers (who are actually nonbelievers according to the words of Jesus). Our Lord and Savior does not want moderates. The politically correct crowd may like moderates but Jesus demands that you be dedicated solely to Him if you are to have your name in His Book of Life. Notice that even with the church which Jesus had the strongest of criticism, He ends His comments with an encouraging call for repentance and restoration (3:19-22). God is patiently waiting for all of us sinners to come home.

### God's Progressive Plan

Listen to Revelation 4:11: "You are worthy, our Lord and God, to receive glory and honor and power, for you created all things, and by your will they were created and have their being." Revelation 4:11 is another way of stating what Isaiah declared in Isaiah 43:7 that man's chief purpose in life is to bring glory to God, our Creator. We fulfill that purpose when we represent Christ in such a way in our lives that we lead others on this pathway to eternal salvation. Even after the Christian church is raptured, God is still reaching out to those remaining souls to repent and turn to Christ. This is another way of saying "it is not all about us Christians." We can be assured, God's plan progresses forward even after the rapture. This is because God is not finished displaying His glory and sovereignty to the world just because the Christian church is no longer in the picture. All of mankind will know God in much clearer details before He is finished with His original creation.

The book of Revelation is certainly not the first time the early church was confronted with "Signs of the End of the Age". Even prior to Jesus speaking of this as quoted in Mark 13:1-31 Ezekiel prophesied greatly about the approaching time for atonement, wrath, and judgment. In Ezekiel 11:9 the Jews were once again warned that their wickedness would have drastic consequences. <u>Why did they not accept the prophecies of Ezekiel?</u> <u>As with today, this was not what the people wanted to hear, so they simply chose to ignore and belittle him.</u> That is why it is so amazing to me that God is always gracious in warning His children prior to sending His wrath. Elohim consistently warns us. However for most, we hear only what we want to hear.

You may wonder why does God acts so patiently with us? Jehovah Jireh does this in order to provide us time to repent of our ways and return to Him. As in prior times, God would be using other nations to be the instruments of His wrath against an unrepentant Israel. Ezekiel 16:58-63 is a wonderful passage about how Israel will finally come to repentance once the Lord has chastened them for their rejection. In Ezekiel 36:22-23 God tells Israel it is because of His holy name that He will deal with them in a righteous manner. In verses 25-28 of that chapter God promises them a new heart. Is that not what God is talking about in Revelations? God uses evil nations for His purpose – to show His holiness to Israel and all the nations of the world. No one gets special treatment. He loves all of us and disciplines each of us. No one nation or groups of people are immune to punishment if they do not follow God in all His teachings. God takes sin seriously and He holds us accountable. <u>As much as the books of Ezekiel and Revelation are about God's ultimate judgment, they also disclose how our Lord graciously extends encouragement and eternal hope to those who will change their hearts and accept our Triune God's offer of redemption.</u>

Occasionally some will raise the question – "Why should we as the Christian church continue to be supportive of the nation of Israel? Did they not crucify our Lord Jesus?" Yes they did. However, what is important for us to remember is that Israel did this as a fulfillment of biblical prophecy (though they certainly did not view Jesus' crucifixion as such). To them, Christ was an unsettling threat to their established order. He said things they did not want to hear and Jesus made them feel unpleasant for things which they enjoyed doing. Although what they did was part of biblical prophecy, this does not lessen their accountability to God. It does however impact our relationship with the Jewish nation. They are absolutely not our enemy. The Jewish Sanhedrin did not do one thing which did not fit into God's plan – on that we can rest assured.

More precisely, the Jews did not murder Jesus. Read John 10:17-18 where Jesus states that no one takes His life from Him but that He lays it down Himself. <u>Our Savior lovingly and willingly gave up His life as full payment for our sin debt. It is *our sin debt* which we should be focused on and not the treachery of the Jewish leaders.</u> These people corruptly sentenced to death a man totally innocent of any charges but that is not the focus of the cross. Bear in mind, this was our Lord's divine mission from the start. Jesus was aware of what *had* to happen. At any point our Savior could have called on legions of heavenly angels to rescue Him. Jesus was *not* sacrificed by the Jewish leaders. Rather our Redeemer offered Himself as the perfect atonement for those who will put their steadfast faith in Him as being the Son of God Almighty (Romans 3:21-26). Without the sacrifice of our Lord's life that day at Calvary, there would be no redemption (and no resurrection). Without redemption, we would all be heading to hell. After all, in the most basic of understanding, Jesus came to save us from an eternity in hell. I know this is blunt talk but sometimes we need to hear the straight truth without any of this ubiquitous spinning which is so prevalent in our world today.

The Jews are our brothers and sisters. God still has a plan for their lives. As such, we are to regard them as being important in the continuation of God's holy plan for His redemption of our world. This Divine plan has been unfolding from the beginning of creation in Genesis 1 on through the end of Revelation 22. It is to offer redemption to all people, from all nations, regardless of heritage, gender, social status, or ethnicity. In view of that, the Jewish people continue to be an instrument of His divine plan on past the part in Revelation chapter 4 where many of us think that the Church will be raptured.

Dr. Doug Sager in his seminar series on Revelation strongly emphasizes the following points. The reason we should continue to support Israel as a nation is that God has never cancelled His original covenant with them. We know this because we can see how God remains active with these people in the following chapters of the book of Revelation. As you read chapter 7 you realize God still has a plan to work out with Israel. Since God Almighty still maintains a relationship with Israel after the Church is raptured, we should take note of this. Simply put, if they remain important to God, then Israel should remain important to the Christian church. This is why we are to support them as a nation. Just as the New Testament is not the replacement for the Old Testament, the Christian church is not the replacement for

Israel. We have our own identity. We are the bride of Christ. We are His Church. Though we are fulfilling the original mission God assigned Israel (to represent Him to the world), God has a plan in His mind for the redemption of Israel, if only they will turn to Him (Ezekiel 16:59-63).

Chapter 9 of Revelation has a very intriguing verse relating to hell. In verse 11 it refers to the king of the demons cast into the bottomless pit. The name of this demon king is Apollyon. Go to 2 Peter 2:4 and read what our Lord reveals through Peter about hell – "For if God did not spare angels when they sinned, but sent them to hell, putting them into gloomy dungeons to be held for judgment..." What is intriguing to me is that we know from the Gospels that Satan's demons roam the earth and inflict a lot of pain and confusion on the people. We also know Jesus often would cast out demons during His earthly ministry. Yet in 2 Peter 2:4 it talks about putting the fallen angels into gloomy dungeons. This gives rise to the speculation that the worst of the fallen angels (represented in 2 Peter 2:4) were immediately sent to Tartarus when they were originally cast out of heaven. The others have been allowed to work through the centuries in conjunction with Satan in this cosmic battle between the forces of good and evil. When the Great Tribulation period comes, it seems the worst of the worst demons will be released as well to wreak havoc on the remaining inhabitants of earth.

### *The Three Levels of Hell*

Contrary to what most of this world believes, nonbelievers will not simply cease to exist. Religious leaders are purveyors of false doctrine when they fail to give significance to God's wrath and final judgment. We are not all going to heaven; many will reside in Gehenna for all eternity (Matthew 7:13-14). The commentary for 2 Peter 2:4 in the NIV Disciple's Study Bible, explains that "hell is not the intended abode of human beings. It was designed out of necessity for the devil and his associates. It is the place of confinement for sinning angels awaiting final judgment." As the result of man's sinful ways, humans who reject God will suffer the same fate as the fallen angels who rejected God in favor of Satan. There are three places of confinement associated with hell. Hades is the first level. It is where the unbelievers go awaiting final judgment. Gehenna is associated with the lake of fire (Rev. 19:20, 20:10, 14 -15). This is the place where unrepentant souls go for the second death (as the result of final judgment). It is much worse than merely being in Hades. Peter used a different Greek word to describe the immediate confinement for the worst offending demons. It is translated as Tartarus. Think of it as the third level of hell. It is reserved for the demons who were too wicked to be allowed to roam the earth when God cast them out of heaven. 2 Peter 2:4 refers to this place. As you know, Satan and his demons have been allowed to roam the earth inflicting their torments on us. These particular angels were so evil that God had to send them to their punishment immediately. The point is: God judges the angels who rebelled against Him and He will certainly punish those of us who likewise reject Him. Remember, when we reject God we are calling Him a liar. That cannot go unpunished.

This idea of a third hell is not farfetched. In 2 Corinthians 12:2 Paul talks about the third heaven. If heaven has multiple layers, it only makes sense that hell has multiple layers. Certainly the people who sacrificed their own children to Baal and Molech deserve far worse eternal punishments than those whom their cultural ties keep them from accepting Christ as their Savior. As already discussed, there may be a timeline for eternal punishment. After the lake of fire, unsaved souls may possibly pass to another level of tormented existence. What is important here is that while we do not know exactly what the dimensions of eternal punishment will be, they will certainly be worse than what most of this world thinks them to be.

We are not without any details though. The book of Revelation gives even more information in chapter 12 about what hell and its inhabitants are like. In 12:3-9 we learn when Satan was cast out of heaven for his rebellion he had a sizable following. As the result of Satan's untamable pride, he took with him 1/3 of the angels. Satan's war with God shows Satan's evil nature. His thirst for revenge against God will claim countless souls. Why? Two reasons: (1) because Satan, in his wickedness, wants to hurt God by separating as many souls from Him as possible, and (2) the devil is working constantly to recruit as many souls as possible in anticipation of the big battle coming against our Lord of Lords and King of Kings. He is hoping greater numerical numbers will be to his advantage.

Elohim allows this because in His original design of man He gave each of us a free will. One might ask, "If our free will is such a part of the rebellious nature of man, why did God give us a free will?" It is all about the process of sanctification. C. S. Lewis explains that "The process of being turned from a creature into a son would not have been difficult or painful if the human race had not turned away from God centuries ago. They were able to do this because a world of mere automata could never love and therefore never know infinite happiness" (Mere Christianity, p. 183). Yahweh wants us to know happiness in its fullest dimensions and He has a plan for just that. Here is what it is. God gives His love unconditionally. He wants our love to be given freely back to Him. Love is a choice, not some indefinable urging which is beyond our control. God wants us to consciously choose Him as the object of our praise and worship. He wants our steadfast faith that He is who He says He is and He does what He says He will do. Without giving us a free will, our faith (and love) would not be a choice. God does not force anything on us. Our God is a God of freedom. He is not some maniacal wizard playing endless games with us for His own amusement. To be precise, this world is a test to see who will respond to the calling of God by what He has placed in our heart. This test puts us in direct opposition to the temptations which Satan presents to our weaker nature. Hence, the battle rages on.

What will hell be like? In various places in the Bible Jesus referred to it as a place which is dark and gloomy, where there will be weeping and gnashing of teeth (Matthew 8:12; 13:41-42). In other areas like Revelation 20:10 and 20:14-15, hell is described as hot and fiery. Either place is inhabited with a crusty cast of characters who will make existence as tormenting as possible. These diverse passages, along with the various words like Hades, Gehenna, and Tartarus, are why I think there are multiple layers of hell. Each will be designed to eternally punish the souls according to what they have done while they were alive. I do not know what will actually be the difference between these levels and I certainly do not want to learn first hand. Whatever hell ultimately becomes for someone, it will certainly not be a continuous party of beer drinking, playing cards and video games.

### *The Greatest of All Battles*

Continuing on we get a summary of the triumphant battle in the spiritual war presented in Revelation 12:10-12. "Then I heard a loud voice in heaven say: "Now have come the salvation and the power and the kingdom of our God, and the authority of His Christ. For the accuser of our brothers, who accuses them before our God day and night, has been hurled down. They overcame him by the blood of the Lamb and by the word of their testimony; they did not love their lives so much as to shrink from death. Therefore rejoice, you heavens and you who dwell in them! But woe to the earth and the sea, because the devil has gone down to you! He is filled with fury, because he knows that his time is short." Good for our side; bad for his. Satan has already been defeated by Jesus' crucifixion and resurrection. First, our Lord and Savior graciously served as the perfect sacrifice for our redemption. Then, to complete the victory, Jesus' resurrection sealed Satan's doom, signifying Christ's dominion over life and death.

As I have stated previously, I love reading various Bible commentaries as I am doing my studies. They often add a higher level of understanding than what I am able to achieve on my own at times. Other times they help to confirm what I feel the Holy Spirit is laying on my heart about some particular passage. Such is the case in the KJVLASB commentary for Revelation 12:12. It covers why God allows Satan to be evil. "God allows Satan to work evil and bring temptation so that those who pretend to be Christ's followers will be weeded out from His true believers." This sounds like the Parable of the Weeds (Matthew 13:24-30, 13:36-43) being played out in real life, doesn't it? This parable and the Parable of the Sower (Matthew 13:3-9, 13:18-23) are the foundational teachings of Christ on which I have based this book. Who are these pretenders? They are the ones who I have labeled as CINO's (Christians In Name Only). CINO's are not a new phenomenon. Our religious leaders have had to contend with them since the first century and, as the book of Revelation indicates, they will be around until the end of times. Nothing is new.

Would it not be simpler for these people to acknowledge God and repent of their sins? Why do these people go through the 7 plagues and the 7 bowls of God's wrath? Revelation 16:9 tells us they refuse to repent. This is hard for those of us who have studied the Word of God to understand. Confess, repent, and seek forgiveness is what we do each day. Why is it so hard for these people to do? They do not repent because most people believe when you die you merely cease to exist; they do not believe in hell. It is amazing to me that most everyone has a concept of heaven but few really believe hell exists. This is one of the greatest achievements of Satan. He has most of the world convinced that you either go to heaven because "God is loving to all" (so a truly loving God could not possibly send so many people to hell), or if you do not go to heaven, you simply cease to exist. As long as Satan can keep a person confused about God's absolute righteous judgment, he wins. These lost souls are willing to cease to exist in exchange for not having to be obedient to God throughout their earthly lives. What a surprise they will get on Judgment Day.

Revelation 20:9-10 tells us of the outcome of the final battle. "They marched across the breadth of the earth and surrounded the camp of God's people, the city He loves. But fire came down from heaven and devoured them. And the devil, who deceived them, was thrown into the lake of burning sulfur, where the beast and the false prophet had been thrown. They will be tormented day and night for ever and ever."

From this scene we move to "The Great White Throne of Judgment". What happens here is proclaimed in Rev. 20:11-15. "Then I saw a great white throne and Him who was seated on it. Earth and sky fled from His presence, and there was no place for them. And I saw the dead, great and small, standing before the throne, and books were opened. Another book was opened, which is the book of life. The dead were judged according to what they had done as recorded in the books. The sea gave up the dead that were in it, and death and Hades gave up the dead that were in them, and each person was judged according to what he had done. Then death and Hades were thrown into the lake of fire. The lake of fire is the second death. If anyone's name was not found written in the book of life, he was thrown into the lake of fire."

## *The Promise*

"Then I saw a new heaven and a new earth, for the first heaven and the first earth had passed away, and there was no longer any sea. I saw the Holy City, the new Jerusalem, coming down out of heaven from God, prepared as a bride beautifully dressed for her husband. And I heard a loud voice from the throne saying, "Now the dwelling of God is with men, and He will live with them. They will be His people, and God himself will be with them and be their God. He will wipe every tear from their eyes. There will be no more death or mourning or crying or pain, for the old order of things has passed away." He who was seated on the throne said, "I am making everything new!" Then He said, "Write this down, for these words are trustworthy and true." He said to me: "It is done. I am the Alpha and the Omega, the Beginning and the End. To him who is thirsty I will give to drink without cost from the spring of the water of life" (Revelation 21:1-6). How can you have a book about redemptive faith without covering this passage? It is the promise to which we hold so steadfastly.

Our reward for being unwavering in our faith that God is who He says He is and He does what He says He will do can be found in Revelation 21:7, "He who overcomes will inherit all this, and I will be his God and he will be my son." To better conceptualize what "this" will mean to us, we should reference the commentary for this verse in the KJVLAS:

(1) eating from the tree of life (2:7),
(2) escaping from the lake of fire (the "second death", 2:11),

(3)  receiving a special name (2:17),

(4)  having power over the nations (2:26),

(5)  being included in the book of life (3:15),

(6)  being a pillar in God's spiritual temple (3:12), and

(7)Nsitting with Christ on His throne (3:21).


Those who can endure the testing of evil and remain faithful will be richly rewarded by Jehovah God.

Not all denominations believe in the plan of Christ rapturing His church prior to the Tribulation Period (Revelation 3:10). If the rapture does not occur, then the church will go through the Great Tribulation Period just like everyone else. All are going to suffer. The church members will suffer at the hands of the antichrist and his pagan government. The nonbelievers will suffer at the hands of none other than the Lord God Almighty, El Shaddai.

Whether there is a rapture or not, why must we believers hold fast to our belief in the Holy Trinity? For whatever your personal reasons, the final reward for all of us is found in Revelation 22:1-5, "Then the angel showed me the river of the water of life, as clear as crystal, flowing from the throne of God and of the Lamb down the middle of the great street of the city. On each side of the river stood the tree of life, bearing twelve crops of fruit, yielding its fruit every month. And the leaves of the tree are for the healing of the nations. No longer will there be any curse. The throne of God and of the Lamb will be in the city, and His servants will serve Him. They will see His face, and His name will be on their foreheads. There will be no more night. They will not need the light of a lamp or the light of the sun, for the Lord God will give them light. And they will reign for ever and ever." Of the things we hope for as believers in Christ Jesus, this picture certainly encapsulates much of that dream.

Reflect on these verses a little further. What do they tell us of the eternal earth and how we will live? For certain, it will have the best of the best of scenery and people. A restored earth, without sin, will be an amazing place to spend all of eternity. Imagine for a moment whatever it is that comes to your mind when you think of the perfect place for you to live. Now imagine that being designed by God, just for you, as a way of Him showing you His eternal love. El Elyon will make it even better than you can possibly imagine. Jesus went away to design this final abode for His kingdom and it will be awe-inspiring (John 14:1-4). It will have the new Jerusalem as its capital city. The description of it in Revelation 21 probably does not do it justice. How do you describe perfection? How do you describe a place beautiful enough to be the home of God? Pristine and magnificent will characterize its splendor. There will be vast countrysides for man's enjoyment and dominion. The part in verse 21:1 about "there was no longer any sea" does not necessarily mean we will no longer have the oceans and the seas. What I think it means is there will be no gulf dividing us from God. His glorious presence will forever be with His creation.

It is my opinion from the study of Scriptures that we will have various roles to fulfill during this eternal existence. I do not get the impression we will be idly sitting around playing harps. The book of Revelation mentions kings, priests, and servants. We will probably have a social structure related to what our deeds were while on this earth. We know God promises us rewards based on these deeds (Isaiah 3:10-11, Jeremiah 17:10). No greater authority than Jesus Himself promises in Matthew 16:27, "For the Son of Man is going to come in His Father's glory with His angels, and then He will reward each person according to what he has done." These rewards most often refer to crowns which we will receive (2 Timothy 4:8, James 1:12). Crowns in biblical times also related to a particular style of life which the bearer got to enjoy. Is it not possible that these crowns will be associated with some type of lifestyle reward? I would not mind being in charge of the horse stables for one of Jesus' great rural estates. Having dogs and cats running around, playing in the hay as the other animals eat would be a most enjoyable life for me. I used to have a small horse farm and evening time down in the barn was always something which I looked forward to with enjoyment. We can be confident that whatever God has us doing, it will be fulfilling and a labor of love.

If we were able right now to remove the element of sin from the world (that being the only change), then this world would most certainly be a very enjoyable place to live and work. In school, students would try to excel and teachers would enjoy helping them discover new knowledge. In business, each would work to the best of their abilities. Companies would compete based on merit and service to the customer. City officials would earnestly look after the welfare of their constituency. I am not going to go so far as to discuss what lawyers might do (I have an active imagination but it does have limitations). Scientists and engineers would help us develop new technologies for managing the resources which God has so abundantly given us. Sports and entertainment figures would go back to pursuing a spirit of excellence and wholesomeness. Each of us would serve our fellowman out of expressions of love and concern for others. We would render to Yahweh all the glory. Do you not think that is what our heavenly Father originally intended?

Now, if we extend this to the eternal earth, imagine how meaningful life will be. There will be no more sickness, no more mental or physical handicaps, no more trickery and deceit. Each thing we do will be of our noblest motives. We will be able to explore the full potential of our creative minds. Work will no longer be a toil. It will be a meaningful expression of our love for God and the goodness of life. If we keep the basic biblical structure of being good stewards of what God has given us, we will all be marvelously engaged in meaningful pursuits. We will be busy helping each other as well as all of God's creatures. Some may have more important roles than others. I can handle that. Certainly those who have devoted this life to being the best witness for our Lord will deservedly be awarded greater honors on the eternal earth. This world today, minus sin and death, is a wonderful place. Add having our Triune God permanently with us, it will be like heaven – which is exactly what it will be.

Imagine the awe-inspiring beauty of a new earth, undefiled by sin and the burden which it has brought on all of creation. There will be long walks along the River of Life. How magnificent will the tree of life be? We will stroll down the lanes of El Elyon's new Jerusalem. The architecture will be beyond anything we have ever seen (or could imagine). The dimensions are mind boggling – Revelation 21:16 – the city will measure 1400 miles by 1400 miles square. How will that be possible? Remember Jesus' words in Mark 10:27, "With man this is impossible, but not with God; all things are possible with God."

We know from the Rev. 22:2 passage that the eternal earth will have nation states (the healing of the nations is mentioned specially). Nations will live in harmony for there will be no trace of pride or prejudice to corrupt our fellowship. We will serve God on the eternal earth. Doing what? Let your imagination run wild? Perhaps we will explore other worlds, other galaxies. The Old Testament books of Genesis, Isaiah, and Ezekiel all contain glimpses into what God intends for us to enjoy as we spend eternity with Him.

I feel certain it will not be a communal existence. Why? I say this because there are so many references to our individual deeds being carried forward into heaven. Both the Old Testament and the New Testament promise us rewards based on our own deeds, not collective deeds. In 2 Corinthians 5:10 Paul writes, "For we must all appear before the judgment seat of Christ, that each one may receive what is due him for the things done while in the body, whether good or bad." Do not fly over these verses without questioning the deeper meaning which is there for us. Stop and contemplate what God is telling us. The NIVDSB commentary on this verse affirms, "An important aspect of future judgment is the assignment of rewards. While salvation itself is a gift of grace, rewards must be earned by faithful living and serving. Often in Scripture the rewards for faithfulness are described as crowns. Rewards can be lost, whereas salvation is secure." This commentary reflects my personal understanding of the judgment of believers as it relates to our future rewards and the security of our salvation.

Jesus' teachings are the main reason why I believe there will be greater roles for some. Christ has many statements which relate to this topic. Our Lord explains to us in Matthew 19:29-30, "I tell you the truth, at the renewal of all things, when the Son of Man sits on His glorious throne, you who have followed me will also sit on twelve thrones, judging the twelve tribes of Israel. And everyone who has left houses or brothers or sisters or father or mother or children or fields for my sake will receive a hundred times as much and will inherit eternal life. But many who are first will be last, and many who are last will be first." <u>Seems rather clear to me that there will be kingdom rulers who will be given authority over others</u>. <u>This status will be given them because of what they accomplished on this earth in His name</u>. The ones who will receive these honors are not the ones who this world currently aggrandizes. The tireless workers for God's holy name will be richly rewarded. Many who are seen today as leaders of government and industry will be placed in supportive roles to those who placed their priorities in kingdom building rather than accumulating worldly wealth and status. <u>As a Christian, I have no problem in seeing myself giving eternal service to my brothers and sisters in Christ</u>. These efforts will not be a burden; they will be labors of love. As with most activities, they will probably require leadership. Being under the direction of those who gave their time and talents serving the Lord makes perfect sense to me. It will be an honor to work under their guidance. I say this because I believe eternity holds abounding challenges for us. It will be a time of joyful pursuits.

To take this a step further, go to Matthew 25:14-30. This is the Parable of the Talents. In verse 23 Jesus says, "His master replied, 'Well done, good and faithful servant! You have been faithful with a few things; I will put you in charge of many things. Come and share your master's happiness!'" To me this indicates those who have produced much fruit in this lifetime will be put in charge of even greater things in the eternal state. <u>This world is a test, so what better way would God have to decide who takes on certain responsibilities on the eternal earth than by how they conducted themselves on the "fallen earth"</u>? Could it be that Jesus is testing our long-term spiritual vision by encouraging us to store up treasures in heaven (Matthew 6:19-20)? Our Lord has a plan for those who have ears to hear.

It makes sense that God rewards us as individuals because God seeks a personal relationship not a collective relationship with us. We are to worship in a corporate manner as an assembly but each is to live as an individual dedicated to Jesus Christ our Lord and Savior. Please do not worry about what we will do. We will have meaningful activity in the service of each other and our Lord. This should not be surprising to any who read the Scriptures because God views work as honorable. It is those who refuse or are too lazy to work that the Proverbs rail against. Perhaps we will be stewards of the land and sea and all creatures thereof (like Adam). Stewardship at its best involves a labor of love. What joy that will be to oversee God's new creation as He intends it to be.

## *In Summation*

Which type of soil are you? Matthew 13:3-9, 18-23 presents us with the reality of kingdom worship. Only a few are receptive to the teachings of our Lord and Savior. Even fewer are obedient enough to be productive. Only a few take the hard road of sanctification which is necessary to make us less like the world and more like our Messiah (Matthew 7:14). Will the angels of the harvest (Matthew 13:30) bring you to the Lord's barns once the reaping starts? Will your life testify that you have accepted Jesus as the perfect atonement for your sins (Romans 3:21-26)? Or will it merely reflect that you had a casual awareness of Him but He never became the guiding force in your life?

Genesis through Revelation reveals God's collection of perfect truths and holy promises. It is said by nonbelievers that the Bible is a series of fables; that our religion is based on myths. If such is the case then what have we to gain from perpetuating it? If it has no real value, then people living in freedom will see the error of its tenets and will simply stop practicing it. The evidence we Christians point to as validating our beliefs will crumble over time. The only problem for our detractors is that the evidence pointing to the authenticity of Christianity keeps increasing rather than diminishing. As man expands his knowledge, it keeps pointing to a Divine Creator. This is the same Divine Creator we know as God Almighty. Only where freedom does not exist do religions with no real essence continue to survive. Freedom is the greatest ally to Christianity, and it is the greatest enemy to false religions.

Our detractors enjoy accusing us of deceiving ourselves and using this mythical God character as a spiritual crutch to fend for our inherent weaknesses. If the Holy Scriptures are untrue, where is the deception and the corollary weakness? The dictionary definition of deception is a deliberate concealment of a falsehood. A deception generally justifies your doing something considered to be wrong for a reason which you consider is right or at least advantageous. Where is our ruse? What things are we to do with the commandments of the Bible? We are to love the Lord our God with all our heart, with all our soul, with all our mind...and to love our neighbors as ourselves (Matthew 22:36-40). In 1 John 4:20 we learn, "If anyone says, "I love God," yet hates his brother, he is a liar. For anyone who does not love his brother, whom he has seen, cannot love God, whom he has not seen. And He has given us this command: Whoever loves God must also love his brother." What is wrong with this? It takes great strength and determination to carry out this command. Should not all religions and world cultures foster such a commitment? Yet not all do. This is to God's glory that we have such beliefs. It is to the betterment of our society that we have such beliefs.

We are also called to be strong and courageous (Joshua 1:6, 18) – two characteristics which really do not go with being weak and in need of a spiritual crutch. We are to fight against evil and injustice (Jeremiah 22:13-16). We are to have a heart for the poor and the oppressed (Deuteronomy 15:7-8, 10, Proverbs 14:31). Christ elevated the status of children and women during His earthly ministry. The King of Kings teaches that each and every human life is precious and we all matter (Psalm 68:5, Matthew 25:32-46). The Lord of Lords encourages each of us to treat others as we ourselves desire to be treated (Matthew 22:39). The Beatitudes instruct us to be humble in spirit, to keep our behaviors under control, to be merciful, and forgiving. Christians are taught to be peacemakers and not to strike out at those who do not accept our beliefs. We are to live righteously, which means to live in harmony with all of God's creation (Matthew 5:3-12). We are taught to have respect for the rule of law and to show ourselves to be good citizens (1 Peter 2:13-17). Everything which God commands us to do is both good for the individual and for society as a whole. Since these are our teachings, where is the evil deception lurking in our religion then to take advantage of someone else's misfortune or stupidity?

Where we get our biggest criticism is not something of which we have much control. Christians are said to be hypocrites. We are also accused of being a poor reflection of Jesus' loving nature. The truth is most of these "so-called hypocrites" are not actually Christians – they are CINO's masquerading as Christians. Like most groups, the fringe of Christianity causes the greatest disturbances. As weird as this may sound, this is where persecution is a good thing. It chases off the CINO's. This is why I previously referenced the KJVLASB commentary for Revelation 12:12. Like the seed which fell on the rocky places, persecution separates these people rather quickly from our ranks (Matthew 13:20-21). Unfortunately for sincere Christians, these are the people who the world thinks of when they criticize our religion. Jesus was wise when He said, "He who is not with me is against me, and he who does not gather with me, scatters (Luke 11:23). By this He means we are to be totally sold out to our faith in Him as our Lord and Savior. Anything less will only result in a poor reflection on His Holy Name. As for Jesus' loving nature, while He certainly is loving, He is also righteous and holy. Christians are called to love, even those who are hard to love. However, being a Christian does not mean we are not to be bold in our plan to live out our faith. It does not mean we have to compromise our Christian values in order to placate the misguided views of our detractors. We are not the world's doormat. Jesus, Paul, Peter, John, and James were filled with love; they also were steadfast in their resolve to live as God originally intended for all mankind to live. Compromising and steadfastness just do not go together. Notice, each time the world wants us to compromise, what they are really saying is they want us to disavow certain of our staunch beliefs and to accept their lax points of view. This is not compromise; it is abdication (and a measure of cowardice for so easily surrendering something which should be a core belief).

Our second source of criticism is actually a badge of honor. The heroes of faith which we have been studying were not without their detractors. The world did not like it that these men confronted it with their decadence and wickedness. How dare they be challenged by people who pointed to their misery as being punishment well deserved? To the depraved, they challenged their contempt for God's Holy Word. To the rich and powerful, they challenged their arrogance and hypocrisy. Great faith carries conviction. Conviction carries boldness. Boldness coupled with a passion for your mission will always send the naysayers into attack mode. This is welcomed criticism. If the world is not criticizing your faith, then your faith has been watered-down. A fervent believer will tell the world the truth when a lie would suit it better.

Nothing the Bible asks us to do is wrong or immoral. It is all edifying, strengthening, and encouraging. Basically most nonbelievers do not object to us believing what we believe but they do not want us to expect them to be obedient to our beliefs. That is their option and God grants them such. Even more basic though, if they know of the fundamental teachings of our Lord and Savior, they resent how these truths make them feel about themselves. Darkness does not like light (John 3:19).

What does God ever ask of me which is not ultimately good for me? Absolutely nothing. Then why do not more people believe the words of the Bible? This is so because this world is a test of man's free will. We are free to respond to the evidence of Jesus Christ as our Lord and Savior or to reject Him and follow some other substitute form for worship (Romans 3:21-26, Rev. 3:10). From the beginning, the Holy

Trinity knew that not everyone (actually only a few) would respond with an acceptance of God's truths. Nothing happens with us that catches God off guard. He knows our tempter. Satan is a very powerful adversary and he has millions of fallen angels to do his bidding. Pride, greed, sexual desires, envy, aggression, and the lust for power are all part of mans' depravity. These work in concert to steal us away from a meaningful relationship with our Holy Creator.

You have to decide if you want to lead a life for the immediate gratification of these worldly cravings or do you want to store up for yourself treasures in heaven. As Jesus teaches us in Matthew 6:19-21, "Do not store up for yourselves treasures on earth, where moth and rust destroy, and where thieves break in and steal. But store up for yourselves treasures in heaven, where moth and rust do not destroy, and where thieves do not break in and steal. For where your treasure is, there your heart will be also." Do you treasure the material things of this world above all other endeavors? This does not mean you are not to like nice things and you cannot enjoy having them. Christianity does not require a vow of austerity. What Jesus is conveying is the encouragement for us to place a greater value on our relationship with God and His people than on anything else of this earth. Where do you stand? Your answer will determine where you spend all of eternity. Choose well.

I have no regrets for having lived according to my Lord Jesus' teachings and commandments. In living by these principles, I have lived a good life. These standards have led me to a quality of life that honors God and blesses me with treasures beyond imagination. I have a precious wife and two wonderful daughters who love me deeply. They have inspired me to be a better man than I would ever have been capable of being without them. My extended family makes me feel important and appreciated. The friends I have made in business and church have truly enriched my life. God has blessed me more abundantly than what I could possibly ever deserve. I know I could not have achieved what I have on my own power. I have had the good fortune of living in the greatest country this world has ever known. I have had the great pleasure of living in the part of our country referred to as the Bible belt. I thank God for that. Some may mean it as a statement of derision, but I take great homage in our fundamental resolve to orient our lives around the inerrant word of Jehovah God, the Almighty God, the Creator of all the heavens and the earth. This heritage has strengthened my soul and given me reason to hope. I strive to live my life by the words of His Holy Book. Therefore I have no regrets.

Life is full of choices and these choices determine our lives. I have thoughtfully considered the totality of my beliefs and I stand steadfastly by them. **I know in my heart that I more than just think the One I worship is God; I "know that I know" our Triune God *is* who He says He is and He *does* what He says He will do.** The members of the Holy Trinity are distinguishable, yet inseparable. Yahweh is my heavenly Father. He is El Elyon, the Most High God. He is my Jehovah Jireh, the Provider of all I need. Jesus Christ is the Redeemer of lost souls and the Savior of the faithful. I know that I know my redemptive faith has set me free of the shackles of sin. At the cross, the Son of God paid my sin debt in full. I trust completely that this man we call Jesus is the Messiah. Furthermore, I know I will live out His promises on the eternal earth. Whenever my spirit is weak, I appropriate enduring strength from the one our Lord sent to the faithful as a seal of His ownership. The Holy Spirit is my Paraclete. He comforts me, guards me, and directs my paths. Christians serve an awesome God! God in three persons, united in the mission of bringing healing to all those who seek Christ Jesus in earnest faith. Our God's love knows no boundaries; His grace is ever present. It is open to all who will call on His Holy Name. It is my prayer that I continue to grow in my love for Him, as He desires. His will is to be my will. His commands are to be my commands. His people are to be my people.

I leave you with one last bit of wisdom. What will matter the most when you take your last breath is not what house you lived in, what car you drove, what amount of money you had in the bank, what position of power you wielded, or what social status you achieved. No, it will be who and what you loved. Think about it. Are you passionate about this man the world knows as Jesus? Is He reflected in your life? Revelation 22:12-14, "Behold, I am coming soon! My reward is with me, and I will give to everyone according to what he has done. I am the Alpha and the Omega, the First and the Last, the Beginning and the End. Blessed are those who wash their robes, that they may have the right to the tree of life and may go through the gates into the city." Be sure of your love for Him, for it will carry you all the way into eternity.

# Appendix I

—⟨⟩—

The Names of God: (from the Blue Letter Bible – Study
    Tools)
El Shaddai (The Lord God Almighty)
El Elyon (The Most High God)
Adonai (Lord, Master)
Yahweh (Lord, Jehovah)
Jehovah Nissi (The Lord My Banner)
Jehovah-Raah (The Lord My Shepherd)
Jehovah Rapha (The Lord That Heals)
Jehovah Shammah (The Lord Is There)
Jehovah Tsidkenu (The Lord Our Righteousness)
Jehovah Mekoddishkem (The Lord Who Sanctifies
    You)
El Olam (The Everlasting God)
Elohim (God)
Qanna (Jealous)
Jehovah Jireh (The Lord Will Provide)
Jehovah Shalom (The Lord Is Peace)
Jehovah Sabaoth (The Lord of Hosts)

Names of Jesus – Root of David, Lamb, Shepherd, Christ,
Immanuel, the Anointed, the Messiah, Faithful and True,
Word of God, King of Kings, Lord of Lords, The Morning

Star, the Redeemer, the Suffering Servant, the Alpha and the Omega, the Lion of Judah

# Bibliography

─────

*New International Version Disciple's Study Bible*. Nashville: Cornerstone, 1998.

*King James Life Application Study Bible*. Wheaton: Tyndale House, 1989.

Blackaby, Henry. *Experiencing the Cross*. Sisters: Multnomah, 2005.

Blackaby, Henry and Richard. *Experiencing God Day-By-Day Devotional*. Nashville: Broadman & Holman, 1998.

Kennedy, D. James. *Why I Believe*. W. Publishing Group, 1999.

Lewis, C. S. *Mere Christianity*. New York: HarperSanFrancisco, 1952.

Luther, Martin. *Commentary on Romans*. Grand Rapids, Kregel, 1976.

MacDonald, William. *Believer's Bible Commentary*. Nashville: Nelson, 1990.

Stanley, Charles. *How To Listen To God*. Nashville: Thomas Nelson, 1985

Stanley, Charles. *Finding Peace*. Nashville: Thomas Nelson, 2003.

Unger, Merrill. *The New Unger's Bible Dictionary.* Chicago: The Moody Bible Institute of Chicago, 1988.

Warren, Rick. *The Purpose Driven Life.* Grand Rapids: Zondervan, 2002.

Printed in the United States
125033LV00003B/2/P